Mobile Learning Cor

D1099407

Mobile Learning Communities explores the diverse ways traveling groups experience learning "on the run." This book provides empirical evidence that draws on the authors' 17 years of continuing research with international occupational Travelers, engaging with workplace learning, globalization, multiliteracies, and emerging technologies which impinge on the ways mobile groups make sense of themselves as learning communities. Dealing with an issue of increasing global significance, this book challenges the simplistic and stereotypical images of traveling groups still found in mainstream media and popular culture.

Mobile Learning Communities brings mobilities and learning communities into a single, comprehensive focus. This text will appeal to scholars in distance education and educational technology, and to researchers in education, cultural studies, and sociology. It will also be of interest to educational instructors, policy-makers, administrators, teacher educators, and pre-service teachers. It tells a vivid story of the experience of mobility through the words of the mobile learners themselves, but also critiques existing notions of learning and suggests ways of creating new educational ltures for all learners and educators.

Patrick Alan Danaher (BEd, BA GradDipTertiaryEd, MLitt, PhD) is Associate Professor in ion Research) in the Faculty of Education at the Too the University of Southern Queensland, Australia.

Beverley Moriarty (DipTeach, BEd, MEd, PhD, AMusA) is Senior Lecturer in the School of Teacher Education at the Dubbo campus of Charles Sturt University, Australia.

Geoff Danaher (BA(Hons), DipEd, PhD) is a Lecturer in Learning Support and the Skills for Tertiary Education Preparatory Studies program in the Division of Teaching and Learning Services at the Rockhampton campus of CQUniversity, Australia.

Mobile Learning Communities
Creating New Educational Futures

Patrick Alan Danaher,
Beverley Moriarty, and Geoff Danaher

Routledge
Taylor & Francis Group

NEW YORK AND LONDON

First published 2009
by Routledge
270 Madison Ave, New York, NY 10016

Simultaneously published in the UK
by Routledge
2 Park Square, Milton Park, Abingdon, Oxon OX14 4RN

Routledge is an imprint of the Taylor & Francis Group, an informa business

© 2009 Taylor and Francis

Typeset in Minion by
HWA Text and Data Management Ltd, London
Printed and bound in the United States of America on acid-free paper by
Walsworth Publishing Company, Marceline, MO.

Library of Congress Cataloging in Publication Data
Danaher, Patrick Alan, 1959–
    Mobile learning communities : creating new educational futures /
    Patrick Alan Danaher, Beverley Moriarty, and Geoff Danaher.
        p. cm.
    Includes bibliographical references and index.
    1. Mobile communication systems in education. 2. Distance education.
    3. Education and globalization. I. Moriarty, Beverley. II. Danaher,
    Geoff. III. Title.
LB1044.84.D36 2009
371.33–dc22   2008043776

ISBN 10: 0-415-99158-7 (hbk)
ISBN 10: 0-415-99159-5 (pbk)
ISBN 10: 0-203-87940-6 (ebk)

ISBN 13: 978-0-415-99158-2 (hbk)
ISBN 13: 978-0-415-99159-9 (pbk)
ISBN 13: 978-0-203-87940-5 (ebk)

For Reanna Kristy Urquhart and Rory Wayne Urquhart
and for Jean Moriarty, Raymond Moriarty, and Alan Moriarty

—Adieu, dit le renard. Voici mon secret. Il est très simple: on ne voit bien qu'avec le cœur. L'essential est invisible pour les yeux . . . .C'est le temps que tu as perdu pour ta rose qui fait ta rose si importante . . . Les hommes ont oublié cette vérité . . . Mais tu ne dois pas l'oublier. Tu deviens responsable pour toujours de ce que tu as apprivoisé. Tu es responsable de ta rose . . .

Antoine de Saint-Exupéry, *Le Petit Prince*, pp. 72-74

Muss es sein? Es muss sein.

Ludwig van Beethoven, Epigraph to String Quartet in F Major, Opus 135

Contents

Illustrations

Tables

Figures

Acknowledgments

The authors are indebted to a large number of individuals and groups, without whose help this book would not have been possible:

- Sarah Burrows (Acquisitions Editor—Education) and Alex Sharp (Editorial Assistant—Education) at Routledge, who provided exemplary support and encouragement
- The anonymous reviewers of the book proposal
- Janice Jones, who created the illustrations
- Emilio A. Anteliz, who tracked down elusive references
- Renae Jenkins, who provided research assistance for Beverley Moriarty
- Peter Hallinan, Ian Kindt, Colin Rose, Rob Thompson, and Doug Wyer, former members of the Australian Traveller Education Research Team at CQUniversity, Australia
- Our fellow Traveler education researchers in Australia, England, Ireland, India, Italy, the Netherlands, Nigeria, Norway, the Russian Federation, Scotland, Spain, the United States of America, and Venezuela
- Máirín Kenny, who helped to collect the 2003 data reported here
- Phyllida Coombes and Geoff Danaher, who transcribed the 1999 and the 2003 data (all 601,722 words of them) reported here
- Our respective families
- Our respective university colleagues, whose interest in our work helps to sustain us
- Cathie Fullerton and John MacDonnell, who continue to welcome us into their respective Australian mobile communities
- And in particular all those members of mobile communities, and the people who provide their formal education, in Australia, Belgium, England, Scotland, the Netherlands, and Venezuela (many of them now our friends), who participated in the research projects and who have taught us so much about mobility, learning, and community.

Acronyms

EFA	Education for All
EFECOT	European Federation for the Education of the Children of Occupational Travelers
ICTs	Information and communication technologies
NESB	Non-English speaking background
OECD	Organization for Economic Cooperation and Development
TESS	Traveler Education Support Service
UNESCO	United Nations Educational, Scientific, and Cultural Organization

Introduction
Mobile Learning Communities

The introduction provides the rationale for focusing on mobile learning communities; locates the book in and explains how it extends the current literature on mobilities and learning communities; outlines the research projects from which the evidence for the book has been compiled and the data collection and analysis techniques framing that evidence; and elaborates the structure of the book.

Mobile Learning Communities: Creating New Educational Futures

Mobility has always been an integral part of the human condition. From the Paleolithic Age onwards, humans have been accustomed to living in groups that move. Individual survival has been inextricably mixed with group sustainability; mobility has operated at the core of fulfilling such basic needs as food and drink, accommodation and shelter, procreation and child rearing, cultural adaptation, and identity and meaning-making.

With the invention of agriculture in the Neolithic Revolution and the expansion of urbanization associated with the Industrial Revolution, the basis of human residence changed radically from mobile to sedentary. Agriculture and industry required large, permanently resident populations to supply the labor and management needed to develop and sustain them. Consequently mobility, which had previously been the only form of residence, became pathologized and even demonized by being associated with such notions as tramps, vagabonds, and persons of no fixed abode. Yet there remained a strong interdependence between settled populations and occupationally mobile groups and individuals, such as in the cases of circuses and fairgrounds, Roma (sometimes called Gypsy Travelers), migrant farm workers, and nomadic pastoralists.

The acceleration of globalization associated with technological advances in the late twentieth and early twenty-first centuries has created a new set of parameters for understanding mobility. There is a growing population of nationally and internationally peripatetic workers, from defense force and diplomatic service personnel to business and information technology specialists to educational and health professionals to aid and development advisers. There is also increased educational mobility, with initiatives such as the Bologna Process designed to enhance opportunities for learning in multiple countries and an increased student body in international schools around the world. Yet, as we explore below, there is considerable diversity of cultural and financial capital among mobile communities, illustrated by the difference between these groups who are largely in control of their mobility and others who are compelled to be mobile for reasons associated with work or dislocation.

These new manifestations of mobility make it both timely and significant to focus attention on that phenomenon. At the broadest level, mobility can be argued as exercising a profound influence on all of us through its creation of unprecedented opportunities for the exchange of goods, services, information, and ideas. At the same time, mobility can be associated with differential kinds of access and power, and can be seen as the vehicle for military conquest, cultural imperialism, and neo-colonialism. This fundamental ambivalence about the meanings and effects of mobility is a recurring theme in this book.

We employ two concepts to frame and fuel our examination of contemporary manifestations of mobility: community and learning. Perhaps as an intended antidote to the perceived alienation and angst of postmodern life, *community* is increasingly appealed to as an idea and ideal that can build enduring relationships founded on mutual interests and respect for diversity at levels ranging from the neighborhood to the planet. Notions such as communities of practice and virtual communities highlight the communal and dialogical characteristics of human existence, with cooperation and collaboration being valued ahead of competition and individualism. As we explore below, the concept of mobile communities yields important insights into contemporary manifestations of mobility.

Learning has always been an indispensable element of mobility. The survival of mobile groups has depended on group members teaching one another, and handing down to successive generations, their culturally situated knowledge and skills, as well as their assumptions and attitudes. From a different perspective, the introduction of mass schooling created additional challenges for both mobile groups and the state, with the latter's insistence on place-based education not necessarily fitting easily into the former's residence patterns. Yet this mismatch has generated a number of educational innovations that can also benefit permanently resident populations.

This book brings together these three ideas—mobility, community, and learning—into an extensive examination of an increasingly significant phenomenon: *mobile learning communities.* This examination is facilitated by the application of several concepts to analyze evidence provided by our own empirical studies as well as those of colleagues. The intention is to link this evidence and our analysis of it to broader questions about learning and living in the contemporary world. Indeed, a key implication of that analysis is that mobile learning communities are effective in making visible and sometimes in disrupting and even subverting binaries such as global–local that can perpetuate existing educational and sociocultural inequities. So a key part of those broader questions and of the creation of new learning futures can be seen as learning from the lessons that can be gleaned from mobile learning communities.

We consider in the next section and in subsequent chapters various definitions and conceptualizations of key terms. For the moment, our working definition of a mobile learning community is of *a group of people who are mobile for sustained periods of the year or of their lives and who recognize in themselves and others a common experience of mobility and a shared commitment to learning for themselves and other group members.*

Three qualifications are appropriate at this point. First, we recognize that some individuals are mobile for a variety of reasons and at different phases of their lives, and we assume that learning is an integral part of their mobility. Second, individual members of mobile groups are likely to vary markedly in the degree to which they see themselves as belonging to a community and/ or as being committed to learning of different degrees of formality. Third, the complexity of community and the human character being what they are, less privileged members of mobile groups are liable to be subject to internal exclusion that can make their experiences of mobility less positive and educationally successful than those of more powerful members.

Despite these qualifications and while seeking to steer around the twin conceptual risks of essentializing (reducing the complexities of subjectivity to a narrowly defined fixed essence) and idealizing members of mobile groups, we argue that such groups can teach all of us valuable lessons in both learning and living in communities. Furthermore, as globalized knowledges and technological developments expand in intensity and influence, these mobile learning communities can and should contribute to the ongoing project of *creating new educational futures* that are more equitable, productive, sustainable, and transformative than the *status quo.*

The remainder of this introduction is divided into three sections:

- A review of selected literature about mobilities and learning communities and of how this book seeks to contribute to and extend on that literature
- An account of our research projects, with data collection beginning in 1992 and with the associated analysis forming the bulk of the evidence presented in the book concentrated on the period between 1998 and 2003
- An overview of the structure and organization of the book.

The Literature about Mobilities and Learning Communities

As noted above, this necessarily selective literature review focuses on two key ideas:

- Mobilities
- Learning communities.

The book helps to extend existing scholarship in this field by exploring in depth and across a range of empirical sites the aspirations and experiences of several mobile learning communities, and by linking those aspirations and experiences with broader questions of policy-making and provision that can help to frame the creation of new educational futures for mobile and non-mobile learners alike.

Mobilities

Mobilities are a diverse and widespread contemporary social phenomenon with emotional, intellectual, occupational, physical, political, recreational, and sociocultural dimensions (Kellerman, 2006; Kukulska-Hulme & Traxler, 2005; Peters, 2005; Sheller & Urry, 2004, 2006; Urry, 1999). While several concepts have been employed to interpret these mobilities, we have identified three key diversities—of manifestation, valorization, and educational provision—as a fruitful way of encapsulating the mobilities literature and of making explicit our intended contribution to that literature.

Diversity of Manifestation of Mobilities

The diversity of manifestation of contemporary mobilities is represented by the following necessarily incomplete list that nevertheless captures something of the wide spectrum of experience of this phenomenon:

- The itinerant sheep-shearing Karretjie or "donkey cart" people of the Great Karoo in South Africa (de Jongh, 2002; de Jongh & Steyn, 2006)
- The movement of teachers from lower to higher socioeconomic status schools in New Zealand (Ritchie, 2004)
- Late nineteenth-century German attitudes to indigenous nomadism in German southwest Africa as an example of national and cultural ambivalence toward mobility (Noyes, 2000)
- Homeless mobility and spatial identities as negotiated by street children in Kampala, Uganda (Van Blerk, 2005)
- An evaluation of Radio C's effectiveness as a specialist medium catering to the nomadic Roma in Budapest, Hungary (Matelski, 2005)
- The worldviews of teenage children of globally mobile professionals (Hayden et al., 2000)

- The post-nomadic identity work of Bedouin who settled in stone houses in Israel's Negev Desert (Dinero, 2004)
- The implications for identity strategies of French international executives working in China for a multinational oil company (Fernandez et al., 2006)
- The migratory aspirations of highly skilled knowledge workers working in such fields as information technology (Ferro, 2006)
- The notion of "neo-nomadism" applied to the development of countercultures by artists, therapists, exotic traders, and bohemian workers seeking to live alternative lifestyles in Ibiza, Spain, and Goa, India (D'Andrea, 2006).

This selection of manifestations of mobilities demonstrates their considerable and dramatic diversity and their global reach in the contemporary world. It highlights also the *constructed, contextualized,* and *contested* character of contemporary diversities. By this we mean that there is nothing "natural" or "inevitable" about mobilities and that they are as much a creation of planning and reflection as any other outcome of human action and endeavor. Furthermore, mobilities vary enormously in their form and impact across the globe and within populations; it makes a profound difference when and where mobilities are enacted in specific places and at particular times. Moreover, mobilities are highly prized by some and devalued, even degraded, by others; it is difficult to discern a national or regional consensus in attitudes and policies toward mobile groups.

Diversity of Valorization of Mobilities

This lack of consensus draws attention to the second diversity that we have identified: valorization. The two opposite ends of the continuum might be represented by the international jet set on the one hand and the urban homeless on the other: mobility is the common denominator but they are very different forms of mobility, with diametrically opposed forms of capital and degrees of access to power and support.

These two mutually exclusive sets of attitudes toward mobility underpin a continuing ambivalence toward people who are mobile. There remains a kind of romanticized idealism of certain forms of mobility, encapsulated in the following extract from the children's classic English novel *The Wind in the Willows* (Grahame, 1961):

"There you are!" cried the Toad, straddling and expanding himself. "There's real life for you, embodied in that little cart. The open road, the dusty highway, the heath, the common, the hedgerows, the rolling downs! Camps, villages, towns, cities! Here to-day, up and off to somewhere else to-morrow! Travel, change, interest, excitement! The whole world before you, and a horizon that's always changing!" (p. 32; see also Danaher, 2000b, pp. 221-222)

This romanticized idealism evokes a kind of envy of people who are mobile, because they have been able to escape from the confines of civilization and the regular routines of capitalist and industrialized labor. Yet this envy is counterbalanced by a fear of the threat posed by mobility to that established order, which leads to a pathologizing of mobility, whereby its *difference* is turned into *deviance*. Thus settled sites often feel uncomfortable when engaging with individuals and groups who move in and out of their communities; these people are "of no fixed abode" and therefore do not have the same emotional and financial investment in the settled sites as permanently resident inhabitants.

This process of pathologizing has created a set of categories that contradicts the romanticized idealism outlined above. These more negative categories constitute the core of sedentarism or anti-nomadism, which McVeigh (1997) defined as "that system of ideas and practices which serves to normalise and reproduce sedentary modes of existence and pathologise and repress nomadic modes of existence" (p. 9) (see also Danaher et al., 2004). McVeigh traced the emergence of sedentarism to "the transition of the *predominant* mode of existence from nomadism to sedentarism" (p. 9; emphasis in original) according to which sedentary residence is associated with civilization (p. 13). For McVeigh, the emergence of the nation state and the project of modernity coincide with pressure for nomads to be settled and assimilated in order to ensure the final triumph of sedentarism (p. 17) (see also Dyer, 2006a).

A striking elaboration of the marginalizing effects of positioning mobility as deficit was presented in the sociohistorical account of Roma and other mobile groups by Lucassen, Willems, and Cottar (1998) (see also Danaher, 2001a, pp. 40-41), who referred to "the inclination to view itinerant groups predominantly as down and out riff-raff" (p. 2), and who identified a clear link among mobility, ethnicity, and marginalization:

> Our knowledge has been severely restricted not only because of historical negligence, but also because of two closely connected paradigms, one which views Gypsies and other itinerant groups as criminal, marginal and poor, and another which focuses almost exclusively on their alleged common ethnic identity and origin. (p. 2)

Thus contemporary framings of mobility are strongly and irrevocably influenced by longstanding ambivalence and in many cases hostility toward the phenomenon, reflected in the passage of the 1994 British Criminal Justice and Public Order Act, which had a significant effect on the policing of Travelers in the United Kingdom (Danaher et al., 2007, chapters 5 and 6). This book's focus on mobile learning communities is not limited to these historically grounded connotations of mobility but it must acknowledge and engage with them. After all, they constitute part of the complex range of challenges and opportunities attending such communities.

Dramatic evidence of the diversity of valorization of mobility presented in this subsection is contained in the contrast between two concepts portrayed in the current literature pertaining to mobility. One concept is "nomadic intelligence," which Fernandez, Mutabazi, and Pierre (2006) posited as a highly developed and late stage of immersion enacted in the identity work of international executives. As conceptualized by Fernandez, Mutabazi, and Pierre, nomadic intelligence exhibits a powerful array of dispositions and skills and is strongly positively valorized:

> This is why nomadic intelligence is not a purely cognitive process nor can it be reduced to righteous mechanics and synaptic connections. It lets itself be taken in and be surprised by events. It is driven by constant curiosity: it embraces unpredictability and overcomes fears of the unknown. It is intelligence as it always looks to the future and rests on past experience. One recognizes knowledge may stem from the unexpected; that ignorance is potentially fertile. Knowledge is no longer about absolute truths. It often becomes experienced knowledge as intuition and "sensitive listening" … develop. (p. 72)

This account suggests that nomadic intelligence is the logical concomitant of a romanticized idealism with regard to mobility. The characteristics of the concept are wholly positive and largely essentialized; despite the implied understanding of knowledge being situated, there is little apparent recognition of the politicized character of that knowledge or acknowledgment of the powerful, even elitist, positions, occupied by international executives. On this basis, we are cautious about applying the notion of nomadic intelligence to our analysis of mobile learning communities—at least not without taking account of some of these broader considerations.

The other concept is spatial identities, elaborated by Van Blerk (2005) in her study of the mobilities of homeless street children in Kampala, Uganda. Van Blerk noted the diversity of purposes for which these children move, especially "in order to escape visible 'otherness,' to access resources that are often realized through street networks, and to search for employment, excitement, or change" (p. 7). She distinguished between "nomadic mobility"—"itinerant movements that are undertaken while homeless" (p. 7)—and "episodic mobility"—"those movements that take place between homeless and non-homeless spaces" (p. 8). While acknowledging that "[n]ot all street children engage in the same forms of mobility" (p. 11), Van Blerk identified the children's three main itineraries as moving "between spaces in the city, between street and non-street locations and between Kampala and other towns" (p. 11). Her account also included some of the strategies used by the children to find alternatives to living on the streets. Her conclusion was that "street children's choice to engage in processes of mobility impacts on their identity" (p. 18), and that:

... for street children it appears to be the length of time spent in particular places that [is] important for influencing identity rather than the distance travelled. These wider temporal engagements influence and (re-)mould the extent to which children are drawn into street behaviours and how they identify themselves and are identified by others. (p. 18)

At one level, Van Blerk's (2005) account of Ugandan street children reflects the opposite end of the continuum in representing mobility from that illustrated by Fernandez, Mutazbasi, and Pierre's (2006) focus on international executives. Instead of romanticized idealism, her study evokes the pathologizing of mobility and its positioning as deviant and as dangerous to the stability of the nation state. The juxtaposition of the two studies therefore encapsulates some of the contradictory images and connotations underpinning the diversity of valorization of mobility.

More broadly, we acknowledge that spatial identities might be considered as essentialized and idealized as nomadic intelligence; certainly there is the conceptual risk of exoticization that accompanies researchers writing about marginalized groups (see also Danaher, 2000a). At the same time, we contend that Van Blerk's (2005) deployment of the concept of spatial identities is more politically engaged and theoretically nuanced than Fernandez, Mutabazi, and Pierre's (2006) application of nomadic intelligence. We also see considerable potential merit in using the intersection between place and space on the one hand and identity (understood as multiple subjectivities) on the other to explore some of the key features of mobile learning communities. That intersection can also inform the identification of possible options in creating new learning futures arising from that exploration.

Diversity of Educational Provision for Mobile Communities

The third diversity that we have identified in relation to contemporary mobilities focuses on educational provision. Table 0.1 represents an overview of the four principal forms of provision—assimilation, integration, segregation, and lobbying—with necessarily selective examples of each form taken from the literature.

Inevitably there are at least three important cautions to note in presenting and interpreting Table 0.1. First, it is not necessarily straightforward to decide whether a particular item is more appropriately located under "integration" or "specialization," and the juxtaposition of these two categories highlights a potential anomaly whereby a specialized program for mobile learners might be integrated within a broader form of educational provision (such as the Brisbane School of Distance Education's former specialist program for Australian show children [Danaher, 1998a]). Second, there is no automatic assumption that the categories closer to the far right column of the table necessarily constitute more appropriate and effective forms of provision for mobile communities; for example, what would seem to be the educational innovations of mobile

Table 0.1 Forms of educational provision for mobile communities

Assimilation	Itinerant farm workers attending a local school in North Queensland for the duration of the fruit picking season (Henderson, 2005)
	Parents sending their children to local schools, sending them to boarding schools, teaching them correspondence lessons, finding non-mobile employment for the duration of the children's schooling, sending the children to live with relatives and attend local schools, and not sending their children to school at all (Danaher, 2001a, p. 255)
Integration	English Traveler Education Support Services (Danaher et al., 2007; Derrington & Kendall, 2004; Kiddle 1999, 2000; O'Hanlon & Holmes, 2004; Tyler, 2005)
	Specialist provision for show children within the Brisbane School of Distance Education (Danaher, 1998a)
Specialization	Adult literacy classes for the nomadic pastoralist Rabari in northwest India (Dyer, 2000; Dyer & Choksi, 2006)
	Berth schools and mobile teachers for children living on Dutch barges (Scholten, 2000)
	Boarding schools for the pastoral nomads of Oman (Chatty, 2006)
	The Camel School Programme for nomadic pastoralist children in Samburu, Kenya (Krätli with Dyer, 2006, p. 17)
	National Schools for Travellers (Kenny, 1997)
	Project SMART (Summer Migrants Access Resources through Technology) in Texas (Meyertholen et al., 2004)
	The Queensland School for Travelling Show Children (Moriarty et al., 2004)
	The Romani School in Adelaide, South Australia (Morrow, 2005)
Lobbying	The Advisory Council for the Education of Romany and Other Travelers in the United Kingdom (Advisory Council for the Education of Romany and Other Travelers, 1993)
	The European Federation for the Education of Occupational Travelers (see for example Kiddle, 1999, pp. 104-105)
	The Gypsy Research Centre in Paris (Liégeois, 1998)
	The Migrant Education Binational Program linking at least 32 Mexican and 10 United States states (Flores & Hammer, 1996, p. 11)
	The National Association of State Directors of Migrant Education in the United States of America (see for example Beck, 2004, p. 229)
	The National Association of Teachers of Travellers in the United Kingdom (see for example Danaher et al., 2007a, chapter 2)
	The Nigerian National Commission for Nomadic Education (Umar & Tahir, 2000)

schools for Nigerian nomadic pastoralists have experienced limited success (Krätli with Dyer, 2006, p. 17). Third and relatedly, debate continues within the literature pertaining to the education of mobile communities about whether integration might also evoke inclusion (Jordan, 2000, p. 254) and whether specialization might signify segregation (Moriarty et al., 2004, pp. 33-34). As we explore in this book, the implications of mobile learning communities for creating new educational futures are complex and contentious rather than consensual and straightforward.

Despite these qualifications, a major theme underlying the diversity of educational provision for mobile communities is the ambivalent, even contradictory, role of the state. On the one hand, most of the examples of lobbying presented in Table 0.1 were established by national governments, sometimes through international cooperation—a situation that reflects the state's overwhelming control of the resources needed to provide formal education. On the other hand, the absence of real educational options for mobile communities encapsulated in the assimilation column in Table 0.1 attests to the power of the state, noted above, in striving to control and settle non-sedentary groups (Dyer, 2006a; McVeigh, 1997). In a real sense, the requirement for new educational futures derives in large part from the failure of current mainstream provision to resonate with the specialized circumstances and needs of learners such as members of such groups.

Similarly, although lobbying is strictly speaking not a form of educational provision, its inclusion in Table 0.1 reflects the ongoing importance of contesting received opinion and conventional wisdom and agitating for new forms of provision that engage with and facilitate the achievement of the specialized educational aspirations and opportunities of mobile and other communities. The envisioning and enactment of new educational futures depend on an openness to acknowledge an existing lack of educational fit and a willingness to consider possible alternative approaches.

More broadly, there are clear links, illustrated in Table 0.1, between pervasive and powerful structuring categories such as class and ethnicity and the kinds of educational provision available to different mobile communities around the world. From this perspective, place-based education—provision that requires learners to be in the same place for most or all of that provision—is complicit with wider forces of social segmentation and segregation within and across nation states. We argue that mobile learning communities simultaneously make that complicity explicit and challenge it, providing the foundation for thinking of additional and hopefully more inclusive and transformative forms of provision.

Learning Communities

Although mobilities and learning communities constitute separate fields of scholarship and literature, they have in common a significant variation on, and a vital challenge to, conventional formal education. While mobilities contest the sedentarist dimension of such education, learning communities question the largely individualistic and often competitive character of traditional schooling. Despite the growing prominence of social constructivist approaches to learning and teaching associated particularly with the Russian psychologist Lev Vygotsky, especially his concept of the Zone of Proximal Development (Vygotsky, 1934/1962, 1978), the default mode of assessment in schools, colleges, universities, and other sites of formalized education remains individual and competitive. This situation leads to a curious mismatch between rhetorical valuing of cooperation and sharing and practical privileging of learning and teaching that divide individuals and assign them to different—and differently valued—categories and ranks. The notion of a learning community is an intended antidote to this state of affairs, as is the growing realization that many learners are disengaged and alienated from formal education, as in the case of Australian university students whose studies represent only one part of their lived experiences (McInnis, 2001).

Kilpatrick, Barrett, and Jones (2003) discerned two distinct approaches to conceptualizing learning communities: highlighting communities' human element and the benefits of community members working together; and curricular structure directed at maximizing understanding of curricular content. Within the first approach, they asserted that "The broadest and most inclusive use of learning communities is to describe situations where an array of groups and institutions have united forces to promote systematic societal change and share (or jointly own) the 'risks, responsibilities, resources and rewards' (Himmelman, 1994, p. 28)" (p. 3). According to the second approach, which is centered on learning communities in educational settings, "Learning communities . . . are seen as benefiting individual learners, rather than the collective" (p. 5). From these two broad approaches, Kilpatrick et al. distilled the following definition that we are happy to nominate as a provisional conceptualization to guide our subsequent investigation of mobile learning communities:

> Learning communities are made up of people who share a common purpose. They collaborate to draw on individual strengths, respect a variety of perspectives, and actively promote learning opportunities. The outcomes are the creation of a vibrant, synergistic environment, enhanced potential for all members, and the possibility that new knowledge will be created. (p. 11)

From one perspective, this working synthesis resonates with the romanticized idealism of mobilities identified earlier in this introduction, whereby mobile learning communities are harmonious, productive, and free from debilitating conflict. From a different perspective, two claimed prerequisites of learning communities might seem to prevent mobile communities from joining the learning community ranks: that they are open systems, whereby "Learning through collaboration with people and groups external to the community introduces new ideas, raises awareness of new practices and exposes community members to new norms and value sets" (p. 9); and that they exhibit "Respect for diversity [that] enhances the learning capacity of a community" (p. 9) and "respecting diversity fosters learning by building a climate of trust and encouraging risk-taking" (p. 9). Given the centuries-old marginalization of many mobile groups and the active role played by formal education in that marginalization, most such groups find collaboration and trust within the group much easier to develop than with outsiders. Yet that development is clearly crucial to broader and longer-term interactions on which the creation of new educational futures in turn depends. This is why the debate about whether educational provision for mobile communities should be focused on integration and/or specialization continues—and continues to be fundamental to the operation of mobile learning communities.

Kilpatrick et al.'s (2003) evocation of learning communities highlighted four associated concepts (three explicitly and one implicitly) that are deployed in different chapters in this book to extend understandings of mobile learning communities. First, *communities of practice* (p. 7) have been defined as "individuals with common expertise participating in an informal relationship to resolve a shared problem or situation that impacts upon their shared futures" (Bowles, 2003, as cited in Kilpatrick et al., 2003, p. 7; see also Lave & Wenger, 1991; Wenger, 1998). The notion of communities of practice highlights members' intentionality, goal directedness, and focus on identifying and addressing perceived problems. While the conceptual shift from legitimate peripheral participation (Lave & Wenger, 1991) to the four dualities of participation versus reification, designed versus emergent, identification versus negotiability, and local versus global (Wenger, 1998) should be noted, our key interest in communities of practice lies in what they can offer us in terms of helping to explain how mobile communities can function as learning communities.

Second, *situated learning* was implicitly identified by Kilpatrick et al. (2003) through their citation of Lave and Wenger's (1991) focus on the concept, which is used to explain how the social relationships assumed to occur in communities of practice constitute the context within which knowledge is acquired and managed. Clearly for mobile communities to be learning communities they must provide a context of relationships, resources, and other elements that make such knowledge acquisition and management possible and desirable.

Third, *social capital* is "defined as norms, values and networks that can be used for mutual benefit" (Kilpatrick et al., 2003, p. 8). Learning communities (and communities of practice) might be presumed to facilitate, and to depend on, the development of social capital, which maximizes the value to community members of the networks and relationships within those communities. While social capital can be seen as not necessarily available equitably and as potentially exclusionary of non-community members, for traditionally marginalized mobile communities it represents a crucial possible vehicle for the generation of counternarratives to that marginalization and for the creation of new and more enabling educational futures for them and other groups of learners.

Fourthly, Kilpatrick et al. (2003, p. 6) identified *lifelong learning* as being, along with "learning opportunities" and "pro-active partnerships," the potential means by which community members "create new knowledge." While in one sense "lifelong learning" might be considered a tautology, on the assumption that learning occurs automatically through being alive, the term is increasingly used to denote sets of both dispositions and literacies that incline and enable individuals and groups to embrace formal, non-formal, and informal learning opportunities in order to enhance personal and collective forms of capital. From this perspective, mobile learning communities clearly need to demonstrate the features of lifelong learning if they are to expand their educational outcomes.

From this discussion it is evident that, like mobilities, learning communities are a diverse phenomenon whose proponents seek to create new forms of educational provision and new educational futures throughout individual lifespans and across multiple physical and virtual spaces (Longworth, 2006; Retallick et al., 1999; Watkins, 2005). Our goal in this book is to extend significantly the current literature on learning communities by highlighting the particular features, constraints, and opportunities of mobile versions of such communities and by linking those elements with some possible new educational futures that reduce the constraints and maximize the opportunities.

The Research Projects

Working in an overall research investigation that began in 1992 and that has continued unbroken since then through data collection and analysis and publication has some significant benefits, including generating a large volume of research data about a number of mobile learning communities and facilitating the authors' growing understandings of those communities. Yet that generation contains its own risks, principally the potential to be overwhelmed by the sheer amount of material. The data forming the evidence in this book have therefore been carefully selected from the period 1998 to 2003 to provide the most detailed information and the strongest argument in relation to each of the eight chapters in the book.

Despite the diversity of research projects reported here, the underlying research methods have had the following common characteristics: they are *qualitative* (in focusing on non-numerical data, particularly the recorded words of participants), *interpretivist* (in seeking to understand how the participants construct their lifeworlds), *phenomenological* (in giving central place in the analysis to the phenomenon of mobility), and *poststructuralist* (in recognizing the partial and personally influenced character of that analysis) (Somekh & Lewin, 2005). More broadly, these methods were directed at helping the authors to fulfill as far as possible the spirit of Anyanwu's (1998) definition of transformative research:

> Transformative research is a systematic enquiry into the real conditions which create oppression or hinder self-determination. It produces reflective knowledge which helps people to identify their situation and in doing so, to change such [a] situation for the better. In this regard, transformative research plays the important role of supporting the reflective process that promotes positive change. (p. 45)

This aspiration of contributing to "a systematic enquiry into the real conditions which create oppression or hinder self-determination" and of "supporting the reflective process that promotes positive change" clearly positions the authors as particular kinds of researchers (hopefully as engaged, interested, and situated as well as reflexive, rigorous, and systematic). It also throws into stark relief the ethical and political dimensions that are present in any research study (Anteliz et al., 2004; Moriarty, 2004). A key element of those dimensions has entailed the desire to avoid the shoals of idealizing, essentializing, exoticizing, and marginalizing mobile communities identified above, and instead to highlight their educational challenges, opportunities, and innovations and to link them with broader possibilities for creating new educational futures that might benefit all learners.

Data Collection

Table 0.2 provides more detailed information about the four specific research projects on which this book draws.

The principal means of data collection was audiotaped semi-structured interviews (and videotaped interviews in 1995), with a prepared interview schedule being used as a starting point but generally giving way to a freely flowing and organic conversation. Quotations from interview transcripts are identified in the book by a combination of project code and year and the speaker's role, so that AC2000 denotes an interview in 2000 with someone associated with the Australian circus community, while DB1999 refers to an interview in 1999 with a member of a Dutch bargee community. Inevitably some data sets within the interview corpus have had to be excluded from

Table 0.2 The research projects

Project code	Mobile community	Location of research	Year/s of research	Details of interviews	Researcher/s
AC	Australian circus people	Speers Point, Swansea, and Sydney, New South Wales; Bundaberg, Gladstone, Mackay, and Rockhampton, Queensland, Australia	1998 to 2000 inclusive	23 interviews with 1 child, 25 adults (including some parents), and 4 home tutors	G. Danaher P. Danaher P. Hallinan B. Moriarty D. Wyer
AS	Australian show people—Queensland School for Travelling Show Children	Brisbane and Southport, Queensland	2003	14 interviews with 20 show children, 6 parents, and 9 educational officials	G. Danaher P. Danaher M. Kenny B. Moriarty
BC	Belgian circus people	Leuven, Belgium	1999	1 interview with 1 adult	P. Danaher
DB	Dutch bargee people	Amsterdam, Rotterdam, and Werkendam, The Netherlands	1999	5 interviews with 2 parents and 2 teachers	P. Danaher
DC	Dutch circus people	Doetinchem, The Netherlands	1999	2 interviews with 2 parents and 2 teachers	P. Danaher
DS	Dutch show people	Heerlen, The Netherlands	1999	4 interviews with 4 adults	P. Danaher
EC	English circus people	Blackpool and Brereton Green, England	1999	2 interviews with 4 parents	P. Danaher
ES	English show people	Exeter and Plymouth, England	1999	4 interviews with 11 parents	P. Danaher
SS	Scottish show people	Edinburgh and Glasgow, Scotland	1999	10 interviews with 2 children and 15 parents	P. Danaher
TT	Traveler teachers	Brussels and Leuven, Belgium; Edinburgh and Falkirk, Scotland; and Bury, Derby, Fleetwood, Hertford, Leeds, London, Manchester, Oxford, Preston, Reading, Rochdale, Sheffield, Totnes, and Wolverhampton, England	1999	18 interviews with 26 teachers	P. Danaher
VS	Venezuelan show people	Caracas, Venezuela	1999	2 interviews with 2 parents	P. Danaher

the book for reasons of space. For example, the interviews with European policy-makers and teacher educators have largely been held over for other publications. The interviews with the two Dutch teachers working with bargee children have been included in order to compensate for that relatively small data set.

These semi-structured interviews were complemented and extended by means of informal observations and individual and collective reflections by members of the research team. Sometimes these reflections were recorded, whether as audiotaped reflections after an interview or as audiotaped discussions among team members during research trips or research retreats. The currency of the data has been maximized by ongoing contact and collaboration with other researchers working with mobile communities and with key members of those communities (for the latter, see for example Currie & Danaher, 2001; Fullerton et al., 2004; Fullerton et al., 2005; Moriarty & McDonnell, 1998).

Data Analysis

The approach to data analysis enacted throughout this longstanding research project has been incremental and iterative, with the analysis being framed and informed by a series of research questions and the application of several conceptual and methodological resources. This approach deployed textual and thematic analysis, with participants' words not being presumed to speak for themselves but at the same time appropriate respect being accorded to the integrity and value of those words. Rowan's (2001) development of transformative textual analysis was helpful as a model for drawing attention to the absences as much as to what was present in the transcripts and for highlighting the importance of identifying whose voices and values were privileged and whose were silenced. Thus the interview transcripts were territories of discursive flow and struggle that encapsulated a broader battle for meaning and understanding in relation to mobile learning communities.

In place of reliability and validity, as a qualitative study this research project was designed to fulfill the four interrelated goals of credibility, transferability, dependability, and confirmability (Lincoln & Guba, 1985; see also Harreveld, 2002, pp. 193-199). Thus, while we would not necessarily expect other researchers to arrive at the same conclusions that we have derived from our data analysis, we hope to have provided a sufficiently detailed audit trail for that analysis to be plausible in view of the evidence that we have amassed – and perhaps even persuasive.

The Book

Now that the key concepts associated with mobilities and learning communities have been introduced, and that the case for interrogating several contemporary manifestations of mobile learning communities and the research projects framing those manifestations have been outlined, we turn to the structure of the book, whose main text has been divided into eight chapters. While all three authors have been integrally involved in writing each chapter, primary responsibility for leading that writing is indicated here:

- Networks and partnerships (Patrick Alan Danaher)
- Lifelong learning: from the cradle to the grave (Beverley Moriarty)
- Technologies and their users (Beverley Moriarty)
- Globalization and interactions with the outside world (Beverley Moriarty)
- The knowledge economy and workplace learning (Geoff Danaher)
- Multiliteracies and meaning-making (Geoff Danaher)
- Communities at risk: building capacities for sustainability (Patrick Alan Danaher)
- Marginalization and transformation (Geoff Danaher)
- with Patrick Alan Danaher leading the writing of the introduction and the conclusion.

In each chapter, the focus is twofold: demonstrating how the selected element of a mobile learning community is enacted in one or more of the communities studied in the research project; and establishing links with current educational practice and suggested implications for enhancing that practice. The conclusion to the book examines at greater length the connections between mobile learning communities and the creation of new and hopefully more equitable, sustainable, and transformative educational futures.

1
Networks and Partnerships

To be effective and sustainable, mobile communities must develop and extend mutually respectful and beneficial networks and partnerships within and outside those communities. This chapter identifies a diversity of strategies by which mobile community members assess and engage in potential opportunities for establishing such networks and partnerships. The chapter also interrogates the crucial impact of those internal and external relationships on community members' access to efficient and equitable pathways into formal, non-formal, and informal learning.

Introduction

Why devote the first chapter in a book about mobile learning communities to discussing networks and partnerships? The answer is twofold. First, the basis of a community is social and emotional connectedness. This connectedness highlights that communities are more than loose collections of individuals, and that their members' aspirations and interests are inextricably intertwined and interdependent. Networks and partnerships act as mechanisms for making those relationships explicit and for helping to strengthen them against potentially competing pressures and priorities.

Second, and building on a point made in the introduction, mobile communities are in many respects marginalized by and from their sedentary counterparts. As this chapter demonstrates, the networks and partnerships that mobile communities create are crucial to reducing the impact of that marginalization and maximizing their effectiveness. From this perspective, expressions such as "safety in numbers," "critical mass," and "from the margins to the center" evoke the range of functions served by networks and partnerships in relation to mobile communities—including their learning dimension.

While networks and partnerships are interlinked conceptually and practically, it is important to differentiate their meanings. Networks are commonly connected with communication and computing systems, and imply generally informal and often extensive relationships among large numbers of participants. By contrast, partnerships signify a formalized and sometimes legalized association among participants, usually with an explicit statement of each partner's intended roles and responsibilities and anticipated benefits arising from the partnership. In combination, networks and partnerships enhance the strength and resilience of individuals as well as of the communities to which they belong, and in the educational arena they maximize opportunities for learning.

From this perspective, networks are not always aligned with partnerships, particularly when participants feel that formalizing their relationships might inhibit their interactions or restrict the benefits of their association. For example, networks understood as waves of resonance and the principle of morphogenic fields (Danaher et al., 2006a) highlight self-organizing systems and cooperative action to which partnerships might be unsuited. On the other hand, partnerships imply some kind of informal network leading to, and providing a framework for, the partnership's existence. Certainly effective partnerships depend on strong and dynamic networks to sustain them in times of tension and conflict.

Specifically in relation to mobile learning communities, this chapter outlines how functioning examples of those communities exhibit complex sets of both networks and partnerships, centered on the intersection between members' mobility and their learning opportunities and outcomes. These networks and partnerships are simultaneously internal and external to the communities, and they are enacted through relationships that are informal and intangible as well as formal and tangible. For the sake of simplicity, they can be visualized as collections of overlapping circles, as in Figure 1.1.

Yet this representation is idealized and formalized, because all relationships are implicitly equal in terms of power, duration, and impact and all participants are assumed to engage and benefit equally. A more realistic illustration of the networks and partnerships in mobile learning communities is presented in Figure 1.2, which uses the rhizomes conceptualized by Deleuze and Guattari (1987) to convey the multiple, non-hierarchical intersections and dead ends characteristic of human social life. Rhizomes are also effective in evoking the highly divergent strengths and longevity of individual relationships and the widely varied degrees of importance that such relationships contribute to the community's survival and sustainability.

A significant theme in the chapter is the impact of formal schooling systems on the networks and partnerships attending mobile learning communities. Such systems, themselves at the epicenter of different kinds of associations, can potentially challenge and disrupt the mobile communities' relationships, resulting in educational disjunctures. Yet they can also extend the learning outcomes of those communities, leading to enhanced mutual understandings that can in turn improve the operations of the schooling systems.

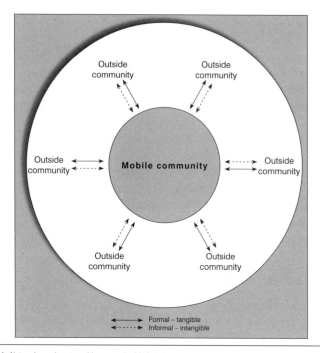

Figure 1.1 Networks and partnerships as embedded circles

Figure 1.2 Networks and partnerships as rhizomes

The chapter is divided into six sections:

- Networks and partnerships in the literature about learning communities
- Networks and partnerships in the literature about mobile communities
- Examples of networks in selected mobile learning communities
- Examples of partnerships in selected mobile learning communities
- Implications for the future education of mobile learning communities
- Implications for broader educational practice.

In particular, the chapter focuses on the strategies that mobile community members use to assess and engage in opportunities for participating in networks and partnerships. Attention is paid also to the effects of that participation on community members' access to and experience of formal, non-formal, and informal learning activities.

Networks and Partnerships in Learning Communities

Contemporary theories of learning such as social constructivism (Vygotsky, 1934/1962, 1978) are predicated on the formal and informal relationships that are also characteristic of networks and partnerships. These relationships clearly include those between learners and teachers, but they also encompass associations among learners, between learners and content, between learners and contexts, and between learners and the media or technologies deployed to facilitate learning. These relationships can be seen as both networks and partnerships. For example, while the interactions between student and teacher in a classroom have an overtly formalized and legalized character evocative of a partnership, their effectiveness often depends on both participants building up the rapport and trust more commonly connected with a network.

The purpose of this chapter is to explore how networks and partnerships are understood and experienced in necessarily selective literature about contemporary learning communities. Two such communities have been chosen: those related to online education and to teacher education professional experience. These are different specific manifestations of a broader phenomenon: the multiple and complex ways in which networks and partnerships intersect to create (and sometimes to constrain) opportunities for learning.

Networks in Online Education

While online education has been critiqued as exemplifying a broader onslaught on university learning and teaching (Brabazon, 2002), and while online learning can be just as disengaging and disempowering as face-to-face encounters, several researchers have pointed to the possibilities of developing lively and enduring communities of learners across boundaries of time and space (Luppicini, 2007). For example, Kehrwald (2007) identified effective strategies for maximizing learner support in online environments, and Kanuka (2002) highlighted ways of facilitating online discussion forums that will generate higher levels of learning.

A prominent theme in the online education literature is different forms of presence. This is not surprising. The absence of face-to-face interactions, particularly in asynchronous online environments, throws into stark relief what is assumed (sometimes erroneously) to be present in face-to-face situations: active and mutual interest and engagement on the part of learners and teachers alike. Anderson's (2004) differentiation among cognitive, social, and teacher presence elicits respectively three interaction modes considered essential components of effective education, regardless of mode: student–content, student–student, and student–teacher (Anderson & Garrison, 1998; see also Danaher et al., 2007).

Clearly presence implies strong and active networks of social connectedness. For instance, both cognitive presence and student presence require learners' direct and ongoing participation in the various elements of online environments, from reading content to interacting in discussion forums to taking part in team-based activities where applicable to completing summative assessment tasks. Similarly, Anderson (2004) distinguished among design and organization, facilitating discourse, and direct instruction as "three critical roles that a teacher performs in the process of creating an effective teaching presence" (p. 274). This distinction highlights the wide range of formal and informal networks to which online educators must contribute if learning outcomes are to be maximized.

The same applies to another significant concept in the online education literature: engagement, understood as active involvement and meaning-making (Danaher et al., 2009; Hafeez-Baig & Danaher, 2007). For example, Herrington, Oliver, and Reeves (2002) emphasized strategies designed to assist online students to suspend disbelief as one key strategy for enhancing learner engagement. Likewise Swan (2001) identified clarity of design, interaction with instructors, and active discussion among course participants as central to students' perceptions of factors promoting their engagement in asynchronous environments. These strategies and factors are posited on the establishment of multiple networks crossing space and time to bring learners into close alignment with one another, their teachers, their content, their contexts, and their educational technologies. Only then can online learning communities function and flourish.

Partnerships in Teacher Education Professional Experience

If we assume that contemporary teacher education is located within multiple and overlapping associations, at least some of which can constitute learning communities (Boling, 2003; Borko, 2004; Lieberman, 2000; Retallick et al., 1999; Swick, 2001), then it follows that the teacher education professional experience, whereby pre-service teachers spend time working with learners in educational settings outside their university classes, can be similarly conceived as a potential learning community. We argue that, for it to do so, effective networks and partnerships that facilitate learning by all groups of stakeholders need to be in place.

Certainly several studies attest to the dependence of the teacher education practicum experience on genuine and engaged collaboration among multiple participants (Brown & Danaher, 2008; Haigh & Ward, 2003; Krieg & Sharp, 2003; Ravid & Handler, 2001; Turner & Sharp, 2006). Interdependent partnerships of varying degrees of formality between university teacher education faculties and educational sites of practice are considered essential to promoting that collaboration (Borthwick et al., 2003; Soliman, 2001; Vickers et al., 2004; Zeichner, 2002). Yet, as Brown and Danaher (2008) pointed out, partnerships are constituted by multiple interests "that are almost inevitably in competition with one another to some extent" (p. 150). This view resonates with the comment by Beck and Kosnik (2002) about teacher education practicum partnerships: "Each group has its distinctive interests and biases" (p. 82). It articulates also with Vick's (2006) historical perspective, whereby issues connected with the teacher education professional experience "are embedded within the framework of assumptions and approaches that have shaped teacher education for over a century" (p. 181).

It is helpful at this point to note Cardini's (2006) conceptualization of educational partnerships in the United Kingdom (see also Brown & Danaher, 2008). That conceptualization is centered on the political dimension of such partnerships, whereby an outward show of democracy and inclusion masks what are often unequal relationships in which power is exercised by one partner over others. Cardini insisted that " … the theoretical definition of partnership has to recognize the issue of power and establish working relationships in which struggle and dissent are discussible and transformable issues" (p. 412). She elaborated this argument by identifying "three fundamental mismatches between theoretical and empirical definitions of partnerships" (p. 398):

> … although collaboration is presented as a main characteristic in theoretical definitions of partnerships, partnerships are spaces where cooperation is very hard to achieve; that although theoretical definitions present partnerships as a cluster of symmetrical and complementary sector partnerships, in practice partnerships tend to show asymmetrical and unbalanced relationships between different members; and finally,

that although the theoretical concept of partnership is directly linked to the idea of social and community participation, in practice partnerships seem to be the instrument to implement top down central policies. (p. 398)

Admittedly Cardini's (2006) focus was on educational partnerships initiated by the British government, clearly far more powerful than any of the partners with which it interacted. There is undoubtedly evidence that mutually respectful and inclusive partnerships can attend the teacher education professional experience (Cleary & Moriarty, 2006; see also Moriarty & Gray, 2003). Nevertheless the point being emphasized here is that networks and partnerships have a political character, that they are not always or automatically successful, and that all participants have to work hard to make them effective. This is certainly the case with the networks and partnerships to be identified in mobile learning communities.

Networks and Partnerships in Mobile Communities

All mobile learning communities exhibit, and depend on, networks and partnerships of varying reach and degrees of formality. These extensive and intersecting relationships underpin and enact the formal, non-formal, and informal educational opportunities that enable members of the communities to learn from and to teach one another and people of fixed residence. This mutuality of interest and diversity of experience have characterized mobile communities from earliest times and are a key element of their determined continuation well into the twenty-first century. This argument is demonstrated here by reference to examples of networks that exist among nomadic pastoralists, and instances of more formalized partnerships evident in English Traveler education.

Networks among Nomadic Pastoralists

The nomadic pastoralists who live and work in several countries in Africa and Asia display multiple kinds of networks of association, both internal and external to their mobile communities. One striking example of this phenomenon is the Bakkarwal people of Jammu and Kashmir in the western Himalayas, near the Indian–Pakistani border (Rao, 2006). Members of this community herd a variety of animals whose care requires them to migrate for a significant part of each year across physically inhospitable terrain shared with other groups competing for similar resources. Patrilineal and generally endogamous, the Bakkarwal live mostly within small family units, enlivened by occasionally larger gatherings such as wedding celebrations.

Within these demographic and socioeconomic contexts Bakkarwal children are socialized, in common with all communities, mobile and others

(Rao, 2006). In addition to the complex array of tasks associated with caring for their families' animals, the children are inculcated from birth into the "[m]anners and [m]orals" (p. 57) of their society. These range from items of clothing and dress to socially sanctioned body postures, reflecting what are regarded as appropriate relationships with, and attitudes toward, other community members and ultimately with Allah, the Bakkarwal being Muslims. The clearly demarcated phases of development from infancy to adulthood constitute sites of informal learning among several networks interior to the community, some segregated according to age and/or gender and others crossing those social categories. The emphasis is clearly on preparing the next generation of pastoralists with the attitudes and skills needed to continue this way of life beside a backdrop of challenge to and competition with that way of life.

It is against this backdrop that the Bakkarwal community's ambivalence toward formal schooling for their children (Rao, 2006) needs to be understood. On the one hand, this schooling, which tends to be state-managed, is regarded as a means of enhancing the children's economic well-being, the parents' security in old age, and the wealth and status of the community at large. On the other hand, some parents fear a perceived link between too much schooling and a child's ill health, occasioned by excessive introspection and worry. There is also some unease about the apparent disjuncture between the community's socialization of its children with its traditional way of life and values and the state's emphasis on a secular—and sedentarist—worldview (a theme that is also explored in Chapter 8). Rao encapsulated this disjuncture as the Bakkarwal children potentially "[g]rowing out of [s]ociety" (p. 61).

This same interplay between networks that are both internal and external to the mobile community and experiences of, and attitudes toward, learning of varying degrees of formality was evident among the Karretjie people of the Great Karoo in South Africa (de Jongh & Steyn, 2006). These peripatetic sheep shearers, descendants of the Karoo's original inhabitants but now Afrikaans speaking, call themselves "*Karretjiemense*" or (donkey) Cart People, "with reference to the donkey-drawn conveyance which carries them and all their worldly possessions when they move between temporary overnight camps" (p. 78). This resilient but potentially precarious lifestyle depends for its continuity on the elaboration and maintenance of a large number of complex networks, summarized as denoting internally "interpersonal relationships" among the Karretjie and externally the relationships associated with "economic and social imperatives" (p. 81). The latter encompass the interdependent but sometimes uneasy associations with farmers whose sheep the Karretjie shear and competition from groups of unionized shearers who come from outside the Karoo. More broadly, these networks both enable and constrain the informal and formal learning opportunities available to the Karretjie: their widely acknowledged skills as shearers are passed down from one generation to the next; yet they are largely invisible to the state, and are therefore excluded from formal schooling unless they eschew their nomadic lifestyle.

Partnerships in English Traveler Education

Partnerships, understood as more formalized relationships between mobile communities and other groups, are represented by the English TESSs, which constitute an enduring and generally effective association between the state and various communities of Travelers in England. The Services "evolved in piecemeal fashion" (Danaher et al., 2007, p. xiv) since the early 1980s, in response to a complex combination of legislative and social pressure and resistance. Varying considerably in terms of composition, size, and duration, the Services combine individualized support of Traveler children with liaising with local schools and developing distance education learning packs for the children to complete when they travel during the summer months.

Inevitably Travelers exhibit a range of perceptions of the Support Services, from engaged and appreciative to neutral to hostile. Nevertheless, according to most indicators the Services have succeeded in developing helpful partnerships with Travelers and a host of other participants and stakeholders (including schools, local education authorities, and other government officials). At their most successful, these partnerships have managed to cut—or at any rate to loosen—the Gordian knot that for generations has positioned mobility and formal education as mutually exclusive phenomena.

One striking example of this kind of partnership in practice has been the Devon Consortium Traveller Education Service (Kiddle, 1999, 2000). Cathy Kiddle (2000), who headed the Service from 1979 to 2002 and is an experienced researcher and author in her own right, highlighted "the importance of outreach work and developing trusting relationships with Traveler families as a prerequisite for the children to attend regularly and achieve high academic standards in school" (p. 269). In addition to the Service's ongoing work with Gypsy Travelers, Kiddle outlined the development of a large-scale project involving school-based distance education for fairground families, with learning packs devised in collaboration with the children's winter base schools. A crucial element was the involvement of the parents, and this was gained and strengthened over time, to the extent that parents became active participants in the Service's training sessions with new classroom teachers.

Kiddle (2000) acknowledged that this kind of partnership is not so easily generated with Gypsy Traveler families, whose mode of mobility and occupations (and associated reception by the broader community) differ markedly from those of fairground families: Gypsy Travelers "do not see an opportunity for power sharing" (p. 273) with educators. At the same time, it is important to take note of, and to take heart from, the hard won lessons learned in the partnership with the fairground families:

> ... a partnership demands power sharing, a mutuality of ground, an exchange between equals. These premises have first to be established before there can be the basis for a partnership. An assumption that the mutuality of ground was the concern for the children's education was insufficient. The two worlds of home and school were often pulling in different ways ... The relevance of one to the other was not necessarily evident to either parents or teachers, and neither could be relied upon to build on the children's learning in one world while they were in the other. (p. 271)

It is clear that the networks and partnerships influencing mobile learning communities involve a great deal of this kind of crossing the boundaries of multiple worlds. Within the communities individuals need to learn and negotiate the often unspoken and usually unwritten expectations of attitude and conduct deemed necessary for the group's continued survival. Outside the communities individuals and groups must engage with a multiplicity of others, from those with whom they are economically and occupationally interdependent to state officials to educational authorities to members of the mainstream population against which they are generally positioned as different, if not deficit and deviant (Danaher et al., 2007; Danaher et al., 2004). In this context it makes sense for mobile communities to enlist the support of both insiders and outsiders in order to secure the best possible prospects for their livelihood and their education alike.

Networks in Selected Mobile Learning Communities

Networks of various kinds and with multiple functions featured prominently in the discourses of the participants in the research projects reported in this book. Sometimes these took the form of small-scale associations among individuals seeking to develop links across the different worlds identified above. One instance was when an English Traveler teacher drew on her connections at a Traveler site to maintain contact with Traveler families who were traveling during the summer months:

> So in the summer I would endeavor to either have the whole [distance education] pack ready to go away with the family, again depending on their pattern, and they would send it back regularly. Or I would send them away a couple of weeks at a time, and then continue to send over the summer, depending on what my network is for getting it there, the delivery. I have a granny who lives on site. She used to be very useful, and works at one of the schools as well, so it's very useful for her to live there ... So she's been very helpful, not only for her own immediate family, but when I had other families up in the yard traveling I could leave things with her, and she would get them back. If people passed

through, she would telephone me and tell me she had them, so we had a good relationship there. (TT1999)

The same teacher discerned a diversity of capacities within Traveler families to exploit available educational opportunities that she linked with socioeconomic status:

> That again depends where in the economic system they are, because, just like in the settled population, you've got those families that are really quite poor and can't afford to miss [working] anywhere. You've got others that are extremely well-off ... and therefore could afford to [stop longer in one place to advance their children's schooling]. Or have a better infrastructure in the family network that they're able to say, "Well, you do that while I go and do this." That is different with each set of families. Some are very supportive, and others are not. You sort of learn [with] who[m] you can say, "Would you give this to the family?" and they will. And others won't. But isn't that the same everywhere? (TT1999)

Effective networks can also occur when individuals change roles, taking with them into their new positions the accumulated knowledge and contacts of previous personas. For example, a female social worker liaising with Dutch bargee families found that her credibility was enhanced by virtue of being a member of a longstanding shipping family, and that the professional networks between the families and her were strengthened by this additional connection of shared experience: "They know who I am. There is no trouble to ask me something ... They say, 'I am here but I have to ask you something'. So it's more informal here" (DB1999). Likewise an English Traveler teacher noted that the relatively small population of bargee children in England "who live on the canals, part of the communication network" (TT1999) needed to take advantage of that network to compensate for their reduced numbers.

At a broader, more macro level, networks are also crucial to building national associations of like-minded individuals and groups working toward a common goal, despite sometimes considerable diversity of backgrounds and approaches. One example related to the various circus communities in England:

> ... we try to encompass everything. Because traditional circus and contemporary circus are all part of the same spectrum—they're just at opposite ends. Basically we're all traveling the same road. The metaphor—we're all on the same motorway, but coming in on different slip routes. We're all going the same way and we should be working together. And we are. Things have changed dramatically in certainly the last five years. There's been a coming together of the professional circus, the circus organizations, the circus training schools, the contemporary

circus network, and the youth circus: we've all been gradually coming together. (EC1999)

The same speaker outlined how such national networks could at times take on an international dimension if other factors were favorably aligned:

So we then decided we'd form the [Network of International Circus Exchange], which we did … It was constituted as a voluntary youth organization, as an umbrella association, with a mission statement which is to promote development in circus arts for, with, and by the people. Built into that there's all the business about lobbying and getting it recognized, providing support networks, facilities for collaborative working. More and more it's become European wide as well, because I'm backwards and forwards quite a lot to Europe. (EC1999)

A different member of an English circus community mused on the strategies (and the associated networks) that enhanced that community's profile and work as well as on the factors that appeared to militate against that enhancement:

… we do, through our social involvement policy, aim to reach as many young people as possible … who would benefit from the experience that we could offer. We don't set ourselves up as knowing who they are. So we work in collaboration with the Social Services and the Community Education Office who do know who they are, and through their youth club networks and through their contact networks we will be brought into a face-to-face situation, if that's possible. (EC1999)

The importance of maximizing the international dimension of networks to promote the learning of mobile communities has a particular focus in Europe, where members of those communities regularly cross national borders. The pioneering work of the European Federation for the Education of the Children of Occupational Travellers (EFECOT) between 1988 and 2004, under the auspices of the European Commission, was very effective in building on existing networks among Traveler communities and establishing new ones. As one member of a Dutch bargee community noted:

… when I found out that a lot of people who navigate internationally, or at least European … [w]e need also contact points in the other countries, and EFECOT could provide me with this network. So I could benefit from an already existing network that I didn't have to build up myself …[S]o I'm very glad that already in the organization that EFECOT existed, and the network was small when I started, but when I see it after 10 years it expanded, and more partners from other countries joined it. (DB1999)

Another Traveler educator associated with the work of EFECOT elaborated the close connection between inter-community networking and a reduction in community isolation, with the prospective benefits of shared understandings and learning opportunities:

> I [can] give you a concrete illustration of it. When EFECOT started organizations linked with the bargee community never had contact with organizations representing the fairground community or the circus community. Now many organizations that we have in the network of EFECOT, they know each other although, they are not working on behalf of [or are] linked with just the bargee community. These cross-links are made—that's a result of the network. That … was, and still is, creating [a situation in which] these organizations don't feel isolated any more, not at a national level, not in the European context. That's I think we may say as a result of working together in this network. (TT1999)

On the other hand, this same educator explained how differences among mobile communities impacted significantly on their respective capacities to take up the educational potential afforded by these kinds of community, national, and international networks:

> … some of the traveling communities are well organized at the professional level. If you see the inland navigation [bargee community] in Europe, they have their professional organization, at a national level, at a European level. This is of course an important advantage because, if you can involve these organizations and if you can convince them of their responsibility vis-à-vis education, this is a big step forward. The same you can say for the fairground communities, but the big problem is that the circus community … and the seasonal workers … are not professional organizations. So there in fact you rely on social organizations, pastoral organizations, who are in the field working for these individual families. (TT1999)

A different Traveler educator, also reflecting on the work of EFECOT, echoed this posited link between networks and a professional approach to educational provision for mobile communities in Europe:

> … between the work of the European Commissioner, the funding of the European Commission, you have a very large network from EFECOT, partners, EFECOT members, and the professionalism position is much … stronger. It's a very professional, high level network, and it's not only a network on paper—it's like a strong family. (TT1999)

Clearly networks wax and wane as circumstances change, and few if any networks are guaranteed permanence. In 2004 EFECOT ceased to function, and there is a concern that the effective work of bringing together previously disparate groups is likely to be reversed, and with it the new understandings of various mobile communities among community members and sedentary residents alike.

Finally in this section, a different dimension of the multiple local, national, and international networks influencing mobile communities was articulated by a member of a Venezuelan show community (VS1999). As the proprietor and manager of a large fairground, he spoke about the interdependence between his organization and members of the public. He also indicated that, while he potentially employed new workers from fairgrounds in other parts of the country, he insisted on training them himself. He spoke as well about the human and non-human networks centered on technology. For example, he took note of what customers said that they wanted in relation to new equipment, and in his annual visits to the technology factory in Italy he sought to collect the parts belonging to the latest equipment, which he assembled on his return to Venezuela. He also noted that changes in currency exchange rates had recently made it much more expensive for him to buy the Italian parts. Thus a single fairground ride is part of a complex web of intersecting and sometimes conflicting networks of relationships, money, and technology.

Partnerships in Selected Mobile Learning Communities

As with networks, so too partnerships were evident with varying degrees of explicitness in the discourses of the participants in this research. A few respondents referred to this concept in the context of their marriages and families. For example, one member of an English circus community reflected on the fortunate complementarity of her husband's and her respective skill sets: " … it's just a partnership. It's just lucky that we fitted in quite well together" (EC1999). Another member of the same community confirmed a finding from our research with Australian circuses, that the professional and personal elements of family relationships needed to be kept separate:

> So even if you had arguments, you still in the end—it doesn't come into it … Your husbands, wives, and partners work together. I know people who actually didn't speak, didn't socialize for years, and [who] worked together … So when they were in the ring and the performance came on, they were professional. (EC1999)

One of the Traveler educators focused on a different perceived benefit of partnerships, which is to provide the respectful insights about particular communities to which members of those communities are oblivious by virtue of belonging to them:

> … we set up … to have an external partner who can offer us a good mirror. Because we are in the middle of it, and then it's necessary for somebody to say, "Hey, hold on a minute. Because do you still have an

idea what's going on there?" … They are offering us in a very constructive way a lot of input …, so not only we will have hopefully good ideas for future evaluation but the process itself now even at this moment has given us a lot of new perspectives [and] fresh ideas to continue. (TT1999)

Another Traveler educator reflected how effective partnerships can be at maximizing shared understandings and reducing personal and communal isolation, even though the latter can sometimes be stubbornly resistant to amelioration:

People came together. People who worked with showmen's children and circus children came together through these partnerships, and what they found out and still find out is that parents and teachers often think they have a problem. They never see that the problem is much … bigger, that they are not standing alone. (TT1999)

Likewise a member of an English circus community with an educational role identified a crucial connection between partnerships and enduring improvement in social attitudes and educational opportunities: "It's looking at developing partnerships between the arts in the broadest sense, the curriculum, the community, and business. It's all about systemic change. The long-term goal is systemic change—that is, changing the establishment's view of how we teach" (EC1999).

While generally endorsing the value of this kind of external partnership for enhancing the educational options of mobile communities, a member of a Scottish show community noted some potential contradictions that resonated with the Gordian knot identified earlier:

It's an interesting thing, Traveler education, because education and our way of life, there is a tension there. It will be interesting to see if Traveler education does become more successful, and I think it should do [so] … Now there's a greater sense of partnership that will improve, and there will be more Travelers getting educated. The thing is of course if they do actually take on higher education, for example. There are many things in that which challenge their own way of life. I've found in my heritage my thoughts are challenged by things I've learned at school … Education will challenge it in a lot of different ways. I don't know if all Travelers realize that. Maybe some of them still think they can either take it or leave it; they can just take what they want. They will affect a generation which is able to benefit. It does more than they perhaps think and it will challenge many of the things that they are told by their parents, the things that are common knowledge or just taken for granted by us. I think all along it will all be a challenge; there will be tensions. It will not be all plain sailing. There'll be give and take. There'll be things lost from it; there'll be things gained. (SS1999)

At the same time, the same respondent acknowledged some significant advances in unraveling the Gordian knot:

> I think it does seem to be developing now in a way which is more conducive to our way of life; it does seem to accept that we have a right to live our way of life if we want to, and they have to try and accommodate it rather than saying, "Settle down in a house and go to school like everyone else, and shut up." Different techniques are being suggested and used. At least they're accepting our right to difference, our right to be who we are. (SS1999)

Commitment to this same unraveling, whereby the intersection between mobility and formal education can be enacted in ways that are complementary and capacity building rather than contradictory, was expressed by one of the Traveler educators:

> I think one of the interesting things about some of the more recent government legislation has been the flexibilities that are occurring from 14 plus onwards for instance, where we can demonstrate a very real linkage and partnership between family-taught skills—if we're talking about showmen's youngsters—and the school curriculum. For instance, there's the ability now to organize a school or a learning experience partly which can be vocational and partly which can be academic. I think [for] Traveler youngsters it's the meeting point—the point where they can begin to see the real relationship and their experiences, and actually how they can complement each other. (TT1999)

Implications for the Future Education of Mobile Learning Communities

This chapter has demonstrated that mobile communities exhibit a large number of internal and external networks and partnerships of widely divergent type and function. Many of these networks and partnerships are connected, alternatively explicitly or implicitly, with various forms of learning, whether that relates to on-the-job training in any of the community's specialist skills or whether that articulates with different kinds of formal educational provision, sometimes initiated by the community (as with the appointment of tutors who travel with the community as they teach the children) and sometimes by the state (as with the peripatetic schools that traverse the community's itineraries, the support services such as in England, or the local schools that some of the mobile children attend).

The chapter has demonstrated also that a diversity of strategies has been enacted by members and non-members alike of these mobile communities to mobilize networks and partnerships with a learning dimension. These strategies have ranged from careful reflection and close communication within the communities about likely partners to working with other groups—some of whom are like-minded and others of whom provide insights gleaned from very different experiences and perspectives—to forming alliances at local, national, and international levels. These strategies are not always successful and they require ongoing commitment and mutual goodwill and trust.

The chapter has explored as well some of the potential convergences and disjunctures that these networks and partnerships help to create through their impact on mobile communities and educational systems. EFECOT was one example of where that impact was largely positive, with important lessons being learned among multiple and very different partners. Yet EFECOT's closure was a timely reminder that networks and partnerships are not necessarily permanent or assured, and that they are always situated in time and place. Recalling Cardini's (2006) conceptualization of the politicized character of educational partnerships, there was also evidence presented that networks and partnerships are not always effective at breaking the Gordian knot that positions mobility and formal education as irreconcilable opposites; often tensions remain and compromises are inevitable.

At this point it is useful to recall Cardini's (2006) articulation of "three fundamental mismatches between theoretical and empirical definitions of partnerships" (p. 398):

> ... although collaboration is presented as a main characteristic in theoretical definitions of partnerships, partnerships are spaces where cooperation is very hard to achieve; that although theoretical definitions present partnerships as a cluster of symmetrical and complementary sector partnerships, in practice partnerships tend to show asymmetrical and unbalanced relationships between different members; and finally, that although the theoretical concept of partnership is directly linked to the idea of social and community participation, in practice partnerships seem to be the instrument to implement top down central policies. (p. 398)

It is crucial to consider these three potential disjunctures if mobile communities are to achieve maximum access to efficient and equitable pathways into formal, non-formal, and informal learning. In particular, and precisely because mobility is positioned as "other" in relation to sedentarism, networks and partnerships attending the learning dimension of mobile communities are potentially at risk of such relationships leading to co-option by and complicity with sedentarism. If this scenario is to be avoided, mobile communities and the many individuals and groups who work with them must develop and extend networks and partnerships that are mutually respectful and beneficial both within and outside those communities. We return to this idea in Chapter 8 and the conclusion, in the form of the suggested principle of articulation.

Implications for Broader Educational Practice

The cautious ambivalence of the previous section is enlivened to some extent by the hopeful optimism communicated by one of the participants in the research quoted in this chapter who was enthusiastic about networks and partnerships in the educational domain:

> The other part [that] I think is very important is that … mobility, not only in … global life, is growing. [The s]tructures of mobile teachers, mobile education system[s], open [and] distance [education] based on certain modules … I think are very useful for the future education, and these small target groups—if it works with mobile groups, you can use it with sedentary clients also. I think one of the things we don't use enough is the special position to offer your special position for general education to read a kind of a pilot garden. That's a pity, and it's also again because most of the [educational institutions] are settled. We do our work, and the organizations around … are not open enough and not political enough to do something. (TT1999)

This proposition resonates strongly with a major theme of this book: that mobile learning communities often enact educational innovativeness and the capacity for creating new educational futures that mainstream educational systems should look to and take account of in the ongoing struggle to regenerate and re-inspire. This is partly because of the respondent's reference to such systems not being "open enough and … political enough to do something." While not all mobile communities are necessarily "open enough" or exhibit the political will needed to stimulate productive change, evidence has been provided in this chapter of the willingness and capacity of many members of such communities to do precisely that.

In writing this, we acknowledge that, as we noted earlier in the chapter, contemporary educational provision is planned and implemented through a complex mesh of networks and partnerships, as in the case of online education and teacher education professional experience outlined above. What the diverse data presented in the chapter have highlighted is three key implications for broader educational practice in relation to those networks and partnerships.

The first implication is the intrinsic analytical utility of identifying and mapping the networks and partnerships associated with specific educational settings and systems. This is central to locating the multiple participants and stakeholders, some more visible and longstanding than others, with some kind of stake and investment in the success of a particular learning institution or project. Devising strategies for establishing and maintaining communication with these participants and stakeholders is also an important part of this process.

The second implication is articulating and reflecting upon the separate and shared interests and aspirations of the members of the educational networks and partnerships. From both Cardini (2006) and the research participants quoted in the chapter it is clear that individuals and groups, whether members of the same community or from different communities, have widely divergent goals, some complementary and others potentially in conflict with the intentions and priorities of others. The broader and more encompassing the network or partnership is, the greater this divergence is likely to be. This is an important element of the diversity of human social life, and it can lead to unexpected synergies and outcomes that can extend understandings and expand the community's critical mass and scale of operations. Yet it can also close down communication and promote fragmentation and fracturing of that same community. While the difficulties should not be underestimated, highlighting and thinking about convergent and divergent interests and aspirations are ways of making such a negative effect less likely to occur.

The third implication is the importance of developing and deploying an appropriate evaluative framework for examining the effects and effectiveness of educational networks and partnerships. Whether explicitly or implicitly, consciously or unconsciously, the participants in the research reported here generally had clear ideas about what a particular network or partnership might—or might not—bring to the potential learning opportunities and experiences of a mobile community. Those clear ideas were based on an assessment of the extent to which involvement in the network or partnership was likely to lead to educational provision constituted in terms of the community's specific patterns of mobility and current learning practices. Such an evaluative framework for the broader educational community would need to interrogate the degree of fit between community members' goals and the likely impact on the attainment of those goals of participating in the network or partnership under review.

Questions for Reflection

- How useful do you find the definitions of, and the distinction between, "networks" and "partnerships" presented in this chapter? How else might we conceptualize the multiple relationships impacting on educational settings and systems?
- What would a map of the educational networks and partnerships in which you are involved look like? Who are the principal players? Who are the less powerful participants? How do you know?
- Which parts of these networks and partnerships have greatest impact on your educational opportunities and experiences? Has that impact been largely positive, neutral, and/or negative? How do you know?
- How would you go about devising a framework for evaluating the educational impact and effectiveness of the networks and partnerships

that are most directly relevant to you? Which criteria would you draw on? How would you measure those criteria in action?

- What do you think about the strategies articulated by the research participants quoted in this chapter in relation to mobilizing various types of networks and partnerships to maximize their learning outcomes? How effective do you consider those strategies to be and why? What other kinds of strategies should they consider mobilizing?
- What do you think of the idea of mobile learning communities as the potential sites of educational innovation with possible implications for mainstream systems? If you agree with the proposition, why might that be the case? If you disagree, why is that so?

Suggestions for Further Reading

Bruggeman, J. (2008). *Social networks: An introduction.* London: Routledge.

Christensen, S. L., & Reschly, A. L. (2009/in press). *Handbook of school–family partnerships.* London: Routledge.

Hadfield, M., & Chapman, C. (2009/in press). *Leading school-based networks.* London: Routledge.

Todd, L. (2006). *Partnerships for inclusive education: A critical approach to collaborative working.* London: Routledge.

Tsui, A. B. M., Edwards, G., Lopez-Real, F., Kwan, T., Law, D., Stimpson, P., Tang, R., & Wong, A. (2008). *Learning in school–university partnership: Sociocultural perspectives.* London: Routledge.

2
Lifelong Learning
From the Cradle to the Grave

What does lifelong learning mean in the context of the lives of mobile community members who move on a regular basis and take with them all or most of the artifacts that are needed for day-to-day living, learning, and earning? This chapter addresses this question by examining the roles that are played by personnel who travel as part of these communities, how those roles are learned, and how they are taught. It also looks at learning that is not specifically connected with traditional roles in a strict sense but which is necessary in order to respond to changing circumstances, attitudes, and interests outside the community.

Introduction

Lifelong learning and community are two concepts that are inextricably linked and mutually reinforcing in mobile learning communities. Mobile learning communities combine the common goals of their members with the ability of those members to contribute in different but complementary ways to the sustainability of the community. They provide a natural context for continuous learning throughout the lifespan. This is largely because they consist of a cross section of people over different periods of the lifespan from infancy to old age who adopt roles that are more complementary than they are common and are learned and taught within the community. Mobile learning communities differ somewhat from communities of practice, therefore, which emphasize common expertise among members as described by Lave and Wenger (1991) and Wenger (1998).

Mobile learning communities, however, are not entirely insular. This is an ancient phenomenon; even when mobility was the only form of living before agriculture was invented, the survival of mobile communities depended as much on an awareness of and a response to outside influence and threat as it did on interactions within the community. In mobile learning communities, therefore, part of the lifelong learning journey of members involves the learning and teaching of roles that respond to changes in circumstances, attitudes, and interests in the outside world.

While access to formal learning and formal qualifications is an enduring problem for mobile learning communities, the context in which members of mobile communities live and work can also be a context that is ideally suited to informal learning that leads to the acquisition of roles and skills to sustain the community and individual interests. It is informative to draw on Kilpatrick et al. (2003) reference to lifelong learning as being formal, non-formal, and informal. The latter two dimensions of lifelong learning provide members with more opportunities to extend both their own interests and those of the community as they live, learn, and earn through interactions both within their community and with the outside world.

The following review of selected literature initially draws on speakers at international conferences on lifelong learning to provide a way forward in identifying researchers into lifelong learning who have developed frameworks that have been drawn upon by many other writers and researchers. Two frameworks that have had wide coverage are the four pillars of lifelong learning, a policy described by Delors (1996) and emerging from the European Union, and the pragmatic conception in common usage of lifelong learning as formal, informal, and non-formal. These frameworks have been applied to a wide range of situations. Their application to different types of mobile learning communities presented later in the chapter is helpful not just in conceptualizing lifelong learning in these situations but also in disrupting and contesting traditional, taken for granted assumptions underlying decisions that lead to the inequitable provision of formal and credentialed learning across the lifespan depending on whether one is mobile or of fixed residence.

Contexts for Lifelong Learning, Earning, and Living

Much of the literature and research that focuses on lifelong learning does not give a definition of the term, either in a more general sense or specific to context, but assumes understanding. Obtaining a definition of lifelong learning that is universal can be as elusive as finding a shared understanding of the term "globalization." It is difficult and not particularly meaningful to speculate as to why this is the case but perhaps more important here to draw on definitions that have been provided by a few key writers or to deduce meaning or definitions from usage in the literature and practice.

André Grace (2006) noted that lifelong learning was an international concept that had its origins just after the conclusion of World War I, was inherently complex, and had a meaning that constantly changed over time. Part of the complexity and the development of meaning over time may be attributable to the application of the concept to a wide variety of contexts. The accumulation of material thus produced could then be regarded as an opportunity to look for patterns across contexts and usage that may not have been explicitly stated in individual cases but become apparent when surveying the field.

Out of this usage emerged several definitions or descriptions of lifelong learning and these have since been referred to by numerous authors. For example, the four pillars of lifelong learning in a policy framework outlined by Delors (1996), and the recognition of lifelong learning as being formal, informal, and non-formal, are now fairly standard in the literature and have been applied in a wide range of contexts. Each application to a different context has the potential to enrich further the already developed understandings as well as to test the extent to which and the ways in which the conception applies to the new context, although perhaps the latter could be considered still to be very much part of the potential and not so much of the reality. Examining what lifelong learning means among mobile learning communities draws out parallels between people who are mobile and people of fixed residence while also highlighting the difficulties that being mobile poses not only for formal learning but also for the credentialing of learning.

The four pillars of lifelong learning as originally espoused by Delors (1996) have been lucidly described by Luck (2004) and Burnett (2008). *Learning to know* involves the acquisition of skills around concentration, memory, and thinking. *Learning to do* is an investment in the future because it relates to the ability to learn and apply skills that will be needed at a later date. *Learning to live together and with others* involves not only respecting other people, which is important, but also a deeper understanding of others' cultures that is steeped in mutual respect and dependence based on a recognition of the ways in which people are similar to one another. *Learning to be* recognizes the importance of education in the all-round development of the person: mind, body, and spirit. It can be argued that these four pillars can be promoted through lifelong learning that is formal, informal, and non-formal in mobile learning communities in and through which members meet most of their needs in terms of learning, earning, and living.

The concept of formal learning possibly needs little introduction because few people would hesitate when asked to define the concept. Regardless of the extent to which an individual has engaged or is engaging with formal education, the most common description given would relate to formalities of structures, such as found in universities, schools, and other institutions where qualifications are gained and students proceed incrementally through levels and even from one institution to another, such as secondary schooling commonly being a prerequisite for entry to colleges and universities. Informal learning as a concept may also be fairly commonly acknowledged, even if the mention of non-formal learning might then bring into question one's understanding of the concept of informal learning.

Commonly accepted definitions of formal, non-formal, and informal learning as described above are found in the literature, with writers drawing on one another, an example being Luck (2004) drawing on Coombs with Prosser and Ahmed who drew upon the seminal work of Smith (2001).

Life-wide learning has also been described as formal and informal (Beddie, 2004), occurring not just in educational institutions but also in community organizations and the workplace, the latter two being much more accessible for mobile learning groups. Others (for example, Tunijnman & Bondard, 2001), as noted by Grace (2006), have also included the home in this list and maintain that optimal progress in literacy is achieved by drawing on all life-wide and lifelong learning experiences.

In such conceptions, a parallel can be seen between formal and non-formal learning in that both are deliberately organized, with the latter falling outside systemic educational mainstream provision but nonetheless being applied to learners who have identifiable and particular needs. Examples of non-formal learning that reach us through advertisements include courses in weight loss or meditation. These advertisements may be promulgated through television or radio advertising, via pamphlets in the mail box or on Internet sites that we visit.

Informal learning, on the other hand, has been referred to as a:

> ... truly lifelong process whereby every individual acquires attitudes, values, skills and knowledge from daily experience and the educative influences and resources in his or her environment—from family and neighbours, from work and play, from the market place, the library and the mass media. (Luck, 2004, pp. 2-3)

The complex interplay of these multiple forces with informal lifelong learning is graphically portrayed in Figure 2.1.

The informal world, as described by Eneroth (2008), is full of unintended occurrences that accumulate to the point where the individual acquires an increasing ability to cope with such isolated incidents. Such capabilities, it can be appreciated, could be helpful when mobile learning communities travel through settled communities that are both different from one another and different from themselves.

This does not mean that formal and non-formal education are separate from the lifelong learning process and that this is the domain of informal education, but that informal learning occurs continuously, almost as a subtext, while formal and non-formal education have stricter boundaries regarding lengths of different experiences and places where this learning occurs. The overlap between non-formal and informal learning is particularly well illustrated in mobile learning communities, as is shown later. Luck (2004), who acknowledged the overlaps among types of learning, particularly between informal and non-formal learning, made the eloquent statement:

> I have always felt that lifelong learning begins in the womb and ends on one's deathbed. All of us are learning all the time just through living and interacting with people, the media, and the environment. This is common sense to me. (p. 24)

Figure 2.1 The multiple forces of informal lifelong learning

Formal learning, therefore, is the easiest to define and has the most consistent usage. It has continued to receive prominence more than a decade after the Delors Report was published because statistics that point to the large numbers of children around the world recently found not to be able to access formal learning and qualifications, even at elementary level, is still alarming (Burnett, 2008). Perhaps of even more concern are the high levels of illiteracy, which confirms that children and adults whose access to formal education is problematic are often not gaining these basic skills by alternative means, such as through non-formal or informal education.

In particular, Burnett's (2008) reference to the 72 million children throughout the world without access to formal schooling in 2000, even though this was a reduction on previous estimates, highlights the relatively inequitable access to schooling by children who are regarded as being on the margins of society. Most prominently regarded as on the margins are children living in parts of Africa, Asia, and the Arab states, particularly girls. The barriers to schooling mentioned by Burnett include residential factors, poverty, ethnicity, and having a disability. Within this list of barriers or included as part of residential factors, we argue, emphasis should be given to mobility because the mobile learning communities that we and others have studied, regardless of options that may theoretically be available to them for schooling, in practice often find it difficult to access those options without relinquishing the mobile lifestyle that families have embraced for generations and that is often central to their identities and meaning-making.

Researching Lifelong Learning Practices in Mobile Learning Communities

Just as lifelong learning practices have been studied in a wide range of contexts with people of fixed residence, the concept of lifelong learning has also been applied to the examination of many mobile learning communities. These communities represent different parts of the globe as well as different types of mobile learning groups, including show or fairground people in different parts of the United Kingdom, Australia, the Netherlands, and Venezuela, Dutch bargees, and circus people in the United Kingdom, the Netherlands, and Australia.

Consistent across all of these studies as well as research involving people of fixed residence in terms of using existing frameworks to examine lifelong learning practices is that frameworks drawn from Delors (1996) and others have been reaffirmed and enriched by the variety of evidence. The use of common frameworks to examine lifelong learning in different contexts also provides independent ways of analyzing data, such that the focus allows some distance to emerge between preconceived or pre-existing prejudices or allegiances and the analysis and conclusions.

Before an examination of the ways in which conceptions of lifelong learning are applicable to particular mobile learning communities is undertaken, there are preliminary considerations that can be tested to determine whether the conceptions more broadly are likely to be appropriate. In order for a conceptual framework to be inclusive of all aspects of life in a mobile learning community, it needs to be able to encompass the full range of interactions that occur not only within the community but between community members and the outside world. Any framework that could not be extended to the examination of outside interactions, for example, would not be inclusive of the full range of interactions and would need to be coupled with another framework, extended in its own right, or not used.

An overview of Delors' (1996) four pillars of lifelong learning gives no cause for concern in this regard. The third pillar, relating to *learning to live together and with others*, when applied to mobile learning communities, is important in its capacity to be applied to interactions outside the community because the continued existence of mobile learning communities depends very much on the ability of members and the community as a whole to gain acceptance by the communities not only through which they pass but also in which they stay for a while and with which they have some financial interdependence— for example, with some groups in entertaining the local people. Respect as well as understanding of the cultures of other people are key platforms of the third pillar, although the extent of this understanding when applied to education might be contestable. Such qualification, however, is just one way in which Delors' framework has been found to be appropriate because it has an inbuilt capacity to extend analysis beyond the descriptive to the critical.

This is important because it ultimately leads to questions relating to "Why not?" when it comes to educational provision for Travelers.

Delors' (1996) first two pillars, *learning to know,* and *learning to do*, are well placed in the sequence because they lead to questions whose answers provide knowledge about how the skills needed for the day-to-day running and ongoing preservation of the community are learned. Similarly, the fourth pillar emphasizes the importance of education in all-round development, which is a logical extension of the questions that could be raised and examined critically in relation to the third pillar, as mentioned above.

While the conception of lifelong learning as formal, informal, and non-formal applies to everyone, a careful examination of this framework in the context of particular mobile learning communities also has the capacity to draw out any imbalances among the three types of learning that may be important when questioning why members of mobile learning communities have traditionally found existing formal educational structures to be difficult to penetrate. This is not to deny the advantages in terms of informal learning that living in these traveling communities can provide, however, as such an examination may provide ideas for how members of fixed communities could benefit more substantially from engaging with informal learning.

The following section of this chapter draws on a range of examples of interactions within mobile learning communities to provide a basic description of how mobile learning communities provide what might be regarded as ideal or fertile ground for the promotion of lifelong learning. The process is extended to a critical examination of how interactions beyond these communities further promote or restrict access to formal, informal, and non-formal learning and education. Using Delors' (1996) and Kilpatrick et al. 's (2003) conceptions provides frameworks for this exploration that have been tried and tested separately in many other circumstances.

The question guiding the exploration is: "What does lifelong learning mean in the context of mobile learning community members who move on a regular basis and take with them all or most of the artifacts that are needed for day-to-day living, learning, and earning?" Most importantly, this examination lays bare the types of assumptions about lifelong learning and mobile learning communities that have created barriers to formal and credentialed learning for people in mobile learning communities, a theme that is considered further later in the chapter.

Interactions affecting Lifelong Learning, Earning, and Living in Mobile Learning Communities

A logical way to present data that represent what we and others have found in relation to lifelong learning in mobile learning communities is to organize the evidence around the four pillars discussed by Delors (1996). Within this overall policy framework it is possible to weave the formal, non-formal, and informal conceptions of education and learning into the response as we examine the question relating to what lifelong learning means in the context of mobile learning communities: "What does lifelong learning mean in the context of mobile learning communities?"

We begin our approach to examining this question by considering the first pillar, *learning to know*, involving the acquisition of skills around concentration, memory, and thinking, at the same time as looking at the second pillar, *learning to do*. *Learning to do* relates to investment in the future because of its emphasis on the ability to learn and apply skills that will be needed at a later date.

Learning to Know and Learning to Do

One commonality among different mobile learning communities is the necessity for participants to learn skills that are specific to their community and type of operation. The differences among these communities emerge when the particular skills that need to be learned are examined. Some of these skills are obvious to outsiders, while other skills are less obvious or perhaps not so readily brought to mind. Often the learning of particular skills could be interpreted as encompassing both the first and the second pillars of lifelong learning, *learning to know* and *learning to do*.

The circus performance is one place where the results of Delors' (1996) first and second pillars are readily visible. Even though aerialists sometimes doubt the extent to which an audience can appreciate just how much skill is needed to perform many of the acts on the high wire, the silence that is kept while a particularly difficult act is executed, the sighs, and the claps afterwards are all evidence that there is some degree of skill involved. These skills are learned and taught within the community. A typical comment by a member of an English circus group was as follows:

> Most of the kids, the best acts and artists are still turned over from the circus families and handed down. Experience from the parents and uncles. As you say, other colleagues help with other people's children in the circus, but they practice together, so that's how they learn the skill. (EC1999)

We also observed many instances of older generations teaching younger people skills that would later be performed in the circus ring and then observed the results in the ring. These skills require concentration, memory, and constant thinking. We also saw the follow through with this informal learning where performers reflected on their performances after the show and helped one another to perfect or refine their skills.

In other situations, however, interviewees talked about informal learning in which there was less emphasis on the direct teaching of skills. For example, in an interview with two Traveler teachers, the comment was made about Gypsy Travelers:

> The girls learn a lot of life-skills at home because they look after the younger siblings and they are expected to clean out the trailer or the house, while Mum relinquishes those activities as she grows older, because some of the families are huge—15 children. (TT1999)

This contrasts with images of parents in the circus teaching their toddler children to balance on their father's shoulders or to learn how to do cartwheels. The children appeared to enjoy this one-to-one learning that in effect oriented them to develop their interests, their concentration, and their memories—skills that would be needed when as toddlers they accompanied their parents in the ring doing very simple, almost cameo roles, and later as they learned and performed more complicated acts and expanded their informal learning contexts to include performers other than their parents.

Learning to Live Together and with Others

Even within the same broad category of Travelers, there are differences in cultures that came out very respectfully in an interview with English Travelers as we focused on the third pillar, *learning to live together and with others*, which involves respect for others and understanding others' cultures that is steeped in mutual respect and dependence based on ways that people are similar to one another:

> The English fairground business is an industry that is a way of life—that is, a traditional way of life. It's handed down from father to son, to son, to son. Now on the [European] Continent, it's a business. If you've got enough money, you can come into the fairground business. No matter how much money you've got over here, unless you're born in the business, you don't go into it, because it's more of a traditional thing. I don't think it's anything that anybody really craves to do unless it's in your blood, to be honest. (SS1999)

Part of learning to live with others in traveling communities involves respecting and learning informally what has been handed down from one generation to the next. For example, two Scottish Travelers remarked:

> We are going to places that my father went to, the same piece of ground that his father went to. We've been given them …

> It's just like an inheritance. (SS1999)

Another example came from discussions with some English show people who spoke about inheriting stalls and the positions that those stalls had on the grounds as the community traveled around. A real sense of pride and possession came through:

> My dad's got a stall which was his dad's, and I'd like that kept in the family, and that position, because obviously we buy our positions at each fair. That was my granddad's position and it's my dad's position, and no doubt it will be my position in time. I'd hate to think that went to anybody else, because that's been in the family for so many years. It is important—I think so anyway. I don't know that everybody feels that way. (ES1999)

Part of learning to live together and with others is also enacted among the members of other mobile learning communities such as within agricultural show communities in Australia. Like their counterparts in other parts of the world, the owners of particular businesses within an agricultural show in Australia or the owners of circuses usually have family histories of attachment and ownership that have also been passed down through the generations. Having come through the ranks, *albeit* associated as well with family position within the community, the more senior members learned what they know from years of informal teaching by their parents and other family or community members, both in relation to learning roles to entertain or deal with the public and in learning to run the business. Inherent in this learning is becoming aware of the positions that people hold within the community and the associated expectations. In comparison with their European counterparts, Australian agricultural show people also learn informally that the placement of stalls at an agricultural show, for example, has a history.

Another dimension of *learning to live together and with others* involves an awareness of changing interests and concerns within the communities through which mobile learning communities travel and where they stay for varying lengths of time to present to the local public. A program and musical director in one of the Australian circuses spoke about keeping up with changing technologies. As she commented:

> You have to keep up with the times where the music and the lighting is concerned. You have to go with the flow there. The day of the old LP [long playing] records are gone. My mother used to use them when I was a little girl. Then you progress to tapes, then to CD [compact discs] players. Now we have mini disks. So now we are up with the times in that department. The lighting—we have intelligent lighting; we just need to find someone to work it. (AC2000)

Being able "to keep up with the times" in order to maintain audience interest is all part of being aware of interactions with the world outside the mobile learning community and understanding the culture of the people who pay to see performances. Ultimately this understanding is necessary for the survival of the mobile learning community.

A more serious example of understanding others' culture is for circuses to be able to respond to concerns or perceptions in some sectors of the broader community that circus animals are exploited or even treated poorly. The financial viability of circuses can depend on the extent to which circus members can draw on an accumulation of informal learning experiences to attend successfully to these concerns. Numerous interviewees commented to the effect that learning never stops and that learning occurs every day.

Some members of Australian circuses also spoke about hierarchies and leadership from what might be regarded as a middle management perspective, in which it was clear that not everyone has a leadership role over others. It can be seen, however, how many of the expectations within these roles can be learned through involvement and observation and how learning to live together and with others within the expectations around these roles helps with smooth operations and creates respect. Reference was made to the tent boss, for example, who "is sort of like a leader of all the boys" (AC1998), while others' leadership positions may have been to be in charge of the canteen or groups of animals. Members would change roles from time to time in their younger years and this would help accumulate knowledge and skills across a range of areas, which was good preparation for the years ahead. A key point that one of the women who had been in charge of different areas at different times acknowledged was the importance of knowing that there was always someone who could teach you and, when you are in charge of others, you get in and do the work with them. This helped to promote respect among community members at different levels of responsibility.

Learning to Be

Learning to be could be regarded as encompassing informal, non-formal, and formal education in traveling communities, even though the particular emphasis might be in different proportions from those of fixed residence communities. As noted above, *learning to be* emphasizes the importance of education in the all-round development of the person: mind, body, and spirit.

While even non-formal learning is also not very evident among mobile learning communities generally, there was some discussion that encompassed this level. Traveler teachers spoke about a community education group that was on site and established a women's group but then went on to say that the attempt had not come to anything. There was also mention of a local community center that had a vehicle called the Alpha Bus.

> … it's Adult Learning something. It's a sort of adult ed[ucation] double decker bus, and it goes around. It could actually come to the site and

give people the chance to use computers or work on literacy and stuff. (TT1999)

In terms of formal education and the all-round development of the person, we found mixed reactions among different groups of mobile learning communities. A common theme, however, was that formal educational provision was either not relevant for Travelers or not responsive to their traveling lifestyle. For example, when talking about Irish Travelers, one of the Traveler teachers commented:

> They feel as though the secondary schools are not offering them the skills they need for the lifestyle they lead. What is the point of going to school and learning Spanish and Geography if what they want to do is brick-laying? (TT1999)

This teacher continued:

> I was talking to some girls last week down on the site here, and both of these girls dropped out of school at around 14. We were just talking about it, and she said, "Well, this isn't what we wanted to learn." They say, even now, "If somebody offered us courses in [terribly sexist, isn't it?] dress-making, cooking, hairdressing—if somebody had offered us those kind[s] of skills in school, we would have stayed." (TT1999)

These teachers then spoke about how they were trying to help traveling families with the education of their younger children and to encourage family attitudes that were positively directly toward education while the children were still very young. Over the years, these teachers had experimented with the way that they provided learning packages to the families and each year discussed with families how the service could be improved. As a teacher from a different part of the United Kingdom commented:

> So every year, we go back and say, "Why didn't it work? What's not done?" So we've now got it honed down. We send work away in three week bulk packs, and that's it, because we find they can't cope with anything more than that. We found that people were getting too much, and if they get too much—it's [counterproductive]. And then it's working with the family to find out when is the best time when they're traveling for that family to do it. (TT1999)

This teacher continued:

> Some families will say they'll do the bulk of the work in the two days when we're in the middle of the fair, because we can't do anything when we're putting it [the tent] up or taking it down. Others will say they'll do it in the morning, and others will say, "No, we'll do it in the evening." But as long as the family themselves [decide] about when it's going to be the

best time for them to do it, it's fine. We are getting children right through to Year 11 and taking exam results. So that's quite good. (TT1999)

Apart from indicating how formal education was part of the overall growth of the person, consistent with *learning to be*, these illustrations are a few of the many examples that we found with Traveler teachers in different contexts who modeled through their own interactions with Travelers who were part of mobile learning communities the importance of valuing other people and attempting to try to understand their culture. In doing this, many Traveler teachers develop a respect for Travelers that is mutual, with increased understanding leading to a heightened appreciation not just of differences between themselves and the Travelers but also of similarities, which is additional evidence of overlaps between the development of the mind in relation to the *learning to be* pillar and *learning to live together and with others*.

We also found evidence among adult learners in Australian circus communities, however, how some attempts on their behalf to gain trade qualifications through institutions that relied on face-to-face delivery were very difficult and steeped in either a misunderstanding of the circumstances of Travelers or a lack of awareness. Skills that some Australian circus members had gained in welding by learning on the job needed to be credentialed and, while they were able to attend some formal classes, they had difficulty in completing their certificates because they had to move with the mobile community rather than staying in fixed locations for the time needed to complete the certificates.

Clearly, the conditions under which many skills, such as welding, are learned informally in mobile learning communities work against members of those communities when it comes to recognition of their prior learning outside their community context or extending or credentialing their learning. Yet this outside context, where the formal, credentialed learning delivered by institutions occurs, cannot replicate the more natural context for continuous learning throughout the lifespan that mobile learning communities provide as members from different parts of the lifespan, from infancy to old age live, learn, and earn.

Implications for the Future Education of Mobile Learning Communities

Many mobile learning communities have a number of features or conditions that could dispose any community quite favorably to success in educational endeavors and long-term sustainability. Learners are readily able to access people around them who can teach them the skills associated with the purpose of their community and which pertain to their own particular interests within the community. They can also contribute to the learning of others. Where members range in age from the very young to the elderly, there is a mixture of fresh enthusiasm, youth, and experience, and members of all ages have the support of extended family and long-term friendships and contacts. They also have the opportunity to learn skills needed in dealing with problems that arise from time to time from having to work every day alongside people with whom they share the circumstances that contain nearly all aspects of their lives.

Informal and life-wide learning, therefore, can be strengths within mobile learning communities, as demonstrated in this chapter and more extensively among the breadth of examples that exist now as evidence and which the examples employed in the chapter represent. This is particularly with regard to learning that takes place in the home and the workplace (which are generally the same place for mobile learning community members), and in some community organizations such as libraries. Eneroth's (2008) description of the informal world, in which the accumulation of unintended experiences equips people well for coping with other unexpected occurrences, is an integral part of the lifelong learning experiences of members of mobile learning communities. Rather than being enclosed within an environment that is predictable and unresponsive to the outside world, the members of mobile learning communities whom we and others have interviewed and observed depend for their community sustainability on being able to adapt to changes in attitudes and conditions on the outside.

To survive long term in their world and in the world through which they travel, members of mobile learning communities need to be able to access formal learning and qualifications, just as members of fixed residence do. This is the one area of life-wide learning that is problematic for these communities. Despite an optimistic view that might hold that there have been relatively successful attempts to improve access and make formal education more relevant to a mobile lifestyle in some places throughout the world, as described in other chapters of this book, better access to formal learning for members of mobile learning communities is quite a long way from the reality. Accessing formal education has been shown to be notoriously difficult for mobile learning communities and this problem of access is repeated among a vast array of communities across the globe as they carry with them most of the artifacts that they need for learning, earning, and living throughout the lifespan.

If access to formal learning were predicated on individuals being part of a community that had all the advantages that representation of a cross section of the community entailed rather than the more restricted teacher–student relationships that predominate in most schooling systems, then mobile communities might be the more advantaged group. Instead, the rich context of their community places members of mobile learning communities at greater risk of educational disadvantage because of difficulty in accessing formal education that predominantly responds to fixed residence as the default mode. For the four pillars of lifelong learning described by Delors (1996) and others to be genuinely adopted as policy that extends to mobile learning communities as well as to people of fixed residence, then the principles and practices of mobile learning communities could be an excellent starting point for reconceptualizing the delivery of formal education more generally.

If informal learning could be valued to the extent to which it leads to the successful acquisition of skills and knowledge that help sustain a community, then informal learning in mobile learning communities would be regarded more highly outside those communities. There is still a need for the formal credentialing of learning and it would be an easy option and even a retrograde step to recommend that informal learning alone is sufficient to sustain mobile communities into the future. Formal educational provision for members of mobile learning communities is an area that has many challenges for systems that have traditionally focused on clients who reside in one place or who move infrequently. In some ways, however, the success of informal learning structures and the existence of other circumstances that favor informal learning in mobile learning communities could mean that the steps to providing ongoing formal education to Travelers, while difficult, could be relatively few in number if given careful consideration.

We suspect that the implications for the future sustainability of mobile learning communities, depending on the extent to which formal, informal, and even non-formal education are each promoted, can be only partially anticipated and not fully realized until formal education and the credentialing of knowledge become a reality for Travelers. In other words, the future becomes more predictable as it unfolds and as successive approximation of the desired goal of Education for All (EFA), as articulated by the Dakar Conference in 2000 (Carr-Hill, 2006, pp. 35-36), is achieved. Mobile learning communities that have gained limited access to formal education that respond to their particular circumstances have found that there have been implications within their communities as a result of the need to adapt to the changes that they instigated. This occurs, for example, where the day becomes more regulated around schooling where previously routines and schedules around travel predominated and determined when the practicalities of schooling were able to occur. Similarly, there are implications for broader educational practice that will emerge as mobile learning communities lay claim to formal education or education systems respond more comprehensively to their distinctive contexts and needs.

Implications for Broader Educational Practice

The concepts of lifelong and life-wide learning, and Delors' (1996) four pillars of lifelong learning, are useful starting points for articulating possible implications of the preceding discussion for broader educational practice. In combination, they constitute specific challenges and opportunities for current and possible future forms of educational provision.

With regard to formal and lifelong learning, increasingly pathways within and across educational sectors are being developed in order to facilitate easier passage through the various conduits for formal education. One example of this facilitation is the increased focus on maximizing transitions in the senior phase of secondary education, including school-to-work transitions (Harreveld & Danaher, 2006-2007). Another instance is the emergence of the Australian Qualifications Framework (Frost, 2006-2007) and its equivalent in other countries, a crucial development if learners are to be able to traverse different educational sectors confidently. At the same time, there is increased recognition of the importance of early childhood education (see for example Anning & Edwards, 2006). All of this suggests an expansion of lifelong learning opportunities, at least in Western countries and at least in ways that further the economic dimension of lifelong learning.

In relation to informal and life-wide learning, there is also evidence of an enhanced recognition of both these dimensions of learning—again at least in Western countries (Danaher, 2008). For example, Findsen (2002) explored the formal, non-formal, and informal learning opportunities accessible by older adults in New Zealand, while Hurworth (2002) considered the effectiveness of the University of the Third Age in Victoria, Australia. Similarly, Kennedy (2004) interrogated the possibilities for knowledge management and workplace learning in complex organizations, while Jackson (2006) analyzed the role played by the British National Federation of Women's Institutes in promoting older women's informal participation in learning. These developments augur well for aspirations to assist the citizenry to engage fully in contemporary social life—yet they also potentially sound some warning bells by those concerned about the knowledge economy subsuming all other ways of knowing (Hargreaves, 2002).

In terms of Delors' (1996) four pillars of lifelong learning, from one perspective they constitute an unexceptional statement of aspirations that might be suggested by many school, college, or university mottos or mission statements. From a very different perspective, they might be seen as encapsulating the key dilemmas and opportunities of contemporary education and social life. Assuredly most if not all educators would be able to use learning to know, learning to do, learning to live together and with others, and learning to be as strong reflective lenses for examining their own practices and their students' learning outcomes. Likewise learners could usefully consider these imperatives as personal and shared aspirations that might constitute powerful navigational tools helping to guide their lifelong learning journeys.

Certainly "from the cradle to the grave" evokes something of the ambivalence that courses through several of the chapters in this book. On the one hand, this expression can be seen as having a faintly insidious tone, similar to the evocation of lifelong learning as life imprisonment (Danaher et al., 2000a. p. 128). On the other hand, the same expression can suggest ongoing support and assistance in using educational opportunities with varying degrees of formalization to achieve individual benefits and simultaneously to contribute to communal goals. Yet, as this chapter has demonstrated, there is something of a disjuncture between the informal, on the job learning engaged in by members of mobile communities and the formal, state-based education system. If that disjuncture exists for mobile community members, it might exist also for other individuals and groups who slip through the cracks in the provision of lifelong learning from the cradle to the grave.

Questions for Reflection

- If we were to remove all signs of formal education as we currently understand it, rebuild our understanding of the concept, and propose models of delivering formal education that considered only the circumstances and conditions under which lifelong learning takes place in mobile learning communities, what would formal education look like?
- Now take this new formal education delivery conception and consider how it could be applied to formal education as it currently stands. In what ways is this new conception of formal education similar to and different from the current application? In what ways and to what extent would the new conception suit people of fixed residence?
- How can we cater equitably for the formal educational needs across the lifespan of both people of fixed residence and members of mobile learning communities?
- What general principles of learning, especially informal learning, that apply in mobile learning communities would be helpful to apply in educational communities where most learners are of fixed residence?
- What are the similar and the different ways in which mobile learning communities and fixed residence communities engage in learning informally?
- In what ways do local schools attempt to embrace some of the advantages of accessing people of all ages to promote the education of the young?

Suggestions for Further Reading

Adult Learning Australia. (2004). The case for life-wide learning. Submission to the Department of Education, Science and Training's consultation paper, *You can too: Adult learning in Australia*. Canberra, ACT: Author.

Chapman, J., Gaff, J., Toomey, R., & Aspin, D. (2005). Policy of lifelong learning in Australia. *International Journal of Lifelong Education, 24*(2), 99-122.

Chisholm, L. (2008). Re-contextualising learning in second modernity. *Research in Post-Compulsory Education, 13*(2), 139-147.

Danaher, G., Moriarty, B. J., & Danaher, P. A. (2008). Lifelong learning journeys on the move: Reflecting on successes and framing futures for Australian show people. In D. Orr, P. A. Danaher, G. R. Danaher, & R. E. Harreveld (Eds.), *Lifelong learning: Reflecting on successes and framing futures: Keynote and refereed papers from the 5th international lifelong learning conference, Yeppoon, Central Queensland, Australia, 16-19 June 2008: Hosted by Central Queensland University* (pp. 113-118). Rockhampton, Qld: Lifelong Learning Conference Committee, Central Queensland University Press.

Gorard, S., & Selwyn, N. (2005). What makes a lifelong learner? *Teachers College Record, 107*(6), 1193-1216.

Jones, H. C. (2005). Lifelong learning in the European Union: Whither the Lisbon Strategy? *European Journal of Education, 40*(3), 247-260.

Windeknecht, K., & Hyland, P. (2004). When lifelong learning isn't enough: The importance of individual and organisational learning. In P. A. Danaher, C. R. Macpherson, F. Nouwens, & D. Orr (Eds.), *Lifelong learning: Whose responsibility and what is your contribution?: Refereed papers from the 3rd international lifelong learning conference Yeppoon, Central Queensland, Australia 13-16 June 2004: Hosted by Central Queensland University* (pp. 389-395). Rockhampton, Qld: Lifelong Learning Conference Committee, Central Queensland University Press.

3
Technologies and Their Users

Technologies have not only had their place in the mobile communities of bargees, circus, and fairground people throughout the history of the existence of those communities but they are also integral and imperative to their operations. From the high wire to the Ferris wheel, the dodgem cars to the barges there would be little remaining in these communities if technologies were removed. Equally important are the ways that personnel and clients interact with and through those technologies. This chapter explores these themes in a way that also shows connections with lifelong learning and how members of these communities seek to guarantee their continued relevance to the outside community and the ongoing existence of their operations.

Introduction

One way in which mobile learning communities distinguish themselves from one another and from people of fixed address is how they learn and interact with and through particular technologies. The flying trapeze, the clown's costume, and the unicycle are markers of the roles learned and played by different members of a circus community, while the appearance of the Ferris wheel at the fairground is a sure sign that the fair or agricultural show is in town.

From this perspective, technology can be understood in terms of applied rather than theoretical science relating to the development of practical arts. The French theorist Michel Foucault has extended this understanding in his concept of technologies of the self—that is, techniques that enable individuals to work on themselves by regulating their bodies, thoughts, and conduct (Danaher et al., 2000b, p. 128). The ways in which these techniques enable humans to develop and interact with assorted forms of technology is therefore an important focus of life in mobile learning communities.

Technologies are significant because they can both enable and constrain mobile learning communities and their members. They can be the basis for structuring routines and all aspects of life. They can enable performance and learning and provide a way of life treasured by their users, especially when applied innovatively or in novel ways. Technologies can be agents of constraint during malfunctions or through inappropriate or outdated use but they can also be sources of learning in such situations, particularly if the users reflect on their efforts. Technologies have increasingly been a subject of interest in recent years regarding the possibilities and constraints associated with formal learning opportunities for mobile learning community members.

The following review of selected literature combined with discussions around findings from our research with mobile learning communities across several continents are guided by the following question. What opportunities for learning, earning, or living do technologies create for mobile learning communities? We identify one category of technologies associated with transport and movement and another with learning and earning. Examination of these categories of technologies provides a background context for understanding how mobile learning communities interact with and through technologies distinctive to those communities. Later we share ideas from different mobile learning communities about how these technologies and their users can enable and constrain the pursuit of learning and earning among members of mobile learning communities and can preserve distinctive ways of life.

We then look at some examples of successful instances in which educational authorities have used different types of technologies to tailor educational experiences for children of particular mobile learning communities. We conclude the chapter by considering how these attempts to educate, together with distinctive opportunities that technologies for learning, earning, and living in mobile communities provide, can help inform a more strategic and integrated approach to the education of young Travelers and have implications for lifelong learning.

Contexts and Technologies for Learning, Earning, and Living

This review of selected literature begins around the practice and use of technologies for learning in an unexpected place. It looks into the classroom of an innovative and inspiring British teacher who does not appear at first glance to have much in common with mobile learning communities. As the winner of the 2005 British Educational Communications and Technology Agency— Information and Communications Technology (BECTA - ICT) award, Tim Rylands has taken his elementary school students on metaphorical journeys just as exciting and exotic as the journeys that people of fixed address might imagine when they contemplate running away to the circus. Rylands' approach to using the *Myst* series of computer games, for which he is perhaps best known in the classroom, is an approach that appeals to different ability levels while it increases engagement in learning, promotes listening and speaking skills, and improves literacy. When young people expand their capacity for literacy, they also learn skills for life.

Firsthand observers of Rylands' teaching (http://www.timrylands.com/) have described his classroom. During a literacy lesson, Rylands might use an interactive whiteboard screen to project the computer game *Myst* so that teacher and students can explore the game together. The children are asked to describe how objects that they see might feel and how they look as a prelude to writing. Teacher and children are so engaged that they can be oblivious to anyone watching (a striking example of flow, which is explored below). Rylands also finds that Google Earth can bring far-flung places within reach but he maintains that these cyber journeys do not replace the real excursion, a point that may be debated by his enthusiastic students. A visit to Rylands' website is recommended. It will be more inspiring and a better description of the impact of his use of technology than we can provide here.

While some children of fixed address may travel through cyberspace with their teachers, children whose parents are mobile travel with their families and, in many cases, with communities that are part of the same occupational Traveler group. Mobile learning communities use a range of technologies, often distinctive to their particular occupational group, for learning, earning, and living but the use of technology has often been seen as presenting almost insurmountable challenges when it comes to the formal education of their children. This is understandable given that mobile communities represent a variety of travel patterns, which makes it difficult to provide access to generalized educational services that are effective for the range of mobile learning communities that need to be serviced.

Included in accounts of good practice in Traveler education, edited by Tyler (2005), however, are Gypsy Travelers, Travelers from particular national groupings, circus, fairground and show people, Romany Gypsy refugees and asylum seekers, New Travelers, bargee and other water craft Travelers, and others such as migratory seasonal workers (pp. ix-x). There is also a wide range of Traveler groups in other countries around the world. More recently, the presence and plight of housed Travelers in London has been recognized (Donovan, 2005), which extends even further an appreciation that all Traveler groups are not alike and therefore that they have varied and specialized needs in relation to their ability to access and take advantage of formal education. This leads to the following question. What does the literature say about how the contexts for learning for children in mobile learning communities differ from those for children of fixed residence who may be taught by people like Tim Rylands and other teachers whom he inspires? What technologies are available in these contexts to support learning, earning, and living for Travelers and their children?

Contexts for Learning

Contexts for learning differ not only between Travelers and people of fixed address but also among different Traveler groups. One of the most basic ways in which Traveler groups differ is in their patterns of mobility. Travel patterns can vary between groups across the year, affecting how long particular Travelers stay in each place, whether, if appropriate, they have a place where they stay for much of the year while not traveling, the extent to which the itinerary is predictable and their purpose for travel (Marks, 2005).

For some groups, such as circus troupes, the most predictable part about their travel is the unpredictability. For example, circus troupes often determine their itinerary according to the presence of other circuses *en route* at the particular time and their acceptance in towns where concerns may be expressed by councils or animal liberationists (Moriarty, 2000). Fairground people, on the other hand, usually have very predictable patterns of mobility, such that their children often celebrate their birthdays in the same place each year. Other occupational Travelers, such as fruit pickers, are guided by the seasons (Henderson, 2005), while the travel patterns of Gypsy Travelers have been described by Marks (2005) as "more complex and variable" (p. 2) than those of other Traveler groups.

Understanding the patterns and circumstances of mobility of occupational Travelers is important for educators, not just for knowing when the children may arrive at a school *en route*, if that is possible, but also for understanding how children of Travelers may feel about attending school, which is so different from their everyday realities (Blaney, 2005). Those realities may normally involve distance education in the context of a Traveler community that lives, learns, and earns together. Children of fixed residence who attend school on a regular basis, however, are more likely to differentiate among those parts of their lives associated with home, school, and work (Hallinan & Wyer, 1998). Awareness of these differences can be important for understanding the opportunities and threats for Traveler children that making friends with children whom they may never see again, or for some time, presents. The traveling lifestyle of many mobile learning communities therefore often challenges assumptions of fixed residence associated with regular schools and the clientele whom they are set up to service. When Traveler children take up opportunities to attend schools for very short periods on their journey, they thus change and contest the demographics of those schools. It is therefore not surprising that Marks' (2005) major report on the use of information and communication technologies (ICTs) among Traveler children in the United Kingdom (known as the E-Learning and Mobility Project, or E-LAMP) focused on ICTs that supported the use of distance education materials.

The ways that mobile learning communities travel from one place to the next varies across groups and also within groups over time. In Australia, many circus troupes originally traveled by train but now use caravans or trailers like fairground or agricultural show people (Moriarty et al., 1998). Technologies for transport have not only been important for getting from place to place but also have been associated with what might be called on stage an "entrance," in which the arrival in town of occupational Travelers is clearly visible. This is important for fairground and circus people, for example, because being noticed on arrival is akin to advertising their shows (Carmeli, 2003, p. 73). Technologies associated with movement for a different purpose include Ferris wheels, dodgem cars, and unicycles. Together with the form of transport used to go from town to town, these technologies help to distinguish and make distinctive one mobile learning group from another as well as from people of fixed residence for whom these particular technologies are not usually part of everyday life. (As an example of this diversity within mobile communities, see Anteliz and Danaher [2000] for an account of the differences between the *carritos chocones* of stationary Venezuelan fairgrounds and the dodgem cars of mobile Australian sideshow alleys [see also Anteliz et al., 2004].)

Other technological groups particularly associated with different mobile learning communities include technologies for learning, both formal and informal, and technologies for earning, such as high wires, show bags, and machines to make ferry floss. While transport and movement could be considered as a group of its own, because it covers so many facets, it is also part of or linked to earning and even learning. Learning and earning are closely related, powerful markers by which particular mobile learning communities live and are recognized.

Technologies for Learning, Earning, and Living in Mobile Learning Communities

Arguably some of the most successful learning within mobile learning communities has been practical, relevant to earning and living within the community, and passed down from one generation to the next without formal recognition of qualifications. Mobile learning communities typically depend for their survival on their ability as a group to provide entertainment or services to the communities through which they travel. To a large extent, they need to be independent as a community, providing among them all of the technologies and skills needed to run their operations. There are few exceptions to this requirement and most are non-negotiable. For example, if someone in the show community is not able and available to operate the Ferris wheel, then one of the main attractions and sources of income is also not available.

The literature about mobility provides many examples of technologies used for learning, earning, and living in mobile communities that are integral for ongoing, day-to-day operations. While it is difficult to divide these technologies into discrete groups, especially when they fulfill more than one purpose, it can be helpful to draw examples from transport and movement on the one hand and the related areas of earning and learning on the other.

The variations that exist among different mobile learning communities in terms of their modes of transport also extend to their living quarters. This is because the trailers, caravans, barges, or other means of transporting the community and their goods are often also the living quarters for those communities while they are on the move. Of course, many other artifacts also need to be transported. These may include circus tents, animals, cargo, fairground rides, and technologies used for amusement in sideshow alley, but it is the different versions of mobile homes that form part of the traveling entourage that are significant because they are often used for multiple purposes associated with learning, earning, and living. Danaher (1998b), while exploring the concept and meaning of "home" to Traveler children, unveiled different purposes for which the trailers or caravans doubling as living quarters were used. These mobile technologies not only transported families and possessions but were also places where families slept, cooked, and ate, socialized, and played and where children completed their distance education lessons, sometimes with the help of their mother, a home tutor, or a parent who combined the two roles. Unless a separate van was kept as a classroom, the family van was traditionally the site of earning (for example, where the parents balanced their books or costumes were sewn or repaired), learning (for example, where children completed their distance education materials), and living (for example, for socializing). While many vans were well-equipped and could be described as a "home away from home," they could also be a hive of competing activities that supported simultaneously a range of technologies and lively interactions pertaining to different parts or even stages of life. As another example of this close relationship between technologies for earning and living that could also extend to the basis of informal learning, de Jongh and Steyn (2006) identified as the key element in their study of the Karretjie peripatetic sheepshearers of the Great Karoo in South Africa "the *karretjie* (cart) cum overnight shelter and a co-residential income sharing entity" (p. 80).

Still other technologies more directly related to formal learning have also emerged differentially among mobile learning communities around the world in recent years. These technologies, including ICTs, have assisted Traveler children's learning directly as well as promoting interaction between the children and their teachers while Traveler families are on the move. Access to these types of technologies has not been endemic among traveling communities in any country, however, and their availability has often been limited to the scope and duration of particular projects that have trialed their use. Nevertheless they potentially offer enormous possibilities for extending the learning of Traveler children and for making formal learning more accessible and consistently available. The key role of technology in "maximising the learning outcomes of the Traveller children so they can fulfil their education potential" has been recognized (Danaher et al., 2007, p. 103) within a context of rapid technological advancement and serious efforts to overcome problems encountered by distance and mobility.

A particular example of these kinds of technologies is Project SMART, a national distance education program for migrant students in the United

States that began in the late 1980s and early 1990s, when migrant educators in Texas expressed concern about the students' lack of educational continuity when their families moved to other states in the summer months (Meyertholen et al., 2004). This is an integrated package of educational technologies, including live interactive satellite televised instruction, live non-interactive televised instruction, delayed televised instruction, and videotaped lessons (Celedón-Pattichis, 2004, p. 200), as well as streaming audio and video, reception via computer stations, and Internet tutoring options (Meyertholen et al., 2004, p. 190). These technologies have been integrally associated with educational practices such as developing a specialized curriculum, devising distance education packs, and hiring and training television teachers. A related initiative is Project Estrella operated by the Illinois Migrant Council, in which 50 high school migrant students each year travel with laptop computers and access online course work (Meyertholen et al., 2004, p. 190). In assessing the overall effectiveness of Project SMART, Meyertholen et al. (2004) encapsulated two of the major themes of this chapter in relation to educational technologies and mobile learning communities. On the one hand, as noted above the issue of access is ever present:

> For example, in many receiving states the only telephone in migrant labor camps is the public pay phone. Computer labs in school buildings are usually closed during the summer months when summer migrant programs are operating in the receiving states. (pp. 190-191)

On the other hand, the most effective technologies are those instantiated in the rhythms and routines of the mobile lifestyle:

> Project SMART is successful because it embraces the lifestyle of the migrant student and seeks to make it a positive experience, rather than a negative one. And Project SMART continues to flourish because it offers a curriculum that is adaptable, universal, flexible, and transportable—all qualities that address the need for continuity in the educational process of migrant students. (p. 191)

It should be acknowledged that not all Traveler children in all places of the world currently learn through distance education or combine this or other alternatives with attending regular school when this is possible. Advancements in thinking and in ICTs have resulted in other approaches, such as the establishment in Australia in 2000 of the Queensland School for Travelling Show Children (Moriarty et al., 2004). This school, which consists of two mobile classrooms that service different routes of travel, combines the advantages of current innovations in technology and the presence of peripatetic teachers who travel the same routes with the provision of dedicated spaces for learning that are more specialized and relevant to Traveler children than the classrooms that many other Traveler children experience in regular schools when they stay for perhaps a week or more in single locations. The school certainly provides more structure and routine for formalized learning than is usually the case with mobile living quarters that double as learning spaces and other activities related to earning, learning, and living. The routines associated with a formal school day also disrupt the traditional opportunities and expectations associated with informal learning *in situ*, in which the children of Travelers learned and practiced skills associated with their parents' occupations and which helped sustain a particular way of life from one generation to the next. It will be interesting to see the outcomes of these changes on the life trajectories of the next generation of these mobile learning communities.

Researching Technologies for Learning, Earning, and Living in Mobile Learning Communities

It is only in recent years that researching mobile communities and, in particular, the education of the children of Travelers, has produced a corpus of literature that has helped us to identify and understand the realities of learning, both formal and informal, for children and adults who travel for all or much of the year. Traditionally this area of enquiry appears to have been largely dismissed by people of fixed residence as not being important. There has also been the difficulty of conceptualizing Traveler groups as an entity with common issues because these groups are so diverse. It is only more recently that the accumulation of knowledge from separate studies into and reports of particular Traveler groups has enabled us to perceive groups of Travelers as mobile learning communities with commonalities across groups and lessons to be learned from one to the other. Research around ICTs and other technologies for learning in the main has proceeded along separate trajectories and mainly with fixed populations, yet mobile learning communities have interacted for centuries with and through technologies particular to them and have sustained their ways of life as a result.

Studies of fairground and circus communities and bargees are examples of this combination of focus on mobile learning communities and the technologies with which they interact. The results have a great deal of relevance for cooperative communities such as schools and classes of students and their teachers both for the ways that they engage and communicate with learners with and through technologies and for the ways that they work together for the common good. Old perceptions are hard to change but it is hoped that better understanding and more positive views are slowly replacing the deficit views of Travelers traditionally held by many people of fixed residence. As technologies for learning become more available to remote and mobile communities and formal literacy levels rise among Travelers with the better educational opportunities that these technologies provide, perhaps understanding will also further increase.

We will shortly look at some examples of how members of mobile learning communities interact with and through technologies and how these interactions promote learning and provide an income. For the purpose of providing the detail and depth of analysis required to investigate how interactions with and through technologies have promoted earning and learning and the continued existence of the community within a relatively small space, we have chosen as our focus the ringmaster of the circus. Coming in from this perspective affords the opportunity to draw on a range of examples of acts, to witness audience involvement and reaction, and to look backstage to make the picture more complete.

Our *entrée* to researching circuses as mobile learning communities was facilitated by a ringmaster who organized most of the interviews that we conducted with individuals and small groups and a large focus group interview, and who provided the opportunity to observe numerous performances as well as life behind the scenes.

The ringmaster at a circus typically presides over a variety of acts whose range depends on the type of circus and the skills of the performers. We have observed and researched circuses, big and small, of the traditional kind that have dominated the scene for the past several hundred years, rather than newer breeds of circuses described by Strickland (1999) that operate without big tops and animals.

Interacting with and through Technologies for Learning, Earning, and Living in Mobile Learning Communities

A useful place to begin examining the ways that circus personnel interact with and through technologies is under the big top at the circus during a performance. The ringmaster is in control of the proceedings and, like a conductor with an orchestra, is acutely aware of the various surrounding elements and brings them together in synchronized harmony, enabling the performers to be presented in the best light and the audience to appreciate the acts that they see. Behind the scenes and between performances the ringmaster can witness the efforts that go into rehearsals, reflections on performances and the refinement of acts, the care of animals, and the making and repair of props and costumes as well as the teaching of skills that occurs from one generation to the next. Over time, the ringmaster can also observe how acts and the technologies used for them change in response to shifting interests and cultures in the wider community, from where audiences are drawn.

The Circus Performance

While audience attention is focused on the performance, there is a range of other activities barely noticeable that accompany the act. Supporting personnel control sound and lighting, security, and distractions at appropriate times depending on the particular act. The ringmaster needs to be aware of all of these support mechanisms in order to get the timing correct and to compensate for when changes occur. For example, the ringmaster knows the order in which the acts are to appear but, if backstage a decision has been made to withdraw an act or change the order of appearance, often the only way that the ringmaster will know is when the music or lights signal the start of a different act. While the sound and lighting technicians interact and communicate with the ringmaster and the performers through technologies appropriate to their roles, the ringmaster uses this information to interact with the audience.

In a similar way, the performers on the high wire interact with one another to ensure a successful performance. They interact with the technologies that are needed in the execution of their act, such as the trapeze and the swings. Even their costumes are part of the act. They also interact through these technologies and with one another to communicate with the audience, even when they take a bow in the middle of the act while they balance on the high wire and hold on tenuously to a piece of rope or wave a hand to acknowledge the expertise of fellow performers and to invite the audience to applaud.

Other acts may involve unicycles, fire, balls, animals, or whips. Whichever acts are introduced by the ringmaster a common element among them is their specialized technologies with which and through which the performers interact with one another, with the ringmaster, and especially with the audience. One way of appreciating the integral role of the range of technologies used is to imagine how a clown, for example, might generate interest from an audience without the unicycle, the makeup, and the costume. The situation would be similar if the acrobats arrived on stage without the high wires hanging above them, without their costumes, and without other props such as hoops. Technologies associated with color, sound, and movement are markers by which these performers are identified, with which they interact, and which form the conduit with audiences. They are, in effect, mediators between the performers and the audience, and without them there would be no interaction.

During the performance, therefore, the ringmaster is in perhaps the ideal position to observe everything that happens in the ring as well as audience reactions and interactions with the performers, mediated by their clever use of technologies. Audience reactions can be read by the expressions on faces, the stunned silences, and excited comments such as "I know how he did that!"

We have often thought that, if teachers could manage to promote a similar level of engagement of their pupils through the use of technologies appropriate to classrooms, then learning would be maximized (see also the discussion in Chapter 6 of the circus's potential role in teaching across several curriculum areas). At this point, those who have visited Tim Rylands' website will have a visual image of how this can occur.

Backstage

It is doubtful whether most audiences at circuses appreciate the amount of skill and practice needed for the successful execution of many acts. It is part of the job of the ringmaster to excite the audience about the feats presented to them and to encourage appreciation and applause. In talking with some performers, even we were surprised by the extent to which acrobats and others like to be applauded and how they remember occasions when the applause was particularly loud or long (AC1998).

When acts are chosen and prepared, consideration is given to audience preferences, social acceptance, and changing tastes. If this were not the case, then very skilled performers who lived for their art could do what they liked but sadly the result could be a decline in audience numbers and even the continued existence of the circus could be in doubt. The ringmaster is in an ideal position to gauge audience reactions, particularly as the job often entails interacting with the audiences off stage as the tent is filling with people or the audience is leaving at the end of a show.

We witnessed one particular example of this attendance to audience tastes and even their education on matters related to the employment of animals in the circus, at a performance in which the ringmaster talked to the audience about how the animals in the circus were treated. There had recently been some potentially damaging media coverage that could have led to declines in attendances that these talks were intended to help address. Audience members were even invited to sign petitions in support of the continued use of animals in circuses. Added to these occasions was the use of a range of technologies to support the interactions of the ringmaster in this educative role.

It is not always wise, however, to continue to use some technologies that clearly have become outdated or culturally unacceptable and again the ringmaster is in an ideal position to observe the relative popularity or decline in popularity of different technologies. With the assistance of a ringmaster in organizing interviews with performers, we spoke with one performer whose words reinforced for us the continuing interplay among technology, performance, and learning while talking about how circus acts had changed over decades and even centuries in response to general acceptance. In the words of the performer:

> There are magicians who put an entire act around cigarettes. They used to produce cigarettes out of the air like that, left, right, and center. In their hands they used to build castles of cigarette packets … and things. Now, of course, cigarettes are not fashionable or socially acceptable, [so] that it's not a big part of the magic world

today. Things like that—a lot of acts have gone because … people who are doing the fakir type acts, you know, where the Indians start sticking needles through their cheeks and sewing buttons on their skin and all that, that's lost its appeal too. Once you would see those sort[s] of acts, but, you know, people develop more taste or ghoulish, gruesome things, not so much. (AC1998)

Leaving one circus ground where we had interviewed a number of individuals and small groups of circus personnel, we drove with the ringmaster to a larger circus one evening, arriving in time to see the second half of the performance and then conducting a focus group interview with many of the people who had just performed. The backdrop to this focus group interview was the high wire, still in place, and several acrobats reflecting on their performance that evening. We also recall the roaring of lions in the background. The senior, more experienced acrobat helped the younger one to identify those parts of the performance that needed refinement and he helped his younger colleague to practice and perfect the act until they were both satisfied with the result. Even in rehearsal, the high wire was the technology that brought the two acrobats together.

In the foreground, the focus group interview was lively and interactive. Part of the discussion highlighted different approaches to learning through technologies connected with varied circus acts. One performer explained how he "started off with the fire eating, then did whip cracking and plate spinning, and knife throwing, balancing, rollerball balancing, and now I'm flying trapeze" (AC1998). Reflecting on this diversity of acts, he mused:

> … you learn a lot watching people. You'd be surprised at how much you learn by just listening to people and asking questions. Most of the acts I do aren't that difficult to learn over time, and as long as you have basic coordination and balance. Most of the acts I do are quite learnable. Things like performing lions, elephants, anything really to do with animals, takes a lot longer to learn—to be very proficient all the time. Because obviously you're dealing with … a lot more different sort[s] of things. Like an animal can do one thing one minute and something different the next, so there's a lot more things that you are careful about. What I do—I'm basically in control of everything I do, so most of the acts that I do almost any person off the street with basic skills could come and learn. It's just a matter of whether they're dedicated enough to [do so]. (AC1998)

This observation reflected an insightful awareness that different circus acts required varied combinations of skills and the application of diverse technologies of learning. The comment also revealed an acceptance of the speaker's appreciation of other circus community members such as those who performed with animals. Clearly the sharing and use of a wide range of artifacts underpinned the deployment of multiple technologies according to purpose and need on the one hand and ability and opportunity on the other.

The use of technologies by circus troupes for earning, learning, and living within a mobile community goes much further than the examples presented here. Aside from the many other examples that could be given to illustrate how technologies can be used to mediate the space among performers and between performers and their audiences, it has also been acknowledged that this type of learning, with all its advantages, comes at a cost, just as it has for the members of many other mobile learning communities.

Technologies to Support the Formal Education of Children in Mobile Learning Communities

Interactions with technologies have both enabled and constrained learning in mobile communities. For example, many children over the generations have learned a range of necessary skills relating to the business side of their communities' operations and their learning has continued to be an important part of their lives as they seek to ensure the ongoing existence of their communities. These opportunities, however, have sat alongside lack of time and circumstances to promote formal learning that is increasingly becoming a necessary complement to the less formal lifelong learning that has characterized life in those communities. Formal literacy levels have not been high in many mobile learning communities that consist of occupational Travelers and their families. Many children in the current generation who may have better access to education have often been availed of these opportunities because their parents lobbied for a better deal or their teachers or educational authorities took an interest in trying new ideas. We now look at a few examples of how different types of technologies have been used by educational authorities to tailor educational experiences for children of particular mobile learning communities.

Lorna Daymond (2005) looks at examples of the development and use of several types of culturally relevant technologies such as books that have been used to gain the interest of Traveler children in the United Kingdom. The first book, entitled *Silly Jake*, was a story told to a young Scottish Traveler boy by his parents. The success of this book in helping the child to read was followed by the production of several other books and eventually of the book *Shaun's Wellies*. These books, which helped to fill a void in the market for culturally relevant resources for Traveler children in the early years of formal schooling, were not just about Travelers, but were produced with the assistance and cooperation of Traveler families. This helped in the case of *Shaun's Wellies*, for example, to ensure that the illustrations were accurate in their detail. An African equivalent of these types of publications were the 17 small books published in Fulfulde, Hausa, and English as part of an adult literacy program for Nigerian nomadic pastoralists, with the pastoralists telling their stories and seeing the books as an effective way of teaching others about their lifestyle and culture (McCaffery et al., 2006).

Attention then turned to how to engage children who were not interested in books with other technologies such as 3D resources that also encouraged literacy through imaginative play. Daymond (2005) explains the employment of a craftsman to design and build mini-caravans that were like Roma trailers that are now purchased by TESSs, preschools, and schools for all children in the early years in the United Kingdom. Daymond regards the technologies more recently developed and currently used in Traveler education as helping to fill one of the biggest gaps in education for Traveler children, that of literacy, including listening and speaking. As in Australia, Traveler adults have often over the generations been more confident with the application of mathematics to their everyday lives than they have been with literacy. Our own research has revealed also the ways in which children of occupational Travelers, such as fairground people, have taught their children to receive money and give change when serving the public (Moriarty et al., 1998, p. 53).

Other examples of technologies to support Traveler families with the education of their children in recent years in the United Kingdom have included the mobile library project, Education on Wheels (Wild-Smith, 2005). Considerable effort has been expended to ensure that resources in these mobile libraries are relevant to Travelers. They include photographs as well as history books, storybooks, and videos. Efforts have also continued to improve access to the mobile library, such that Travelers who were first-time library users develop the confidence to use libraries along their routes and the associated technologies. The expansion of technologies in modern libraries means that Travelers who, with their children, access mobile or fixed libraries have open to them the wide and ever-expanding learning opportunities that contemporary ICTs enable and the opportunity to expand and regularly to update their own use of ICTs for learning, complementing the many other types of technologies for learning and earning found in their own environments.

One similarity between these examples of recently developed technologies for learning among Traveler children and technologies used by circus performers is their ability to gain the interest and intrigue of those whom they were intended to engage. The next step in improving educational opportunities and outcomes for young Travelers will be to maintain this momentum and engagement in learning so that the effects are cumulative and sustainable.

Implications for the Future Education of Mobile Learning Communities

We began this chapter with this question. What opportunities for learning, earning, or living do technologies create for mobile learning communities? To some extent, we have approached the task of answering this question in the context of the opportunities afforded to members of mobile learning communities as they go about their daily lives, learning from one another and interacting with technologies that are essential for the ongoing operations of the community.

We have seen that a number of initiatives have been undertaken through the innovative use or development of technologies to address problems in educating children in mobile learning communities. To date, these attempts have reacted to the less than ideal circumstances in which most Travelers find themselves when it comes to the formal education of their children. This is largely because schools are designed to service primarily children of fixed residence. It is difficult for those schools to address the educational needs of children who not only travel for all or much of the year but who also belong to a range of mobile learning communities that have different travel patterns and quite different needs. Even distance education has proven difficult.

While attempts to address these problems more recently through the use of varied technologies have been disparate and generally uncoordinated, a collation and review of these efforts might now be timely and help to promote a more strategic approach to the education of the children of different mobile learning communities. Some efforts, such as the establishment of traveling schools and even mobile libraries, could provide the impetus for deciding on the bigger picture direction that Traveler education could take. Other initiatives, such as the production of culturally relevant resources, could impact on pedagogy. Together, these approaches, technologically akin perhaps to hardware and software, could provide a framework for encapsulating the breadth and depth of the varied techniques currently being used, in order to capture those elements that have been shown to enable learning in mobile learning communities and to address elements of constraint.

Efforts will need to be ongoing, reflective, responsive to, and inclusive of the communities that they are intended to serve. Perhaps someone, somewhere, will even tap into the ideas and technologies that Tim Rylands has used to engage his students and to improve their literacy levels.

Implications for Broader Educational Practice

Formal educational provision has sometimes been associated with an enduring ambivalence toward the place of technologies in promoting student learning. On the one hand, a celebrationist discourse is encapsulated by Kuzma's (2000) depiction of "[t]echno-optimists" (pp. 183-184). On the other hand, Kuzma's reference to "[t]echno-skeptics" (p. 184) reminds us of Hodas's (1993) account of "technological refusal" in schools by teachers who consider technology a distraction or even a threat to learning (see also McDougall, 2004), and also of cultural critic Neil Postman's construction of "technopoly" as "the surrender of culture to technology" (1993).

A contemporary manifestation of that ambivalence is the doubt expressed about the educational impact of the social practices associated with an extensive array of current technologies, ranging from mobile phones, SMS messaging, and MP3 players to online communities and wikis such as Facebook, MySpace, and YouTube associated with Web 2.0 to massively multiplayer online games like *Everquest* and *Second Life* (Delwiche, 2006). This ambivalence and doubt are reflected in the distinction between the older generation of digital immigrants and the younger generation of digital natives (Prensky, 2001), which can be seen as a particular representation of concerns about a digital divide separating particular communities within and between countries.

We see some aspects of this discussion as essentialist (for example, there are as many differences among digital natives as there are between them and digital immigrants) and even elitist (given the concentration of technologies associated with being a digital native in a relatively small proportion of the world's population). At the same time, the more extensive and inclusive definition of technologies provided at the beginning of this chapter has enabled us to analyze several of the technologies associated with mobile learning communities in ways that suggest a cautious optimism about the place of such technologies in formal education more broadly.

This cautious optimism is expressed for us in terms of three current issues in the ongoing debate about the purposes of education and its links with contemporary living. We argue also that these three issues are among several defining elements of the technological uses and applications of effective and sustainable mobile learning communities. The first issue is *problem solving*. The focus group interview with the circus performers cited in this chapter highlights how for them the technologies of their earning functioned also as the technologies of their learning and their living as they identified and analyzed problems and worked individually and collectively to solve those problems. So too with the technologies available to many young people today—at least in some parts of many developed countries. These can be seen as facilitating a problem solving approach to learning and life that requires engagement and commitment—two prerequisites of a productive and future-focused citizenry.

The second issue is *interaction and meaning-making*. If they are to survive, let alone to engage in learning, mobile communities must use and adapt technologies in ways that allow them to interact in meaningful ways with one another and with the non-mobile communities that they encounter and from which they derive significant aspects of their personal and group identities. Effective classrooms are also spaces in which interaction and meaning-making should be explicit intended learning outcomes. Technologies such as those associated with Web 2.0 can be harnessed to make such interaction and meaning-making more accessible and interesting to many contemporary learners and to equip them with dispositions and habits that can benefit them and others throughout life.

The third issue is *flow*. This refers to the idea, proposed by psychologist Mihaly Csikszentmihalyi (1998, 2003), that someone who is fully immersed in an activity experiences a feeling of energized focus, involvement, and success. There is a clear conceptual link between flow and mobility that highlights the importance of members of mobile learning communities being fully immersed and successful in their formal and informal learning, related to a wide range of activities from a daring trapeze act to dismantling and setting up complex machinery in sideshow alley to planning the most efficient itineraries of nomadic herds. Likewise flow evokes an intellectual fulfillment and a sense of awe and excitement that most educators would wish to see in their learners and themselves. While flow has been associated with recreational online games, its potential link with promoting learning in online environments is strong (Pace, 2007) and provides a compelling argument for seeking equivalent opportunities in face-to-face education.

Understanding technologies as applied interactions between the self and multiple environments, as outlined at the beginning of the chapter, thus helps to explain why and how mobile communities use such interactions to engage in learning, earning, and living in multiple contexts that are sometimes favorable and sometimes hostile to their mobility. Their success in enlisting various kinds of technologies to keep their communities efficiently on the move provides an object lesson for educators desiring to deploy technologies for maximum effectiveness in their learning and teaching sites and situations. Technologies can be inaccessible, alienating, and even disabling; they can also create new, exciting, and otherwise unavailable opportunities for mobile and non-mobile learners alike to experience achievement and to make meaning.

Questions for Reflection

- What are some of the key connections and relationships among the technologies for learning, earning, and living for mobile communities explored in this chapter? What are equivalent and different connections and relationships among technologies for non-mobile learners and their communities?
- In what ways can teachers be compared with circus ringmasters? What could teachers learn from ringmasters that would help them to interact and engage with their students? What limits might there be to the analogy?
- What possibilities might there be for enhancing literacy through the use of computer games in class? How might this approach impact on the learning of Traveler children who happen to be in the class with non-Travelers during these lessons? What are the advantages and

disadvantages of using this approach to teach literacy to non-mobile learners in classrooms?

- What is your position on the digital natives/digital immigrants distinction? If it is valid, what can teachers do to move from immigrant to native status? What other ways of thinking about technological use in contemporary education might be relevant and useful?
- Is there a digital divide in technological access between mobile and non-mobile communities? If so, what causes it and what might be done to reduce it? Are other kinds of digital divides significant in influencing contemporary educational outcomes?
- What do you see as the roles and responsibilities of technologies in facilitating the effectiveness of mobile learning communities? Are there any risks to that effectiveness posed by particular kinds or uses of technologies?

Suggestions for Further Reading

DiGiano, C., Goldman, S., & Chorost, M. (Eds.) (2008). *Educating learning technology designers: Guiding and inspiring creators of innovative educational tools.* London: Routledge.

Januszewski, A., Molenda, M., & Harris, P. (Eds.) (2007). *Educational technology: A definition with commentary.* London: Routledge.

Kukulska-Hulme, A., & Traxler, J. (Eds.) (2005). *Mobile learning: A handbook for educators and trainers.* London: Routledge.

O'Neil, H. F. Jr., Perez, R. S., & O'Neil, H. F. (Eds.) (2002). *Technology applications in education: A learning view.* London: Routledge.

Ryu, H., & Parsons, D. P. (Eds.) (2009). *Innovative mobile learning: Techniques and technologies.* Hershey, PA: Idea Group.

4

Globalization and Interactions
with the Outside World

This chapter on globalization and interactions with the outside world picks up and extends on the point reached in the chapter on technologies. One of the underlying tensions in much of the discussion in this chapter is the idea that mobile communities that can appear inward looking and almost self-sustaining also need to be aware of and respond to particular challenges presented by the outside world. It is more than the imperative to remain viable, however, that can lead those communities to adopt a more globalized perspective and to promote interactions with the outside world that are beyond what they regularly do. The chapter, through its exploration of the ways that these communities respond to and interact in a globalized world, broadens readers' understandings and interpretations of bargee, circus, and show communities.

Introduction

Globalization, like lifelong learning, is a concept that has been defined and used in many different ways. It has had political, economic, technological, and sociocultural connotations; it has been associated with both optimistic and pessimistic prospects (just as we found with technologies in chapter 3) and conspiracy theories. There have also been different approaches to understanding the effects of globalization, which also differ from the view that regards globalization as an outcome of particular events. Just as it can be helpful to acknowledge the contribution of early Travelers and explorers in initiating interactions with people well beyond their communities and views of the world and in being the first agents of change, it can also be helpful at the other end of the spectrum to consider how far we have traveled in the past decade with conceptualizing globalization and interactions with the outside world, depending on context and empirical evidence.

There is no doubt that the perceived effects of globalization have engendered disagreements and created debates and that some of these will continue into the future. Regardless of the origins of the debates and their influence on perceptions that fixed residence and mobile communities may have of each other, it is likely that what is perceived as an increasing pace of change associated with globalization and the different rates at which people absorb and cope with associated adjustments impact at least in part on the extent to which the benefits arising from globalization are recognized and embraced.

This chapter takes us on a journey, ultimately unfolding through our and others' examinations of contemporary mobile learning communities and their interactions with and responses to the outside world, and leading to a broader understanding of those communities in an increasingly globalized world. Our argument is that, while an economic dimension of these interactions exists, this is only part of the picture for these communities as they promote interactions beyond their own *milieux* while continuing to do what they regularly do in their own contexts and in the process retaining their cultural roots.

From the political, economic, cultural, and technological dimensions of globalization that are discernible in the review of selected literature, we turn in particular to cultural and political considerations to explore the effects of globalization on the educational prospects and futures of mobile learning communities with whom we and others have interacted through our research. This approach is intended to complement the emphasis in chapter 3 on technologies and their users, which did not have globalization as the central focus, and is supplemented by the recognition that economic viability needs to be maintained for self-sustaining mobile communities. Several surprises may be in store for many readers as we explore the following questions. In what ways do mobile learning communities respond to and interact with a globalized world? What is the impact of those responses and interactions on their educational prospects and futures? For the moment we leave readers to reflect on the challenges as well as the possibilities that globalization poses for the education and cultural sustainability of many traveling communities. In particular, we highlight the underlying tensions in those communities among self-sustainability, the need to interact with the outside world, and the positive impact that globalization can have on broader educational practice.

Contexts for Learning, Earning, and Living in a Globalized World

We noted in the introduction the profound and endemic influence that globalization has had on all of us, leading to opportunities for the exchange of goods, services, information, and ideas at unprecedented levels. As noted above, globalization is commonly regarded as having political, economic, technological, and sociocultural dimensions that, depending on context and perspective, are regarded as impacting positively and/or negatively on life, educational prospects, and educational futures.

Initial access to communities beyond our own has had varied origins and purposes, with inroads made via means such as military conquests and cultural imperialism that perhaps promoted among local communities feelings of fear and self-protection rather than welcoming interest toward Travelers. It is understandable, then, how members of groups might find collaboration and trust easier to develop in their own communities than with people outside those communities. In order to maintain their economic and cultural viability, and perhaps also fueled by the pace of change, mobile communities have had to reach out and to understand their fixed residence counterparts.

We turn now to what might be termed the roots of globalization in the realization that the idea crept up on the world slowly and over a long period of time, despite the term itself being introduced much more recently. We then look at some of the main ways in which globalization has been defined and used in the literature, and at how we have applied it in this chapter to understand the ways in which mobile learning communities have interacted with the outside world and the perceived effects of some of those interactions.

The Roots of Globalization

We know that the first communities were not settled in one place and that their existence as hunters and gatherers depended on their being mobile. The development of agriculture meant that many nomadic communities became settled. Those individuals who left their communities and led the earliest explorations or who joined expeditions that went to far-off lands, regardless of whether their motives related to future sustainability, adventure, or curiosity, must have engendered mixed feelings among those who stayed behind.

In any age, the way in which Travelers or even explorers are regarded is influenced by history and by personal and shared experiences and views of the world. The pathways that lay ahead of the early explorers consisted of many unknown human and environmental factors. Knowledge of these uncharted places grew during the journey and was disseminated when the explorers returned with stories, artifacts, flora, and maps that they had drawn. Explorers met people on their journeys who did not know that visitors were arriving. The first time that these other communities saw anyone from outside was a moment that must have changed their outlooks forever, as suddenly there existed the possibility or even the fear that strangers could arrive at any time.

One such category of early Travelers was the Roma groups who went to England in the 1500s (TT1999). These people left Northern India in about 1000 A.D. and traveled through other parts of Europe before reaching England. While it could be argued that globalization had its roots back when Travelers first began trading goods and services, the term was not introduced until the middle 1980s (Hoogvelt, 1997). Like the terms "lifelong learning" and "technology," "globalization" has been used in many different ways, making understandable Beck's (2000) claim that the word has been, and will continue to be, misused.

One way of interrogating the concept of globalization is to recognize that part of the difficulty associated with the term is not just that its dimensions can be variously defined but that those dimensions are linked by complex sets of interactions whose relationships have not yet been definitively or empirically measured or established. The gain in the momentum of globalization since the late 1900s, which has been associated with unprecedented technological advances, has added further complexity.

Dimensions of Globalization

Several interconnected dimensions of globalization can be discerned in the literature. These pertain to politics, economics, culture, and technology. The different ways in which the term "globalization" is applied, however, relate not only to which dimensions are used or whether globalization has a predominantly positive or negative effect but also to whether globalization is itself the result of other forces. As with lifelong learning, the way in which the term has been used has depended to a large extent on the context. Sometimes the different interpretations of globalization have been the subject of debate and lengthy theorization; at other times users of the term have applied it to a particular interpretation and set of empirical evidence. When consideration is given to how far we have traveled in our understanding of the concept in recent times, the approach in this chapter is to examine how evidence gathered by us and others from mobile learning communities at a number of locations across the globe increases our understanding of those communities as they respond to and interact with a globalized world. Of particular interest is how these communities interact with people outside their communities in ways that appear to go beyond what they normally do and that enable them to respond to opportunities and challenges that they meet on their way, particularly in their efforts to work toward better educational futures for their members.

Bartlett et al. (1997) emphasized the political dimension of globalization, writing about early explorers as mapmakers who refused to accept the limitations imposed on them by other people, and as people responsible for shifting borders and progressively widening boundaries. The authors also reflected critically on snapshots of their own lives to date after recognizing that they had reached their shared interest in globalization by coming from very different starting points and angles. This reflected another attempt to use theoretical understandings of globalization to apprehend practice better and then to comprehend the theory better by reflecting on practice.

Theorists continue to vary in their preference for relating to globalization as a predominantly positive or negative concept. For example, Bigum, et al. (1993) and Menzies (1994) articulated pessimistic views about the effects of globalization, whereas Danaher and Wyer (1997) took an optimistic view. This dichotomy reinforces the point that caution needs to be taken when comparing outcomes that are derived from different contexts.

In the context of research into mobile learning communities, Danaher (2001b) identified debates around whether globalization can be considered helpful or harmful, whether it results in a loss of cultural distinctiveness, whether it prolongs marginalization or promotes empowerment, or even "whether it is a servant of the market or a harbinger of culture." To understand the effects of globalization on mobile learning communities, it is necessary to examine how those communities respond to challenges and interact with a globalized world. On the surface it may appear that one of the main reasons behind the necessity to interact in this way is to remain economically viable, but examination of the evidence indicates a more complex picture. There are indications that some of the dichotomies raised by Danaher (2001b) are beginning to be contested by some members of mobile learning communities in their interactions with other mobile communities and with what might be regarded as the outside world. These are explored later in this chapter.

Researching Globalization in Mobile Learning Communities

By definition, to study the concept of globalization in mobile learning communities demands that researchers conduct interviews with Travelers and people connected with traveling communities in vastly different locations around the world. Comparing data collected from different locations as far from one another as Europe, Latin America, Africa, and Australia encourages comparisons to be made across data sets, with similarities and differences emerging in some unexpected places that broaden understandings of mobile learning communities and of the interactions that those communities have with individuals and organizations from the outside world. As alluded to earlier, however, it is important not just to compare the results or conclusions drawn in different studies but also to acknowledge the different contexts that are likely to have impacted on those results.

The act of conducting interviews with members of mobile communities could itself be regarded as a globalizing influence as interviewers and interviewees inevitably learn from each other and broaden their understandings and interpretations of the political, economic, technological, and cultural dimensions of each other's lives. The act of interviewing and the research projects with which it is associated, therefore, could be regarded as a vehicle for promoting globalization.

The following examination of interactions promoting globalization between mobile learning communities and the outside world generates ideas that emerged from interviews that might surprise the readers of this book. During their interactions with interviewers, who themselves are part of the outside world from the perspective of mobile community members, interviewees from different parts of the globe and representing diverse groups, such as bargees, circus, or show people, revealed some highly powered interactions with members of their own communities who extended the boundaries of previous generations as well as directly with state or international organizations that most people never experience. Disregarding for a moment the difficulties that members of mobile learning communities typically have with accessing formal education, the level of involvement of some members of these communities with powerful organizations should itself command respect from those outside those communities. The evidence is drawn from our own interviews as well as reports from investigations undertaken by other researchers representing countries different from our own. The rigor and trustworthiness of the overall conclusions are increased when the results of these independent sets of results are drawn together.

Interactions Promoting Globalization Between Mobile Learning Communities and the Outside World

The interactions that are examined in this part of the chapter relate predominantly to the sociocultural and political dimensions of globalization, as indicated earlier. This approach complements the emphases on financial viability or economics and on technologies in other chapters.

The evidence for these two dimensions is presented together in relation to the two questions. In what ways do mobile learning communities respond to and interact with a globalized world? What is the impact of those responses and interactions on their educational prospects and futures?

In What Ways do Mobile Learning Communities Respond to and Interact with a Globalized World?

In Europe particularly, members of mobile learning communities, including children, are often multilingual. The necessity to interact with people outside their community could be regarded as being facilitated by the ability to speak different languages. Conversely, the necessity to interact with a globalized world could be seen as the catalyst to speak in and maintain several languages.

Interviews with Dutch circus people revealed that when circus people in Europe remain for at least one year with circuses in other European countries this allows sufficient time to learn another language (DC1999). Similarly, most circus children in Europe could speak two languages and sometimes they shifted from one language to the other in the one sentence.

Interviews with other European Travelers highlighted the extent of their international itineraries. For example, Dutch bargees revealed that they traveled through a number of countries throughout Europe, including not only the Netherlands but also Germany, Belgium, northern France, and Switzerland (DB1999). It emerged from these discussions that Dutch Travelers also adopted other languages as a natural part of their culture. One of the Dutch show people, for example, spoke about having stayed in Prague and Israel and even for a year in the Czech Republic (DS1999). Being able to communicate in the Czech Republic was not a problem; he could speak German.

Likewise Scottish show people spoke about fairground communities traveling to foreign locations to present their shows. This was seen as an opportunity to visit other places to present their shows where traditionally fairs were not located. Singapore was seen as a lucrative market but other places such as Africa and Malaysia were also visited and communities were away for five months at a time (SS1999). Traveling by boat was also now seen as viable and many younger people were prepared to go further afield. Mention was made of the relative ease with which such travel could now be undertaken and how travel companies could organize the transport of Travelers' gear in a package deal. Reference was made to the days when:

> … [I]f you traveled two or three hundred miles down in England you were going far, because the vehicles you had weren't capable of going too far. In those days you had four or five loads for one roundabout; well, they can take one now. That's a different story, because the expense on the boats to get over there, it's viable. (SS1999)

This ease of travel that has been experienced in recent times by some fairground people is not restricted to members of mobile communities. Globalization has, however, enabled mobile communities to get the best from both worlds; they can retain their cultural heritages and traditions within their communities and also see and experience parts of the world that their forebears could not. As a Scottish show person said with measured understatement, "It's a wide world" (SS1999).

What is the Impact of those Responses and Interactions on their Educational Prospects and Futures?

One of the changes in attitudes relating to globalization was that in Europe members of traveling communities were seeing themselves as members of a much larger community of the traveling occupational population, rather than predominantly as bargee, circus, or fairground people (DS1999). This more global perspective was regarded as a positive step. While retaining their particular cultural heritages, different mobile groups could also celebrate and find camaraderie in a shared culture.

Another influence on this more global outlook was the formation of the European Community. The Community made traveling much easier because of the disappearance of borders that formerly presented complications. The observation was made that Travelers who once stayed within their own countries progressively widened their scope until their itineraries covered much of Europe (DS1999).

When EFECOT was in its early days, one of the policy-makers was invited to France to conduct a presentation at a conference organized by UNESCO (TT1999). He also visited the UNESCO headquarters in France on several other occasions. Recognizing that (the now disbanded) EFECOT was really a small player on a big stage, he was keen to collaborate with other national and international representatives of people who are mobile to put the education of mobile people on the UNESCO agenda, especially given UNESCO's commitment to Education for All.

One mobile community in Europe that successfully lobbied for specialized educational provision for its children aged between three and a half and six years was the Dutch bargee families. Scholten (2000) reported that there were 450 children in this age range who lived on ships with their parents, meaning that these children were unable to attend kindergarten or elementary school on a regular basis. These children's older siblings generally attended boarding school during the week. While it was not mandated that the younger children had to attend school, the reality was that they did not have the early educational opportunities of other Dutch children, meaning that, by the time that they attended school in the year that they turned seven, they were already behind their counterparts. As a result of the efforts of the parents of Dutch bargee children, the first berth school was established in 1967, quickly followed by others. The berth schools in Amsterdam, Rotterdam, and four other towns are all networked, such that the collaboration among these schools helps ensure that the attendance and progress of bargee children are tracked in the system.

In Europe then, as on other continents, one of the reasons why representative members of mobile learning communities initiated contact with the outside world beyond their regular involvement with those communities was to lobby for a better education for their children and other community members. This has also occurred in Australia (AS2003).

Australian show people have enacted several political, economic, and social tactics to campaign for improved educational opportunities (Moriarty et al., 1998). Parallels can be drawn between these tactics and dimensions of globalization, which can then be helpful in trying to gain a more encompassing and unified understanding of the concept of globalization. The political tactics included gaining support for the continuation and expansion of the existing educational program provided for show children, at first close to home and then increasingly higher up the political chain. Even then, the importance of working in the interests of show children from the different Australian states was recognized. Importantly, it was found that the social tactics employed by show people helped them to maintain their distinctive culture, which in effect meant that mainstream educational approaches would be culturally inappropriate. For example, if their children had to attend day or boarding schools with other children, then they could become disengaged from their own communities. The same people also employed economic tactics in order to maintain a viable financial base. One way that this was done was by shifting the emphasis from using people to entertain the crowds to using technologies, thus responding to changing interests among the general public. This research, therefore, applied and developed theories around political, economic, and sociocultural tactics that paralleled dimensions of globalization, pointing at the same time to the complexity of relationships among these dimensions.

Kiddle (2000) also noted the concern of Gypsy Traveler families in England who, while recognizing the importance of education for economic sustainability and therefore wishing to take advantage of moves to promote access to schooling for children of Gypsy Traveler families, were worried that the globalizing aspect of schooling could result in a loss of cultural distinctiveness. In response to this concern, some parents sent their children to school but insisted that their children still learned family cultural traditions. Other parents, who perhaps perceived an even greater dichotomy between going to school and maintaining their cultural practices, refused to send their children to school.

Implications for the Future Education of Mobile Learning Communities

This chapter began with a promise to take you on a journey in order to explore the following questions. In what ways do mobile learning communities respond to and interact with a globalized world? What is the impact of those responses and interactions on their educational prospects and futures? Our journey has involved tracing different types of routes taken by different groups of mobile people from the early explorers to contemporary young Travelers who have created new maps for their own communities. We could also have taken you on metaphorical journeys, but you have already been there when we explored together the work of British teacher Tim Rylands and his students in Chapter 3, which focused on technologies and their users. We could also have taken you to India to see whether the call for Education for All has been realized there, but you will be going to India in Chapter 7 when you explore communities at risk. Our journeys on this subject could fill a lifetime. The recognition by international organizations such as the United Nations Educational, Scientific, and Cultural Organization (UNESCO) that mobile learning communities exist in many parts of the world opens up possibilities that globalization has the potential not only to sustain but also to enrich these communities.

One of the most powerful and empowering outcomes of globalization that we found in mobile learning communities was the realization in Europe, particularly by members of bargee, circus, and fairground communities, that they were really part of a much larger community of occupational Travelers. To see similarities where once you saw differences makes the world seem a much smaller place. The realization by members of these communities that what they share complements their differences is a legacy of the now disbanded EFECOT.

As with Australian show people who lobbied successfully for a better education for their children, it can be argued that the efforts of EFECOT members to put the education of different groups of mobile communities on the UNESCO agenda effectively sought to reduce the negative impact that globalization can have on the education of mobile groups and to increase the potential positively outcomes of such globalization. By drawing attention to their common disadvantage in terms of formal educational provision, these mobile learning communities are more likely to achieve outcomes that improve their educational prospects and futures while enabling them to maintain their cultural distinctiveness, both in relation to one another and more broadly.

The pace of change under globalization can vary enormously from very slow changes over a long period to relatively substantial changes in a short time frame. The connections that mobile learning communities in Europe have been able to make relatively quickly in recent times with UNESCO, a long-established, international organization that is committed to Education for All, appear quite striking for outsiders in particular and may even have been surprising, given the traditional and endemic poverty of access to education by Travelers worldwide that could have disabled attempts at high-level interaction. It could be said that the political dimension of globalization in this example has helped not only to sustain but even to invigorate the cultural dimension. Rather than cultural heritages of individual Traveler groups being lost in these exchanges, any fears that this might happen may have been overridden by positive outcomes and optimism for the future of traveling communities, both individually and as a group.

The opportunities taken by some fairground people in Europe to travel abroad to present their shows demonstrate how the cultural dimension of globalization can intersect with the economic dimension, although the latter was not a particular focus of this chapter. Firstly, it is necessary to have the financial ability to travel such long distances. Secondly, it was apparent from the conversation with two Scottish show people that the maintenance of one's cultural heritage evident in the distinctiveness of what these Travelers had to offer citizens in Singapore, for example, was an integral part of what made the effort financially viable and even rewarding (SS1999). This is an example of how globalization can promote the continuation of one's cultural background rather than enact a cultural blur that reduces cultural distinctions to the point of losing much-valued heritage. The implication, however, is that continued acceptance and economic viability and rewards depend either on the newness to other groups of what Travelers have to offer, necessitating the continuation of their mobile status, or on an affinity that develops with local Singaporeans as the newness of what they have to offer fades.

Globalization, therefore, has enabled the concept of mobile learning communities to move onto a world stage in recent years in ways probably never previously imagined. Similar occurrences, *albeit* on a smaller scale, have happened in Australia, with unprecedented results. The Queensland School for Travelling Show Children is a beacon for mobile learning communities in Australia and elsewhere, even though work still needs to be done to achieve more for this group of children as well as parallel situations for children in other mobile learning communities. Even so, globalization has already had a positive impact on the educational prospects and futures of these and other children as success stories are conveyed to other mobile communities.

Implications for Broader Educational Practice

Being able to conceptualize different groups of mobile learners as exhibiting important commonalities while retaining their cultural distinctiveness can be effective in uniting the diverse groups of learners who compete for access to educational resources because such commonalities mean that there are fewer groups to compete for the same resources. The hope is that this will lead to greater appreciation and less fear, and that the more pessimistic conceptions of globalization identified by Danaher (2001b) and Danaher and Wyer (1997) will be set beside more optimistic views. In the past, mobile learners were separated from the lives of learners of fixed residence, even when they sat together in the same classrooms. If the positive experiences of sharing culture and educational aspirations with other traveling groups highlighted in this chapter could be transferred to individual classrooms, schools, and education systems, then the sharing of educational resources might be regarded as possibilities for everyone rather than as the division of already limited opportunities.

The pace at which globalization has impacted on everyone in the past decade, underpinned by continual advances in technology, changes in economic stability, and political and cultural forces, suggests that the future needs to be embraced positively by all parties not only as they interact within their own communities but also as they embrace the outside world. The alternative, which is for groups to attempt to insulate themselves from others in order to protect what they have always had, has no future. This is because no-one is immune from the effects of globalization. It could be argued that young people lead the way with technologies and the effects that ICTs have on their lives and with their abilities to look outwards. They are unlikely to accept or even understand a world that lives in a past that they have never known. It is to be hoped that the centuries-old marginalization that many mobile learning communities experienced through very limited or no access to formal education will be replaced by further collaboration and the development of trust that leads to more enriching educational experiences for all.

Questions for Reflection

- Think about the organizations or political forces in your part of the world that could be considered to promote the equivalent of the EFA aspiration of UNESCO. Which are these organizations? What are these forces? How have they gone about effecting change in education at the local level?
- What have been the effects of globalization on the educational opportunities and cultural practices of Travelers through your community and the people who live there permanently?
- What effects—or perceived effects—of globalization have people in your community feared in the past 10 years? Have these fears been realized or sustained?
- Over the past 10 years, what have been some of the positive effects to emerge from globalization that have been evident in your community?
- What challenges lie ahead and what optimism does globalization promise for the future of your community and the people who travel through it?
- What can your community learn from others that would help it to meet the challenges of globalization and to embrace the future with optimism?

Suggestions for Further Reading

Burbules, N. C., & Torres, C. A. (Eds.) (2009/in press). *Globalization and education: Critical perspectives* (2nd ed.). London: Routledge.
Chi-Kin Lee, J., & Caldwell, B. (2010, in preparation). *Changing schools in an era of globalization.* London: Routledge.
Elliott, A., & Lemert, C. (Eds.) (2009/in press). *Globalization: A reader.* London: Routledge.
Lingard, B., & Rizvi, F. (2009/in press). *Globalizing educational policy.* London: Routledge.
Munck, R. (Ed.) (2009/in press). *Globalization and migration: New issues, new politics.* London: Routledge.
Spring, J. (2008). *Globalization of education: An introduction.* London: Routledge.
Stronach, I. D. (2009/in press). *Globalizing education, educating the local: How method made us mad.* London: Routledge.
Turner, B. (Ed.) (2009/in press). *Handbook of globalization studies.* London: Routledge.

5

The Knowledge Economy and Workplace Learning

Increasingly work is understood as a mobile activity, displaced from some fixed location within a factory or shop and mobilized across a range of sites such as the home, online, and overseas. The forms of learning that take place within these mobile workplaces are similarly complex and shifting. Creating viable workplace learning practices for the mobile lifestyles characteristic of the contemporary knowledge economy is a significant challenge for educational provision.

Introduction

The focus of this chapter is the challenges and opportunities that the emergence of the knowledge economy provides for mobile learning communities. We are particularly interested in exploring these communities' workplace learning practices in relation to this new economic environment.

Different mobile communities respond to the challenges of the knowledge economy in a variety of ways. Indeed, certain mobile communities have emerged in response to that economy. An example is the large number of native English speakers who have moved to countries of a Non-English Speaking Background (NESB) to teach English. The market for such language teaching is driven in part by an understanding that English is the international language of business; accordingly both children and adults in countries such as China, South Korea, Vietnam, and Thailand are keen to learn the language, creating opportunities for Britons, North Americans, Australians, and people from other English-speaking nations.

Traditionally, many mobile communities have emerged to support an agrarian economy. This is true particularly of the traveling fair, which has links to livestock markets and the sale of other agricultural and horticultural produce. Other mobile communities have been employed in the movement of livestock, such as nomadic pastoralists. Accordingly, it would seem that a profound shift is required within such mobile communities to move from engaging with an agrarian to a knowledge economy. At the same time, however, this shift is associated with a transformation within the agrarian economy itself, wherein the commercializing of knowledge becomes a significant feature. So while the context remains the same in dealing with agrarian-based societies, the kind of work taking place and the skills that are valued have been transformed by the knowledge economy. For example, biotechnology is now a significant part of rural industries.

In other cases, the emergence of the knowledge economy in certain countries has created shortages of labor in other industries that have created a demand for mobile workers. In Australia, for example, the rise of the knowledge sector of the economy has created labor shortages in horticultural industries, and guest workers from Pacific Island nations have come in to fill these positions. Without such mobile labor, the harvesting of certain crops would be in peril.

Other mobile communities are defined by their removal from the knowledge economy. Traditional traveling communities, such as the Romany Gypsies, pursue a lifestyle that depends on complex literacy practices that are nevertheless viewed negatively by the broader society (Levinson, 2007). And while Ireland has experienced significant economic transformation to a contemporary knowledge economy with considerable investment in information technology, the Irish Traveler community is characterized by cultural traditions that are marked by its distance from, rather than its integration into, this economy (Kenny, 1997).

Furthermore, in certain cases a mobile community is defined by its rejection of, and its desire to escape from, the contemporary knowledge economy. While work in this economy is characterized by being indoors surrounded by ICTs, certain Travelers seek open spaces as an antidote to what they perceive to be an artificial and highly pressured environment. New Travelers in Great Britain, for example, are seeking to "drop out" from this society.

The chapter is divided into five sections:

- The knowledge economy and workplace learning in the literature about learning communities
- Concepts and issues that relate to the impacts of the knowledge economy and workplace learning on mobile communities
- Evidence of the knowledge economy and workplace learning in selected mobile learning communities
- Implications for the future education of mobile learning communities
- Implications for broader educational practice.

The Knowledge Economy, Workplace Learning, and Learning Communities

The idea of the knowledge economy can be understood in the context of shifts in work practices over the last century. It is framed within the categorizing of industry within three broad areas: primary industry, referring to activities tied directly to work performed on the natural environment, such as mining, fishing, and agriculture; secondary industry, based on the conversion of the raw materials of primary production through manufacturing into finished goods, such as motor vehicles or processed foods; and tertiary or service industries that focus on promoting human capital, and that include sectors such as education, government services, and ICTs. A knowledge economy refers to the role of information and education services in facilitating economic production.

The knowledge economy does not simply involve the development of new knowledge but also the "more effective use and exploitation of all types of knowledge in all manner of economic activity" (Houghton & Sheehan, 2000, p. 1). While knowledge has played an important role in economic activity throughout human history, the degree of the incorporation of knowledge and information into the economy now is such that it has profound structural and qualitative effects on the character of economic practice. Thus, Houghton and Sheehan (2000) viewed the rise in the knowledge intensity of economic activities, driven by the impact of the exponential growth of ICTs such as the Internet on business and community life, as a defining feature of the knowledge economy. The other defining feature that they identify is globalization, marked by a reduction in the barriers to both foreign investment and trade in goods and services along with the deregulation of financial and product markets, which has contributed to escalating capital flows among developed nations.

The knowledge economy involves a range of different forms of knowledge: knowledge of markets; knowledge of goods and services; knowledge of financial planning; knowledge of ICTs and systems. The knowledge economy is focused on global networks and partnerships that are equipped to respond flexibly and quickly to transformations in market conditions. Within the knowledge economy, the language of "market forces" comes to prevail as a framework for making sense of different aspects of life: education, for example, is understood as a global market that offers various challenges and opportunities.

Rifkin (1995) explored the implications of the emergence of the knowledge economy for workplace learning and training. Japanese workplace models that are team-based and cooperative rather than hierarchical have been particularly influential in shaping the new production systems characteristic of the knowledge economy. Rifkin cited one Japanese manager explaining the process of sharing information with workers:

> One of our most important jobs is to make all of our employees willing to cooperate fully, and to make them want to continually improve themselves. To achieve this, it is necessary for us to provide all kinds of information equally to everyone ... Every employee has the right of access to "all" computerized information within the company. (p. 98)

The company Google, which itself has played a tremendous role in the generation of the knowledge economy, epitomizes the new, open workplace. At the company's Googleplex in California, gourmet meals are supplied free of cost through 18 cafeterias, and employees are encouraged to play games and exercise freedom of expression as a way of helping to fuel creativity and innovation (Wright, 2008, pp. 16-17).

Universities play an integral role in creating the conditions of possibility for a knowledge economy. In some ways this has compromised their role as a community of scholars; rather, they have come to function more as a manufacturing plant producing knowledge workers. Contemporary universities are challenged to achieve economies in processing students while simultaneously maintaining the traditions of scholarship and inculcating the joy of learning to those who pass through their gates. It is difficult, for example, to reconcile those traditions and that joy with the World Bank's (2002) encapsulation of the principal characteristics of *Building Knowledge Economies*, in which universities are intended to be active participants:

> Continuous, market-driven innovation is the key to competitiveness, and thus to economic growth, in the knowledge economy. This requires not only a strong science and technology base, but, just as importantly, the capacity to link fundamental and applied research; to convert the results of that research to new products, services, processes, or materials; and to bring these innovations quickly to market. It also entails an ability to tap into and participate in regional and global networks of research and innovation. (cited in Kenway et al., 2004, pp. 336-337)

One dimension of the knowledge economy has been what Cookson (2002) called the hybridization of higher education, with a growth in distance education based on the use of ICTs to complement face-to-face teaching.

Conceptualizing the Knowledge Economy, Workplace Learning, and Mobile Communities

In shifting the focus to a consideration of some of the theoretical resources connecting the knowledge economy and workplace learning with mobile communities, we explore a range of concepts and approaches that help to articulate the tensions and opportunities that such connections bring about.

Situated Knowledge

First, while the emergence of the knowledge economy is bound up in processes of globalization, it is important to recognize the ways in which knowledge practices are situated, contextualized, and associated with cultural values and relations of power.

The value of such situated, localized knowledge for sustaining mobile communities was highlighted by one of the most devastating catastrophes of recent years. When the tsunami struck coastal communities in places by the Indian Ocean on December 26, 2004, it was reported that casualties among local animal species were relatively few (Williams, 2005). For example, herds of elephants began to move out of coastal areas before the tidal waves struck and sought refuge on elevated land. Similarly, sea Gypsies called the Moken in the Andaman Sea off the coasts of Burma and Thailand survived the disaster by retreating to an elevated part of their island (Simon, 2005). On the other hand, many Western tourists in places like Phuket in Thailand were unaware of the impending disaster and unfortunately suffered the consequences.

Knowledge about the tsunami was recorded elsewhere: scientists in Hawaii detected evidence of a massive earthquake in the Indian Ocean, but they were unable to warn the threatened communities of the approaching wave. While there are a number of early warning systems within the relatively prosperous countries of the Pacific Rim, at the time of this event it was considered economically unviable to locate such a system in the Indian Ocean.

The tsunami disaster teaches us something about knowledge: its movement and its value. In contemporary Western culture, scientific knowledge such as seismology has a particularly privileged value, evident in the economic investment in such knowledge and its location in significant learning institutions such as universities. In the language of the French sociologist Pierre Bourdieu (1990), such knowledge has both economic and cultural capital.

The localized knowledge of the sea Gypsies, on the other hand, has relatively little economic and cultural value within the global knowledge economy. Such knowledge clearly derives from situated learning (Kilpatrick et al., 2003; see also Lave & Wenger, 1991; Wenger, 1998), has been accumulated over centuries of experience in this region, and is passed on through an oral culture, so that an understanding of a tsunami and the signs from the sea heralding its arrival took on the status of a myth. CBS journalist Bob Simon (2005), who did a report for the television current affairs program *60 Minutes* on their survival story, commented:

> It's their intimacy with the sea that saved the Moken. They're born on the sea, live on the sea, die on the sea. They know its moods and motions better than any marine biologist. They're nomads, constantly moving from island to island, living more than six months a year on their boats. (2005, n.p.)

While such knowledge has, from the perspective of a media network such as CBS, some value in terms of its exotic appeal and resonance within the genre of miraculous survival story, its enduring significance at the global level is likely to be limited, much less than that generated by marine biologists. After all, the sea Gypsies live a largely subsistence existence within an outpost in the Indian Ocean—Simon (2005) comments that they are, "of all the people of the world, among the least touched by modern civilization" (n.p.). Thus they have much less global impact than a multinational company drawing on developments in marine biology to aid medical research, for example. Indeed, their exotic and marginal status means that the Moken lack access to the forms of validated knowledge that might transform their lives in ways that derive value within the prevailing logic of this "modern civilization," and the knowledge economy that accompanies it.

A significant feature of privileged and powerful forms of knowledge is their capacity to overwhelm and colonize other forms of knowledge. Foucault (2003, p. 179) discussed how in France during the eighteenth century there emerged processes that allowed bigger, more general or more industrialized knowledges, or knowledges that circulated more easily, to annex, confiscate, and take over smaller, more particular, more local, and more artisanal knowledges. Foucault viewed this as a period in which knowledges, rather like the bodies in which they were situated, were disciplined, involving their selection, normalization, hierarchization, and centralization (p. 181).

From Discipline to Control

Within the context of the knowledge economy, while there are still tendencies to take over smaller, localized knowledges, rather than centralization what is more evident is the dispersal and dissemination of such knowledge throughout the global market place in the interests of economic activity. In this context, the emergence of the knowledge economy can be understood to some extent in relation to the transformation from a disciplinary society to a society of control. Foucault (1977) is a writer who is credited with articulating the relations of power and the forms of knowledge that characterized a disciplinary society. Bodies and minds were carefully molded and quietly coerced through training and habit to form effective workers for the industrial factories that were characteristic of the disciplinary society that emerged in Western countries in the nineteenth century. At the same time, taxonomies of knowledge emerged across diverse scholastic fields such as economics, biology, linguistics, medicine, and so forth that focused on securing the health, fitness for work, and appropriate educational status of the populations of these countries. The disciplinary society was structured around relations of power, which worked the body at a microphysical level, and forms of knowledge, which were designed to manage populations, focusing on the physical, social, and moral health of people.

Changes associated in part with the emergence of the knowledge economy have transformed the disciplinary society from the closed, closely regulated world represented by the factory to a more open system of control (Deleuze, 1995). In what Deleuze called the society of control, work is much more mobile and fluid but still subject to intense pressures. This transformation could be represented metaphorically through drawing on images associated with banking and finance. The financial model connected with the disciplinary society was represented by the bank, a solid, dependable looking edifice where one's savings could be stored and accumulate steadily and where credit in the forms of home and other loans required careful management. The financial model associated with the society of control is represented by today's incredibly complex system where vast sums of money are traded through a myriad of funds and financial instruments and people in Western cultures are accustomed to living off credit cards and generating significant debt. When this system faces difficulties, as it did with the credit crunch in the sub-prime mortgage market in the United States of America in late 2008, the global implications can be enormous.

This complex global financial system highlights the importance of information in the contemporary knowledge economy. Forms of knowledge are no longer so much focused on managing populations and producing goods and services, as occurred in the disciplinary society, as traded as commodities, representing marketable goods and services. For example, knowledge in an emerging field such as biotechnology might be used in the creation of new markets for different fuel sources, just as a knowledge of a new development in literacy teaching can be used for expanding education markets.

Another analogy for making sense of this new economy is to think of the effect of new media technologies in creating a voracious and insatiable need for content. The media of a few decades ago consisted of a limited number of radio and television stations, a few film studios, and some newspapers and magazines. While the number of television and radio stations has expanded exponentially over recent decades, the generation of online environments through the World Wide Web and virtual worlds such as Second Life means that contemporary culture is thoroughly saturated with media. Accordingly, a challenge for contemporary media is supplying sufficient content to feed this monster. Thus, a focus of the contemporary media economy is on producing knowledge and content workers capable of generating the information, news, commentary, and entertainment needed to sustain this environment.

This escalation of media technology points to a further dimension of the knowledge economy: the rapidly shifting character of work. A characteristic of the disciplinary society was relatively stable patterns of employment, such that a worker routinely remained in the same field of employment throughout his (for it was customarily a masculine role) working history, gradually ascending the ladder of career progression. In the contemporary knowledge economy, an individual is expected to have a number of jobs and career options throughout her/his working life, moving between and across fields such as education, media, information technology and systems, government, and business. Rather than knowledge workers being tied to a single company, it is increasingly common for those workers to operate as consultants outsourcing their skills, and indeed for professionals in fields such as multimedia and finance to telecommute, working from an office in their home.

Systems Thinking

While this transformation from a discipline to control society has its problematic character, as Deleuze (1995) highlighted, the thinking that accompanies this change might be viewed more positively. This change from discipline to control is analogous with a transformation from mechanistic thinking to systems thinking, associated with the ideas of Capra (1996). Much of the knowledge that impelled the processes of industrialization depended on a kind of mechanistic thinking that broke things down to their component parts. For example, the periodic table identified the different chemical elements that comprised various substances, while engineering focused on fitting the parts of machinery together in the most efficient manner. This paradigm of knowledge formation entailed constructing taxonomies, evident for example in the classification of plant types in biology, and also led to binary oppositions as a way of making sense of differences.

The systems thinking paradigm is focused rather on interconnectivity; instead of breaking objects down to their components, it is a case of considering their place in a system that is greater than they are, studying how their operation produces effects that influence other parts of that system. A famous example can be extracted from chaos and complexity theory, where the fluttering of a butterfly's wings in South America can set off a series of reactions that eventually leads to a typhoon in Japan. Thus the focus of this thinking and the forms of knowledge that it produces are more concerned with connections and resonances than with discrete parts.

This shift has important implications for mobile communities. Within a mechanistic worldview, knowledge about different social groups (that is, parts of the social whole) was generated through various forms such as surveys and ethnographic studies. Such knowledge shaped the way that these groups were viewed and treated by various institutional authorities. Indeed, it meant that central institutions were authorized to generate knowledge about certain demographic groups who were regarded as problematic, because of their otherness or some dimension that was perceived to threaten the health and welfare of the society. The binary oppositions that were constructed distinguished between us and them, settled and nomadic, lawful and lawless.

Within a systems thinking worldview, the focus shifts to considering how the knowledge generated about a particular group and the consequent treatment of this group affect the social body as a whole. Rather than making Travelers the object of knowledge produced by institutions authorized to speak on their behalf and to make judgments about their welfare, systems thinking is attuned to considering how the knowledge perspectives of mobile groups have their own place in shaping their actions and those of others. Systems thinking is mobile in the way that it moves among different perspectives and forms of knowledge.

A mobile learning community such as a circus provides an example of systems thinking in action. The circus is a complex, interconnected system consisting of different parts and perspectives: the audience, performers, animals, ringmaster, caterers, and so forth. As the circus staff take on multiple roles and responsibilities, they are able to understand the system from different perspectives and consider how a change or disruption in one part will affect the overall performance. In other words, rather than thinking and operating independently they work interdependently.

The advantages of mobile and flexible thinking and knowledge-making in facilitating processes of self-transformation are eloquently expressed in these words of Foucault:

> After all, what would be the value of knowledge if it resulted only in a certain knowingness, and not, in one way of another, in the knower's straying afield from himself [sic]? There are times in life when the question of knowing if you can think differently than one thinks, and perceive differently than one sees, is absolutely necessary if one is to go on thinking and reflecting at all. (as cited in Rothwell, 2008, p. 9)

This thought pattern recalls the way in which mystics in ancient times sought to wander into the desert in order to attain a fresh perspective. Such nomadic patterns of thought, in which the knower strays afield from her/himself, seem to be important in confronting the challenges facing the world today.

It is possible to imagine the emergence of mobile knowledge workers working across a range of fields responding to the challenges of the twenty-first century. They might conceivably be involved in rehabilitating damaged ecologies on land and in the ocean, networking isolated communities through new ICTs, or forging links among diverse cultural groups dispersed across a wide geographical region. Such workers could also be involved in generating alternative energy from diverse sources to support the needs of society in an environmentally sustainable manner. They could be involved in moving across the pathways of interconnection that bind the world and the planet. Accordingly, the literature presented here points to possible greatly empowering futures within the knowledge economy for mobile communities.

Forms of Capital and Social Fields

Another conceptual lens for making sense of the impact of the knowledge economy of mobile communities emerges from the work of Bourdieu and his ideas of different forms of capital and social fields (1990). That is, a social system can be divided into various fields, each with different roles and positions, approved forms of conduct, and forms of value. As we move through life, we go from the formal educational field to assorted occupational fields (such as business, law, and government) and come into contact with different cultural fields (sporting, religious, music, and so forth). Bourdieu made sense of actions within these fields along a continuum ranging from the autonomous pole to the heteronomous pole. At the autonomous pole, actions are driven by the values of the field itself. When we speak of something being good in itself, such as "art for art's sake," or learning a difficult foreign language as something of value in itself, we are identifying with the autonomous pole of the field. When we speak of something being valuable not in itself but because of its worth as an economic generator, we are identifying with the heteronomous pole of the field. For example, an anthology of challenging poetry might be valued within the autonomous pole of the literary field because its experimentations with form and thematic complexities adds to the overall value of literature. However, a bestseller might not offer much literary value but be very significant in generating profits for publishing houses and the author, and therefore contribute at the heteronomous pole of the literary field.

The knowledge economy tends to emphasize the importance of the heteronomous pole in its focus on the economic value of forms of knowledge. That is to say, the focus is not on knowledge as a good in itself but rather in terms of its commercial potential. In part, this focus reflects the growing managerial ethic that has accompanied the massification of higher education in Western societies. Students are understood as consumers purchasing an educational product (degree qualifications) that they can trade for a lucrative career. Furthermore, the focus on research produced from universities and research centers is increasingly on commercial applications.

More broadly, the distinction between autonomous and heteronomous values can be related to the distinction between high and popular culture. Within contemporary Western communities, it has become quite conventional to distinguish between high cultural forms such as opera, ballet, theatre, and literary fiction and popular cultural forms such as rock music, film, television, and sports such as baseball. While high cultural forms lack the mass appeal and therefore the economic power of popular culture, they are regarded as culturally significant and worth investing in because of their elevating and educational value.

Many mobile communities are influenced by these cultural distinctions and use them to make sense of their activities and reach an audience. In some cases they challenge the distinctions, showing how the boundaries between high and popular culture, and between autonomous and heteronomous values, are malleable and shifting. While Shakespearean plays tend to be regarded as high culture today, for the strolling players who performed his works in the sixteenth and seventeenth centuries they were regarded in many cases as popular entertainments. Similarly, opera was regarded as a popular cultural form in Italy in the eighteenth century but is now marked as designating high culture. On the other hand, the circus tends to be regarded in Western countries such as Great Britain, the United States of America, and Australia as a popular cultural form, but in Eastern Europe it is regarded as a high cultural pursuit with an equivalent status to opera and ballet.

Given that distinctions between high and popular culture are malleable, it might be thought that they are not so very important. However, these distinctions influence the ways in which audiences interact with and make sense of a performance. If you are conditioned to understand circus as high culture, your appreciation of the routines being performed and the skills in human movement being displayed is different from a situation in which you go to the circus for some popular entertainment. The distinction impacts on the kind of workplace learning and training that take place within these communities.

The Knowledge Economy and Workplace Learning in Selected Mobile Learning Communities

Findings from our interview data, supported by information about other mobile communities, indicate that the workplace learning that occurs in such communities can have more general resonance. A Dutch circus teacher, for example (who is also cited in Chapter 7 from a different perspective), described teaching skills such as acrobatics as "a diving board to your future" (DC1999). He identified three aspects of this form of workplace learning: (a) working together; (b) being in balance; and (c) trust. There is a connection between being in balance physically and mentally. And there is an act of balancing in the relationship between one's own performance and that of others. There is then a focus on creating a harmonious work environment in which one performer's trust of others becomes an important part of being able to work together. In this way a traveling occupation like the circus can provide a resonant model for teaching life skills for the broader community.

This focus on circus having an educational role for society at large points to a particular tension concerning the extent to which circus arts ought to be seen as the preserve of members of that community versus the degree to which these skills deserve to be shared more widely. An important figure in this debate is Reg Bolton (2004), who pioneered the use of circus with disadvantaged youth as a social medium in the 1980s. He established what became known as new circus, distinguished from traditional circus by, among other things, not featuring animal performers. New circus sought to demystify the aura attached to the circus arts, seeking to make these skills accessible to everyone, irrespective of their ability or profession.

The workplace learning of the circus can assist other Travelers. A good example is the backpacker Travelers who are forming an increasingly significant proportion of the global tourism and travel market. In order to supplement their savings, backpackers aspire to develop a range of workplace skills that might earn them income. It is quite common to see public areas in large cities transformed into stages for buskers performing circus acts such as juggling, stilt-walking, and fire-eating. It is conceivable that they have developed such skills at circus schools or through less formalized training. The relative portability of the circus equipment, and the capacity of the acts to resonate with different cultures throughout the world, make this an attractive option for backpacker Travelers.

These Travelers also play a significant role in sustaining small regional economies through their willingness to take on work that, for a range of reasons, might not be attractive to the citizens of these areas. Fruit picking, for example, because it is a seasonal activity with little prospect of permanent work, can face problems in attracting the participation of fixed residents in the areas in which it takes place. As such, backpackers who move into the area on a temporary basis to pick fruit or to perform other agricultural work in order to shore up their savings for further travel can play a vital role in sustaining the livelihoods of farmers and the regional and rural communities of which they are a part.

A further significant impact of mobile communities upon the global economy has been the phenomenon of guest workers, people who move into another country that is experiencing labor shortages and who save money to send to their families back home. In certain cases guest workers respond to seasonal demands and adopt a peripatetic lifestyle in the host country; in other cases their residency is more fixed, responding to long-term shortages in labor. In certain situations the legal status of these guest workers is problematic, and they live with the threat of having their status as illegal aliens exposed. Over recent years, examples of guest workers have included Polish trades people working in the United Kingdom and France, and Mexican and other Central American nationals taking menial jobs in the United States. This global movement has resonated within popular culture over recent years. Movies such as *Syriana* (Gaghan, 2005), *Fast Food Nation* (Linklater, 2006), and *Babel* (Iñárritu, 2006) have explored the challenges and opportunities facing guest workers as they seek to adapt to different cultural contexts.

One considerable benefit that guest workers offer is in terms of the remittances that they send back to their families in the country of their nationality. As the families' situation is often desperately poor, these remittances are very important in sustaining their livelihood. The money also helps to build localized economies. It has been estimated that every dollar of remittance money generates three dollars in the local economy. For very poor economies, remittances can be much more effective than aid money in reaching the affected people on the ground and providing the seeds for improving their circumstances. However, guest workers are subjected to suspicion in the host country out of concerns that they are taking jobs from local people and/or driving down wages.

In many cases it is the character of the occupation of the traveling community that shapes their contribution to the knowledge economy and workplace learning. The armed forces constitute a very considerable traveling community, as personnel are transferred between posts in their own country and dispatched abroad on operations. The armed forces are equipped to deal with the logistical challenges of moving people and equipment across vast distances in short time frames. Accordingly, the armed forces can be said to constitute a global knowledge economy in terms of sharing ideas and intelligence and providing the physical and cultural infrastructure for social and economic renewal.

Like other sectors of the contemporary knowledge economy, Traveler occupations are subject to an escalating culture of managerialism, where the focus shifts from one's own particular enterprise to a higher order managerial role that involves overseeing others. One English circus family lamented this loss of personal involvement, comparing their business to a gas station franchise in which they would have meetings with circus managers around the country, watch the performance, and give pointers (EC1999).

Bourdieu's (1990) distinction between the autonomous and heteronomous dimensions of a cultural field, discussed earlier in this chapter, is relevant here. The focus on the heteronomous dimension would seem to fit in with the values of many occupational Travelers, who are accustomed to tailoring their knowledge and skills to commercial outcomes. At the same time, the attraction to the autonomous values of their lifestyle and art creates a certain tension, which was articulated in the response of a different English circus Traveler:

> ... the word is in the name, "show business". So we have to make a show and make [a] business ... We have to take money because we have to live, and [to] support and improve your standards, you need money unfortunately ... It would be very nice just to concentrate on our art, but we need the money. Some people say, "I'm not interested in that". Yes, of course you'd have to [be]; both [are] important. (EC1999)

The concept of show business indicates how the art of the circus as an autonomous value cannot be considered separate from the heteronomous value of earning a livelihood. A challenge for this community, then, is to reconcile economic and cultural or lifestyle values associated with the autonomy of their art. While it is evident that a circus performer's commitment to her art is bound up with other non-economic dimensions of life, such as traditions, values, and belief systems, this needs to be balanced with sustaining one's economic livelihood.

As elsewhere in the knowledge economy, the scale of enterprise plays a significant role in shaping the role within Traveler occupations. While small-scale circuses or fairground businesses require people to perform multiple roles, acting as Jack or Jill of all trades, as that enterprise grows larger it enables greater specialization. Inevitably, it tends to be the smaller scale enterprises that are most vulnerable to the swings and roundabouts in the wider economy.

These changes also impact on what might be understood as a traditionally romanticized view of traveling communities, the idea of moving into a town, parking on the village green, putting up posters and spruiking the act, and then moving on. One English circus family mentioned how various constraints had forced them " … to evolve into this business orientated commodity" (EC1999). Costs such as insurance and increasing overheads, along with competition from other sources of entertainment, have shaped this change in outlook. Hence business studies have become an important asset in contemporary Traveler occupations.

Within contemporary late capitalist knowledge economies, competition among occupational Travelers becomes ever more intense. The ready availability of credit is a significant aspect of this culture of competition, as is the close proximity in which members of an occupational traveling community operate. Thus if a joint on the fairgrounds is observed to be very successful in attracting customers, others of that variety will be set up. Circuses are also renowned for planning their itineraries with a view to maximizing market share. Understanding where the competition is and what they are offering is part and parcel of the knowledge economy: knowledge equates to a competitive advantage and therefore money.

Performance-based mobile communities are faced with various challenges associated with social and economic developments in contemporary cultures. Concerns about public liability in case accidents occur and the prohibitive cost of insurance are one threat to their livelihood. Another relates to issues involving the size of operations and economies of scale. A Scottish fairground operator compared the situation with supermarkets attempting to corner the market and force out smaller businesses (SS1999). Large theme parks using the latest science and technology are challenging the viability of the smaller traditional fairground operations. In this context, occupational Travelers are also conscious of the challenge posed by other forms of entertainment, such as computer games. This position was eloquently expressed by a different Scottish fairground Traveler: " … the public's getting more sophisticated now … They want wine, women, and song now. We can't provide that" (SS1999).

One response has been for these fairs to become savvier. Rather than expecting the public to come to them, they move to where particular events like a town's gala week or a large folk festival or New Year celebrations are occurring and provide a sideline attraction. Instead of being an attraction on their own, these fairs are seeking to feed off other events. Thus their mobility remains an advantage in comparison with static theme parks and they are able to respond proactively to a cultural *milieu* in which staging large public events and festivals is regarded as an effective way of responding to the challenge generated by other forms of entertainment.

One advantage is a tradition among occupational Traveler families of working as an economic unit. A Scottish fairground Traveler found that, when his family ran a restaurant, it was done in much the same style as operating various fairground attractions (SS1999). The parents worked as business partners, and the children were encouraged to leave school as soon as possible to become part of the business. In seeing themselves as business people, fairground families were conscious that this distinguished them from other Travelers.

Creating appropriate spaces for effective learning is one of the significant challenges for mobile learning communities. One English Traveler educator spoke about the need to replicate classroom conditions within the caravan to assist the Traveler children in concentrating (TT1999). While outside was the playground where the children were free to run and play, inside the caravan was a place for relaxation and quiet study. That certain Traveler communities have a tradition of immaculately kept cut crystal glassware and bone china was advantageous in the sense that it maintained that space as a site where the children were acculturated to remaining still. When working with Traveler children, this educator would rearrange the furniture, the bookcases, and so on to create spaces that were enclosed, so the children fairly quickly settled down to the routine of concentrating within those spaces.

One challenge for traveling communities is to complement their cultural traditions with workplace training. Among Roma girls, for example, is a cultural tradition of wearing jewelry and creative hairdressing. Accordingly, careers in the beauty and hairdressing industries would seem to be quite a natural fit for these girls. Besides doing dedicated training courses in these areas, an English Traveler educator recommended the complementary role of a broader education to equip these young women with the skills to compete in the market place (TT1999).

In relation to the corporate memory dimension of the knowledge economy, one role for traveling communities is to be recognized as guardians of their own cultural heritage—as keepers of their flame. This enduring corporate memory across many generations is a distinctive feature of many traveling cultures. One English Traveler teacher said that it was like becoming experts in their own cultural knowledge: " … if you want to do a book about Gypsies and Travelers, you go to Gypsies and Travelers … " (TT1999).

An issue here is who speaks for whom. There is a tradition in education that aims to inculcate forms of expert knowledge. Thus a scientist might spend a great many years developing a specialized knowledge of marine creatures that accredits her to speak as an expert in that field. Traveling communities have in many cases been the subject of such expert knowledge. Scholars in fields as diverse as anthropology, linguistics, genetics, and geography have made Travelers an object of their studies. Mobile learning communities have a situated interest in challenging this practice, empowering Travelers to speak for themselves (see for example Kiddle, 1999) and to become acknowledged as the experts in their own forms of cultural practice and knowledge. This aspiration broadens out the concept of workplace learning; beyond being a site for acquiring artisanal and technical skills, the workplace might also be understood as a site involved in the acquisition of cultural knowledge.

Museums and archives play an important role in preserving the corporate memory of traveling communities. As for the most part these communities have been oral cultures, there tends to be relatively little written material produced by their own hands. In cases like this, photographic traces, voice recordings, and ephemera such as costumes and pieces of equipment can be important.

What constitutes intellectual property is a central issue of the knowledge economy that has particular implications for mobile communities. Two significant issues relating to the performance skills of occupational Travelers are the degree to which they can be codified, on the one hand, and the extent to which they have copyright, on the other. Music and written performance pieces, such as plays or sketches, can be preserved and codified through being inscribed in musical notation and written text. As such, they can be made available to others and performed in different contexts in the future. But no such system of notation exists for other performance routines, such as a dance choreography (although here music can provide some guide) or a particular juggling or acrobatic act. Even in the absence of notation, these acts have a particular vocabulary. In such cases, the acts are passed down from teacher to learner. Indeed, this tradition shows the significance of the oral culture of Travelers in preserving and carrying on performance arts in cases in which written records are not available. Contemporary video technology has impacted on this dimension of performance literacies by providing visual records of the act.

Copyright is another source of contention. Although there is no formal regime of copyright protection of acts, there is an informal kind of copyright in the particular 'signature' that a performer brings to the act. As an English circus performer said: "… nobody copies it because it's yourself" (EC1999), while a Dutch circus performer stated: "Sometimes they copy the music, the tricks, but not the feeling" (DC1999).

In other words, each act has a distinctive sensibility that resists imitation. This point was taken up by an English circus teacher who observed: "I don't think I've ever seen an act that has been copied. I've seen an act that has resonances …" (EC1999). So although the precise feeling of an act cannot be copied it can resonate with others so that it can develop and branch out. As this circus teacher acknowledged, all art makes some reference to what has come before.

Indeed, this acknowledges one of the significant contributions that a mobile community such as the circus can make to the globalized knowledge economy: promoting an experience that resonates across all boundaries in a way that is genuinely interconnective. As the same English circus teacher remarked:

> The physicality of circus is a shared, common experience. Maybe if you get to one or two technicalities, but in general we share that physical commonality. And this is why I talk about the common psyche of circus. You could go to the middle of Africa or you could go to the middle of Australia, and I was friends with the Aborigines. You can juggle, and that's an instantly recognizable form that people can relate to. There's an instant understanding of what you're doing. That seems to happen time and time again. So there must be something in prehistory where people have this common physical understanding that you were talking about as presocial communication. I would firmly believe that. (EC1999)

While the contemporary knowledge economy involves very sophisticated ICTs to link the world as a market place of ideas and commodities, these words remind us that the ties that bind us in common humanity are basic, embodied resources.

Implications for the Future Education of Mobile Learning Communities

In terms of the future educational opportunities of mobile learning communities, the knowledge economy and workplace learning have a number of significant implications. From one perspective, these communities might have a sense that "our time has come"—that the flexible forms of knowledge, economic practices, and workplace learning protocols that they have traditionally practiced are becoming less exceptional in a mobile world. The focus on values associated with the adaptability, innovation, and interconnectivity of knowledge systems suggest that this might be the case.

On the other hand, there is a concern that mobile learning communities will continue to have to accommodate their practices to suit the knowledge economy and workplace learning protocols of sedentary communities. The focus on becoming credentialed through having the appropriate qualifications and certificates from formal educational and training institutions does impose constraints on occupational Travelers. And the formalized knowledge economy can work against the interests of the informalized knowledge networks and cultural traditions of certain mobile communities.

Implications for Broader Educational Practice

The experience of mobile learning communities in relation to the knowledge economy and workplace learning also has important implications for broader educational practice. One issue has to do with the ramifications for schooling and education generally in an increasingly borderless, mobile world. The challenge for sedentary educational institutions such as schools and university campuses is to respond meaningfully to this context. It seems that, rather than expecting students to come to them and fit in with their routines and protocols, these institutions will need to design packages and accommodate themselves to the routines and protocols of a culturally diverse and geographically dispersed student population (see for example Danaher et al., 2009).

Thus the tendency toward work experience, practicum placements, and internships for school and university students might well act as a model for future educational practice. At the same time, it does seem that the theoretical knowledge provided by educational institutions will continue to be valued. Certainly, given the enormous challenges that the world faces in relation to issues such as climate change, sustainable energy, food and fuel provision, and managing ecological stresses, an investment in research and development will be an increasingly significant part of the global knowledge economy. Such an investment will need to come from private as well as public funding, and much discussion will be required to create an effective infrastructure and environment for the production, distribution, and consumption of innovative research and development across worldwide knowledge networks. The cooperative approach that we have seen evident in the research and development that takes place in mobile learning communities such as circus schools, performance troupes, and carnivals, where parties work on innovating with new acts and attractions, might provide a model for an effective implementation of that infrastructure and environment.

Questions for Reflection

- What opportunities and challenges does the emergence of the knowledge economy pose for mobile learning communities?
- What implications does the emergence of the knowledge economy have for relationships between mobile and sedentary communities?
- What forms of workplace learning take place within mobile learning communities?
- What lessons might the workplace learning practices of mobile communities have for sedentary communities and educational institutions?

Suggestions for Further Reading

Cookes, P., & Piccaluga, A. (2006). *Regional development in the knowledge economy*. London: Routledge.

Evans, K., Hodkinson, P., Rainbird, H., & Unwin, L. (2006). *Improving workplace learning*. London: Routledge.

Fuller, A., Munro, A., & Rainbird, H. (Eds.) (2006). *Workplace learning in context*. London: Routledge.

Kenway, J., Bullen, E., Fahey, J., & Robb, S. (2006). *Haunting the knowledge economy*. London: Routledge.

Rooney, D., McKenna, B., & Liesch, P. (2009/in press). *Wisdom and management in the knowledge economy*. London: Routledge.

Van Woerkom, M., & Poell, R. (Eds.) (2009/in press). *Workplace learning: Concepts, measurement and application*. London: Routledge.

6
Multiliteracies and Meaning-Making

Mobile communities are often configured as being at risk in terms of basic educational outcomes such as literacy. Because their travel challenges the routines of standard educational provision, there is a fear that they will fall through the cracks of that provision and be party to a cycle of illiteracy across generations. By contrast, the concept of multiliteracies engages with the complex and multiple arrays of literate experiences that these communities generate as they interact with various social groups, forms of technologies and creative practices. This chapter explores the ways in which this multilterate perspective provides a framework for making sense of the rich learning experiences of mobile communities.

Introduction

This chapter on multiliteracies and meaning-making focuses attention on the cultural values of mobile learning communities. These attributes are keys to Travelers sustaining their distinctive cultural identity whilst also communicating effectively with a range of different people using a diversity of media. Multiliteracies and meaning-making, then, are integral to mobile learning communities in conserving their past, enriching their present, and ensuring their future.

In spite of what we see as its constraining features as a practice of governance, we contend that multiliteracies add value to mobile learning communities. Such literacies can operate as an important sense of empowerment to these communities, enabling them to be immersed in a culture of learning and the world of reading and writing that can translate to improved work and lifestyle opportunities. Furthermore, multiliteracies play a considerable role in affirming and sustaining the identities of traveling communities, helping them to articulate their shared traditions and to draw on their cultural heritage as a rich and enduring resource bank or living artifact. In these terms, multiliteracies are bound up with authentic learning, associated with the real life scenarios with which Travelers are confronted on a daily basis.

This chapter consists of the following five sections:

- Concepts relating to multiliteracies in the literature about learning communities
- Discussion of the literature relating to multiliteracies within mobile communities
- Examples of different forms of multiliteracies in selected mobile learning communities
- Implications for the future education of mobile learning communities
- Implications for broader educational practice.

Multiliteracies in Learning Communities

A review of the literature concerning literacy reveals much debate and contestation in relation to the term. Breier (1997), for example, identified the concern with using "literacy" in the singular as privileging one form—that is, "schooled literacy" (p. 202). Beyond focusing on the plural, "literacies," Breier also drew attention to "literacy events," defined by Heath as "occasions in which written language is integral to the nature of participants' interactions and their interpretive processes and strategies" (1982, as cited in Breier, 1997, p. 2002).

Multiliteracies can be understood as an attempt to pluralize the concept of literacy further, reconstructing the form of literacy pedagogy in response to a valuing of cultural diversity along with dramatic changes in media and communication technology. The term "multiliteracies" is most commonly associated with the New London Group, so-called because of a meeting of group members in New London, New Hampshire, United States, in September 1994 that resulted in a seminal paper in the Spring 1996 issue of the *Harvard Educational Review*. The term emphasizes the connections among "Linguistic Meaning, Visual Meaning, Audio Meaning, Gestural Meaning, and Spatial Meaning." In their synthesis of the concept, Bill Cope and Mary Kalantzis (1996) contended that "The term 'Multiliteracies' highlights two of the most important, and closely related changes" (n.p.) associated with contemporary transformations of personal and public lives, cultures and communication practices. "The first is the growing significance of cultural and linguistic diversity" (n.p.). "The second major shift encompassed in the concept of Multiliteracies is the influence of new communications technologies" (n.p.). From the perspective of this chapter, the concept of "multiliteracies" functions as a theoretical navigational tool for exploring the meaning-making practices and communication strategies of mobile learning communities.

The educational paradigm for making sense of the way in which multiliteracies shape the meaning-making of mobile learning communities, we argue, is constructivism. Constructivism focuses on the learners' active involvement in making meaning and constructing models of world.

Accordingly, the emphasis is not on the knowledge that the teacher has but rather on the learners' needs and worldviews. As Twomey Fosnot (1996) commented:

> Learning is a constructive building process of meaning-making that results in reflective abstractions, producing symbols within a medium. These symbols then become part of the individual's repertoire of assimilatory schemes, which in turn are used when perceiving and further conceiving. (p. 27)

By its very character, the traveling lifestyle of mobile learning communities inculcates a distinctive repertoire of assimilatory schemes, associated with, for example, spruiking to an audience, sizing up a situation and responding appropriately, visual art, and a sense of space and movement. We explore these assimilatory schemes, or literacies, throughout this chapter.

Contextual and supporting factors shape the conditions in which learning communities construct their meanings. Biggs (2003, p. 27) indicated the role of these factors in his concept of constructive alignment, a marriage between a constructivist understanding of the nature of learning and an aligned design for teaching. The critical components of such a constructive alignment include, apart from curriculum content, teaching methods, and assessment procedures, the climate that teachers create through interactions with students and the broader institutional climate consisting of rules and procedures that teachers have to follow (p. 26). These factors are particularly significant in relation to mobile communities and challenge the way in which educators can create an effective constructive alignment that accommodates the routines and values of those communities.

While multiliteracies is an enabling concept to make sense of the plurality of different communication practices in operation today, its semantic connections with the term "literacy" mean that it cannot be entirely removed from the governing role that that concept has played in shaping the language learning of people for more than a century. This principle is particularly important when considering the language education of mobile learning communities. In Foucauldian terms (Burchell et al., 1991: Foucault, 1977), literacy can be recognized as a very significant form of self-governance. Through becoming a literate citizen, a person exerts governance over her/himself and is able to communicate in ways that are socially sanctioned and valued. So, while literacy is a means to becoming an autonomous, self-governing individual able to exercise reason and make rational choices, this autonomy is subject to internalizing the codes and norms of the society in the manner in which one speaks and writes. This understanding of literacy explains why governments of various political philosophies invest so much weight in basic educational aptitudes such as the three Rs: reading, writing, and arithmetic. For governments of rightwing philosophies, literacy tends to be understood as a significant value in developing social cohesion and also national competitiveness: it is believed that the greater the proportion of literate citizens the more effective the country will be in competing in the international market place, even though according to Luke (1993) there is little evidence in any country in the Organization for Economic Cooperation and Development (OECD) of a direct relationship between literacy levels and economic productivity (p. 13). For governments of leftwing beliefs, literacy is regarded as an instrument of social inclusion, enabling the marginalized members of the community to become more integrated. Indeed, it is through literacy that the state is sanctioned to intervene directly in the lives of its subjects: through ongoing testing, monitoring, and treatment of those considered at risk.

Historically, literacy has been used as an instrument to determine who does and does not belong within a particular society. For example, in the early twentieth century, Australia used literacy tests as part of its practice of immigration restriction known as the White Australia Policy. Policemen, who in some cases had limited literacy skills themselves, were charged with testing the literacy of people suspected of being undesirable immigrants (Monsour, 2007). While initially the standard of spoken and written English was simply one of many aspects reported on by the police and immigration authorities, by 1917, influenced in part by concerns about "illegal aliens" during World War I, literacy in English had become a mandatory requirement for citizenship.

Part of the way in which literacy functions as a governing force is through the generation of ongoing crises (see also Warmington & Murphy, 2004). Thus institutions involved with government, business, education, the media, and so forth are continually raising concerns about standards of literacy, citing fears about falling below international benchmarks, about children falling through the cracks, indeed about the debasement of language owing to various factors, such as rap music lyrics, advertising, and text messaging. Such crises serve to keep literacy alive as an issue of concern, something that can never really be resolved. This lack of resolution keeps open the discursive space within which literacy speaks. Accordingly, in considering the discursive space of literacy we should consider questions such as:

- On whose behalf does it speak?
- What interests does it serve?
- With what objects in mind?

Multiliteracies in Mobile Communities

These questions need to be considered even when the issue of literacy seems, ostensibly at least, to be much more benign than in the case of a discriminatory practice like the White Australia Policy. Over more recent years, various policies have been adopted around the world to improve the standard of mobile communities' literacy rates. In the United Kingdom, for example, Traveler children who entered mainstream school were given a special literacy hour with Traveler teachers focusing on this aspect of their school work. Literacy has also been one of the main concerns of the mobile Queensland School for Travelling Show Children, with consideration being given to night classes in literacy for the adult show members, particularly the men, whose skills in this area have often been lacking. Indeed, within this school there is an aspiration to break the cycle of illiteracy passed on from generation to generation.

In many respects, these are laudable aims, and, as the writers of this book, we have witnessed the excitement and enthusiasm of Traveler children exposed to the world of books and reading. However, such exposure to literacy is accompanied by a range of tests and measurements, the effect of which can be to mark Traveler students as routinely falling below the norm and therefore relatively failing. An educator at the Queensland School for Travelling Show Children, for example, was concerned about the effects of literacy testing on the morale of the show community, who might expect immediate improvements in their children's performance relative to the norm (AS2003).

Historically, the language of Travelers has been subjected to suspicion from social authorities because of its perceived connection with criminality. Reynolds (2002), for example, traced the emergence in sixteenth century England of what he calls a "distinct criminal culture of rogues, vagabonds, gypsies, beggars, cony-catchers, cutpurses and prostitutes ... united by its own aesthetic, ideology, language and lifestyle. In effect, this criminal culture constituted a subnation that illegitimately occupied material and conceptual space within the English nation" (p. 1). Here, then, there are links made among a distinctive language, criminality, and an illegitimate use of space associated with mobile communities such as Roma.

Such concern with a criminal class threatening the proper order was revisited in Henry Mayhew's reportage of the London underworld during the Victorian era. While Mayhew's (1862) study of London labor and London poor was ostensibly focused on addressing the moral habits of London's inhabitants and their fitness for work in the rapidly emerging industrial society, he introduced his subject not with a discussion of poverty, laziness, or ignorance but in terms of an ethnographic classification of the world's population into distinct races, the wandering and the civilized tribes, along with an intermediate group. While the civilized were marked by their submission to social norms, including recognizing property rights and through acquiring wealth making themselves respectable, the wandering hordes were viewed as frequently having a different language from that of the more civilized portion of the community, and that they had adopted with the intent of concealing their designs and exploits from the latter.

Mayhew's (1862) point about the differences in languages concerns us in this chapter. Not merely was the language of the wandering hordes divergent but also it was regarded as being intended to conceal those hordes designs and exploits from the bearers of civilization. In Halliday's (1976) terms, the wanderers, like their counterparts in the sixteenth century, employ an anti-language, a form of expression that challenges the rules and conventions of authorized linguistic practice (see also Bakhtin, 1981, 1984).

The movement toward literacy can be understood in part as a means of controlling such tendencies toward anti-language. Literacy represented a properly codified national language, a form of communication that was normalized and standardized and that could be absorbed through pedagogical practice. Thus the role of literacy in the mass schooling movements that emerged through Education Acts in countries such as Britain and Australia in the 1870s was very important. These Education Acts made schooling compulsory and free. They can be understood as a program to promote the values of civilization throughout the social body at large.

Along with the invention of race and civilization, nineteenth century ethnography generated the distinction, within a nation, between two characteristic ways of using space: occupying it in settlement; and wandering over it. Civilization, in its distinction from the wandering hordes noted above, is identified with sedentarism (McVeigh, 1997). Insofar as the national space had come to be imagined through a vast range of mapping devices, the nomadic tribe was the antithesis of civilization. It was constituted as a barbaric space, a nomadic life, within the heart of civilization.

The concept of civilization is important here. The perceived need to find a word to express the idea of a civilized mode of life originated in France in the mid-eighteenth century as part of the Enlightenment project. From France, the word "civilization" was exported, jostling and overlapping with "culture" and replacing "Bildung" in Germany, "civilita" in Italy and "civilità" in England (Duckworth, 1994, p. 5). Hence the concept of civilization was bound up with the constitution of a settled, temperate, social order, and associated as Mayhew (1862) makes clear with a sedentary lifestyle. Thus, while it is conventional to distinguish civilization from barbarism, it is also distinguished from nomadism.

Formalized education consists of an institutionalized intervention through curricula, forms of pedagogy, assessment, and associated policies and practices into the interaction between cultural contexts and the behaviors of individuals and communities. These cultural contexts, and the behaviors that they influence and are influenced by, are more or less rigidly structured and fixed and yet are also subject to change. Formal education intervenes in these contexts and behaviors, which might be understood as forms of cultural patterning, in order to achieve certain outcomes.

Focusing on the experience of English Gypsy communities, Levinson (2007, p. 5) noted that, while a commitment within education to improve the literacy levels of individuals from marginalized groups is often perceived as a means of empowering the disempowered, this tends to overlook wider cultural repercussions. He notes how many minority groups have come to define themselves in opposition to the dominant group, manifested in the rejection of mainstream cultural forms. In this sense, Gypsies' eschewal of literacy can be understood as a form of boundary maintenance (p. 8).

Multiliteracies in Selected Mobile Learning Communities

In turning to the interview data, it is evident that the mobile communities with whom we spoke use their language, multiliteracies, and meaning-making apparatuses in various ways for different ends. In relation to the boundary maintenance to which Levinson (2007) referred, Travelers use language to engage the world on their terms and to negotiate complex and shifting relationships with one another and settled communities.

Discourses and Vocabularies

In some ways the language of Travelers can be understood as a discourse—that is, a particular way of speaking based on shared experiences and regularized relationships. In certain situations, this discourse can involve a specialized vocabulary relating to the equipment used in the Travelers' occupations. Fairground Travelers, for example, have a range of words relating to their joints and rides, while Dutch bargee workers have a specialized vocabulary relating to loads, cargo, and navigation.

In other cases the specialized vocabulary relates to conserving a traveling community's cultural heritage. A Traveler education officer in the UK recollected a member of the Romany culture speaking about going into some woods and meeting his grandmother, who "told him this magical, secret word that was not supposed to belong to the sedentary population" and that was regarded as "a privatized word" (TT1999).

Constructivism

It is evident that Traveler educators draw on principles associated with constructivism in designing their programs and packages. For instance, a European educator interpreted constructivism in the context of open and distance education, or just in time learning: "What do I need, as a learner, to know? How do I need to know it? When do I need to know it?" (TT1999). For mobile learning communities, this approach raises certain challenges. There is an issue, for example, of whether the educational structures are sufficiently flexible to accommodate such learning needs. Furthermore, the increasing focus on needing formal educational qualifications places pressures on accommodating the mobile lifestyle of Travelers. In addition, the context in which increasingly educational institutions such as universities and some schools are becoming commercial enterprises concerned with the bottom line of economic performance compromises the extent to which they are able or prepared to invest learning and teaching resources in an area like Traveler education where there is likely to be limited financial return.

Another European Traveler educator drawing on constructivism described occupational Travelers as "autonomous entrepreneurs" (TT1999), a term that serves to emphasize their personal investment in their lifestyle and business. For such Travelers, situated learning and authentic learning are very important. In other words, the Travelers need to appreciate the ways in which formal learning connects with their everyday lifeworlds and practices. An example of authentic learning from the middle ages was the masters and apprentice model, when skilled masters acted as role models for apprentices learning such skills as how to paint. It is evident that in many mobile learning communities—for example, the circus—artistic and performance skills are passed on according to this model from generation to generation. A Belgian circus teacher endorsed the interviewer's articulation of the way that constructivism informed the work that the teacher carried out with the young performers: "'We've got this task; we've got this performance next week or next month. What are we together going to do to make it our own?' That's constructing in the people's own framework, cognitively and … creatively and emotionally," adding that "I think it can be good when it fits … you …" (BC1999). Constructivism, in other words, is focused on fitting the learning with the learner in authentic, meaning-making contexts.

Languages

In certain cases, the movements of Travelers across international borders create challenges in relation to interacting in different languages. For younger Travelers, there can often be what might be called "a universal language of childhood" that enables them to interact with other children. Research supports the claim that younger children often find it easier than adults to learn other languages as their own native language is not fully formed. An eloquent example was a Dutch circus child who referred to "My daddy, meine mutti" (DC1999), mixing the English word for "father" with the Dutch word for "mother."

However, it is evident that proficiency in English as a unifying global language is a significant asset for NESB Travelers. One Dutch fairground worker revealed that he learned English from United States movies and television shows and also from his interest in buying vintage American cars that required him to travel to the United States on a regular occasion (DS1999). On the other hand, an English circus proprietor indicated that he regarded the language classes in German and French as being the most valuable part of his secondary grammar school learning, as these equipped him to communicate effectively with colleagues on the European continent (EC1999). Indeed, as gifted circus performers come from around the world, and particularly from prestigious circus schools in Eastern Europe, Russia, and China, it becomes necessary for everyone professionally engaged in this environment to develop some degree of multilingual fluency.

Animal Literacies

For certain traveling communities, interacting with animals and engaging with what might be called "animal literacies" is extremely important. Indeed, such interaction helps to transform our understanding of animals, enriching our appreciation of the complex communication strategies that they employ.

A particularly moving example of how mobile learning communities create possibilities for engaging animal literacies involves the story of Christian the Lion, which became a global hit on YouTube in 2008 (retrieved September 29, 2008, from http://au.youtube.com/watch?v=adYbFQFXG0U&feature= email). It involves two young Australian men who in 1969 traveled to London and bought a lion cub from the Harrods department store. At that time it was common for young Australians to travel to England—for many the home country—as a rite of passage into adulthood. Thus expatriate Australians and New Zealanders formed their own mobile learning community engaging with the cultures of the United Kingdom and Europe and taking on various jobs as they moved around the country. They were forerunners of today's global backpacker travel market.

The famous department store Harrods boasted that it was able to sell anything that a customer asked for; when a lady asked for a camel, the sales assistant is reputed to have replied, "One hump or two, Madam?" When the Australians saw the lion cub who came from a zoo confined to a small cage, they bought him and named him Christian. He lived with them in the basement of a furniture store in the King's Road in Chelsea where they worked and exercised in a nearby church graveyard and park, where he enjoyed playing soccer. When Christian became too large to continue his city life, he was shipped to Kenya and released back into the wild. When the two Australian men announced their intention to travel to Kenya in the hope of seeing Christian, they were informed that he hadn't been seen for some time. However, the day before they arrived, he was seen again. And, after several hours searching, the two companions spotted Christian. The films show him pausing, then recognizing the pair, and breaking into a joyful run as he rushes to them, jumps up, and affectionately licks their faces.

An Australian circus performer who had an act involving poodles spoke about the importance of making it a game, because once they had learned the routine of the act they were really keen to do it. She added: "And they just love the audience response ... : clap them on and they get all show-offy ... I've had ones that couldn't wait to get out there in the ring and show off ... " (AC1998).

The issue of having animals as part of mobile communities has become considerably vexed. Certain mobile communities emerged through their work with animals, such as the nomadic pastoralists in Africa and the stockmen and shepherds in the Americas and Australia. For traditional circus communities, the role of exotic animals such as lions, elephants, and monkeys has been an integral feature of their appeal. More recently, animal liberation groups have protested about the presence of such animals in circuses, arguing that the cramped conditions in which they travel are inhumane. They have been influential in having animal-based circuses prohibited in certain places.

Some traditional circuses have responded by seeking to show that their treatment of animals has been very humane and by promoting the benefits of animal acts for a variety of reasons. For example, children in many cases encounter these animals for the first time through the circus. They learn firsthand about the animals and acquire a sense of their size, strength, dexterity, and conduct. Furthermore, it is evident that special bonds emerge between the performers and the animals with which they interact. The trust and complex communications that emerge between lions and their tamers, elephants and their handlers, and horses and their trick riders broaden our understanding and appreciation of the bonds between human and non-human animals. A Dutch circus Traveler, for example, spoke of a horse becoming bored with the ballerina routine that he was performing so he learned new tricks (DC1999). And a Scottish fairground Traveler recalled a forebear from some four generations ago acting as a horse whisperer for a circus (SS1999). On the other hand, a Scottish fairground Traveler with circus connections recalled an elephant called Jumbo who used to let himself loose and wander about the town when his handler, her uncle, was away. As soon as he heard his handler's voice, Jumbo would get himself back and stand in the tent (SS1999).

Mathematical Literacies

Occupational Travelers develop considerable skills in numeracy from a young age. Children in fairground and circus families tend to be inducted very early into the business lives of their communities, and become adept at handling money and supplying the correct change. This is true also of so-called tinker Travelers and hawkers. Indeed, as these traveling businesses grow, their members develop an impressive financial literacy, calculating the benefits of investments in acts, pieces of equipment, and other aspects of their workplace. One English fairground operator observed a gendered dimension to this financial literacy, with females tending to take the role of maintaining the accounts and bookkeeping (ES1999). For guest workers who send much of their earnings back to their families in their home countries, such financial literacy can be the key to a future free from poverty.

Beyond such business skills, a mathematical literacy is also evident in certain circus skills. One English circus school teacher demonstrated how an afternoon of juggling can be a most effective and practical way of teaching the principles of physics such as gravity, centrifugal forces, flight, and parabolas (EC1999). Because of the means by which through their acts and workplace management the circus becomes a practical laboratory of spatial awareness and manipulation, it seems an ideal context for teaching these geometric principles to students in ways that maintain their interest and engagement.

Indeed, because the circus involves a synthesis of a range of artistic forms and performance principles, it can operate across the academic curriculum and break down disciplinary boundaries. As an English circus teacher commented: "Name a circus skill; I'll put it into a curriculum for you" (EC1999). Rather than pigeonholing techniques into discrete disciplines such as theatre, dance, and music, circus involves a creative fusion. As such it promotes a common language. Thus French, Dutch, and English children are able to interact meaningfully because they share a common language of juggling, for example.

Geographical Literacies

Because of the character of their traveling, mobile communities also develop a practical geographical literacy. They tend to become familiar with a great many more locations and regional variations than do settled people. One Australian show child recalled identifying his birthday with a certain place, as that would occur when the show arrived at that location as part of its regular annual routine (AS2003). Such regular travel also enables mobile communities to take advantage of local attractions and to develop a wide array of interests and talents: surfing, swimming, snorkeling, skiing, sailing, rodeo riding, and so forth.

Musical Literacies

A very significant literacy among Travelers relates to music. The distinctive musical heritage among traveling communities such as the Roma has resonated throughout the world. Indeed, music itself is a traveling force, and it is interesting to consider the various musical currents that are mixed within different cultural contexts. New Orleans, for example, has a very rich musical culture forged from the different traditions that have been carried to that location: jazz, blues, country, and so forth. And the port city of Liverpool in England welcomed sailors bringing in United States musical records, which influenced the emergence of the Mersey Beat movement that brought with it the Beatles in the 1960s. Thus, when thinking of different cultural multiliteracies, we should consider not only the ways in which communities travel across different locations with their own traditions and cultural movements but also the ways in which cultural movements such as music, dance, theatre, and language are carried by Travelers across diverse locations, producing different local inflections and hybrid mixes.

Artistic Literacies

Many Travelers also exhibit considerable artistic literacy and flair. Fairground attractions often depend in part on their visual appeal to attract customers, so skilled fairground artists are in considerable demand. It is interesting that such a literacy also involves certain colors being regarded as superstitious. For the show community in Australia, for example, green is considered an unlucky color, and this was taken into account in the design of the uniform of the Queensland School for Travelling Show Children (AS2003).

In certain traditional traveling communities, the literacies and dispositions that have developed over long periods of time tend to become closely associated with roles such as gender. Among Roma, for instance, skills in hairdressing and dressmaking are regarded as the females' preserve (TT1999). While such fixed gender roles might seem stereotypical and perhaps even prejudiced from the perspective of other communities, recognizing such traditional roles is important in building trust with these Travelers.

Spatial Literacies

More generally, a characteristic literacy among traveling communities relates to their sense of movement. This facility is observable at a range of levels: individual bodily movement, movement of people, and movement of the community itself and its equipment. At the level of individual bodily movement, mobile performing artists such as circus performers or members of traveling dance and theatrical troupes exhibit considerable grace and dexterity as part of their acts. The daring and beauty of the acrobats, flying trapeze artists, and dancers compel attention. While such accomplishments might seem to be beyond the capacity of most of us, certain circus schools are actually concerned with demystifying this aspect of their acts, focused on showing that most people can develop such dexterity of movement with the appropriate training. A Belgian circus teacher mentioned that even the act of falling over was valuable in terms of teaching children how to react appropriately to different situations, giving a good answer to a bad situation (BC1999).

Organizing the effective movement of people through the space occupied by the mobile community is another important consideration. A good example is the circus, which goes from town to town spruiking for spectators. The circus must be adept in creating a sufficiently large spectator space to accommodate the audience in a context where tickets tend not to be prebooked but are available only at the door. Beyond that, the procession of acts must be orderly and carefully timed to keep the show moving at an engaging rate. In traditional circuses the ringmaster has a very important role in maintaining this flow between acts, and his or her sense of timing and capacity to respond to unexpected delays or impediments to the production need to be assured and convincing. Indeed, the ringmaster is crucial to keeping the audience entertained as sets are put up and taken down to suit the different elements of the circus performance (AC1998).

In the case of fairgrounds, an important literacy relates to attracting customers from within the movement of people down the concourse of sideshow alley. Again the importance of effective spruiking is considerable. Then the different attractions such as fairground rides need to be organized effectively to enable people to queue, participate in the ride, and move off without hindering others. Thus fairground operators become adept at organizing space and moving people through it in an orderly manner (AS2003; ES1999).

At a macro level, the erection and dissembling of the rides, joints, attractions, and, in the case of the circus, the big top require considerable finesse and teamwork. Given the premium of space among Travelers, they tend to develop a considerable facility for portable living, such that everything is packed away as efficiently as possible. Such mobile communities often travel together in convoys, and develop the logistical skills to transport their members and equipment across considerable distances and often varied terrain. One Australian educational official who dealt with the show community commented approvingly of the sheer "loose coupling" that keeps the show on the road and running smoothly in the face of the great number of challenges confronting them (AS2003).

Such lifestyle challenges mold the values and dispositions of mobile communities in significant ways. There is a focus on the practical issues needed to sustain the mobility of the operation. One Australian teacher recruited to the traveling show school mentioned that a key difference that he found from his experience in sedentary schools was that what he called " ... the *Days of our Lives* drama that goes on in the staffroom[s]" (AS2003) in such schools seemed much less important: the office politics and gossip among staff.

Given such challenges of the mobile lifestyle, skills in flexibility, adaptation, and improvisation are very important. In cases where the mobile community might be far from any settlement, the capacity to develop makeshift solutions to keep the vehicles going until something more permanent can be found is an important asset. This means that the degree of surveillance and supervision of employees and others in the mobile community tends not to be as stringent as it can be in sedentary communities. An Australian Traveler educator remarked on this article of faith in terms of "… recruiting hard and managing soft …" (AS2003). While much time and effort needed to be invested in recruiting teachers with sufficient skills in adaptation and flexibility, it was important to manage the teachers softly, empowering them to deal with the situations that arose without feeling too constrained by bureaucratic guidelines.

Multiliteracies and Branding

In certain situations, traveling groups can emphasize their reputation for exoticism as a canny marketing move. It was a tradition for strolling players and circus performers to change from their normal clothes to their performance costumes before they entered a town or city (Carmeli, 2003). That meant that they arrived in the place dressed as exotic entertainers who stood out in terms of their difference and glamour. An English circus teacher said of this tendency: "… I think that's exquisite marketing. Looking again at branding and how the personnel department try and choose people who live their brand. In a way that's what circus is about; it's choosing people who will live that" (EC1999). This perception extends to the high end circus productions. When one approaches a Cirque de Soleil performance, for example, one knows that it will be a high quality evening of entertainment with lavish production values.

Play

A crucial element in fostering the multiliteracies of traveling groups is play. Indeed, while many circus and carnival children learn the acts and are part of the performances from a very young age, these communities tend to emphasize the value of play in providing a balance in their life. A Dutch circus parent, for example, noted how her daughter, already an experienced performer, needed time to play. She reflected regretfully on the experience of school children unable to play because of hockey, violin, and horse riding lessons: "They have all kinds of lessons and they cannot play, they've no time to play, and I think they should play" (DC1999). This view was endorsed by an English circus teacher, whose words are worth citing at length:

> Life is serious. You're an adult now; stop playing. My wife says it to me, 'When are you going to grow up and stop playing?' The deeper you get into adulthood, the more rejection you have if you're seen to be playing. So by the time we become adults, the educational system knocks the play element out of us, and we forget how to play. So it's very interesting that circus is perceived as play, very much, by the educational establishment, by adults … It's not play, and it's extremely focused. There's a lot of physical and mental hard work in just learning to juggle, for example. There is so much to be gained from going through the actual process

of learning that. So, what I'm trying to say is, yes, it is play, but play is work, and we should not forget how to play. (EC1999)

This is an important insight in the context where childhood in settled communities is increasingly devoted to scheduled activities such as tennis and piano lessons or soccer training. It is perhaps ironic that it is mobile communities where the children work from a young age that are conscious of the need to devote time to unscheduled and freely structured play, besides acknowledging the role of play in learning complex skills and arts.

Stories also play a very important role in developing the language skills of young children. A British circus educator recounted the role of storytelling in teaching preschool children:

Because they're just beginning to come to terms with concepts, they're listening to stories, and I think in this world we live in the art of storytelling is one that's diminishing because of the media; we don't need to sit and listen to stories. So we always in our young classes have a central story. Then to be able to take ideas and to take them in different directions and create ideas around those stories. (EC1999)

This teacher remembered children who could not read or write and who were experiencing coming into the theatre class and learning through improvisation: "... [H]ere, because they're allowed to exploit their creativity, they can throw their ideas onto the stage, they can improvise, and then create through improvisation" (EC1999).

Multiliteracies and Habitus

Bourdieu's (1990) concept of habitus, referring to relatively enduring attitudes and dispositions attuned to the cultural fields through which people move, can be applied to the development of multiliteracies among mobile learning communities. Habitus can here be understood in terms of how the traveling lifestyle shapes the values and identities of people at both individual and wider social levels, molding their forms of conduct and literacies. This idea was encapsulated in the words of a Scottish fairground Traveler: "There's a way of life and there's an attitude to life which goes with our lifestyle, and which can survive it" (SS1999). While such a habitus involves enduring values, it can be open to transformation through forces such as education and reading. The same Scottish Traveler, the first member of his family to attend a university, commented:

I liked education; it was a break. I do appreciate the background I have, but it was a kind of refreshing break from the life. I could be two people, and I liked the fact that I could move about. Once I learned to read I found books to be a comfort, they could take me to many places. (SS1999)

Thus reading afforded another form of travel to complement the speaker's family's occupational mobility, suggesting, however, that reading was able to take him to places that the fairground could not.

At the same time, this displacement of the speaker's fairground habitus through being "two people" created tensions: "… when you are brought up with a certain mental attitude, with a certain kind of cultural standard, as it were, you do feel the tension in yourself anyway" (SS1999). The reflections of this Traveler were insightful in suggesting the forces operating in shaping the enduring cultural values of a mobile community. While transforming a tradition of oral culture through embracing the world of reading can be refreshing and empowering, such an experience also involves a tension within this habitus.

Language use and intonation are significant aspects of the Travelers' habitus. For example, Scottish fairground Travelers have a particular accent that distinguishes them from their compatriots. Also fairground Travelers tend to speak loudly in order to make themselves heard above the surrounding noise. For Travelers who have experienced settled life, this linguistic facility enables them to move in and out of different roles, as was encapsulated in this comment: "I can put on my Traveler accent when I want to, [and then] come back and just be an ordinary Edinburgh person more or less" (SS1999). The importance of such a distinctive linguistic habitus in reinforcing a sense of community was expressed simply by another Scottish Traveler: "You want to be among your own people. They talk the same language as you" (SS1999).

Important here is a sense of the ownership of language. This was movingly expressed in the case where an English TESS collected pictures and anecdotes from a group of clients and produced a book based on their experiences. One of the Travelers, a man in his mid 30s who was formally illiterate, initially expressed little interest in the book. Even though he recognized the photographs, he assumed that the accompanying words had been thought up by somebody else, and therefore had little connection with him. When a young girl from the mobile community, who had received formal education, began reading the text and relating his experience, the illiterate Traveler suddenly made a connection, recognizing "that a book can mean something to him" (TT1999).

Multiliteracies, Assertiveness, and Fearless Speech

A significant aspect of Travelers' multiliteracies relates to their capacity to assert their distinctive identity in order to secure the interests of their communities. In part, this assertiveness is a cultural characteristic forged from the University of Life. As a Scottish fairground Traveler commented: "There's no college which you go to for that kind of thing: our assertiveness training" (SS1999). From about the age of five, children are spoken to as if they were adults. They become accustomed to speaking to adults, not only as equal but also often on first name terms. Such assertiveness was an important factor in the Australian traveling show community's negotiations with politicians and education bureaucrats in order to secure their own mobile school (AS2003). It has also been a factor in challenging prejudiced views directed at mobile communities. An English Traveler educator expressed this view in these terms: "We've had to find ways that will be listened to ... and there are different ways for different people" (TT1999). So assertiveness plays a role in gaining a voice for mobile communities (see also Kiddle, 1999).

That Travelers are accustomed to putting on roles and playing out personas assists them in articulating this distinctive voice. Indeed, it might be argued that in some cases Travelers are part of an enduring tradition of fearless speech that is crucial to sustaining open and reasonably democratic societies. Foucault (2001) wrote about the concept of "Parrhesia," a Greek term referring to frank or fearless speech. Foucault explored significant figures such as philosophers and dramatists within ancient Greece and Rome, and the role of fearless speech in empowering people to face others in more powerful positions and to challenge decisions that might have negative consequences. Foucault discussed on what basis these figures had a right to speak so frankly. In the case of Socrates, for example, this right was accorded on the basis he made "a true concord in his own life between his words and his deeds"; that is to say, he lived up to any "fine words however freely spoken" (p. 99). For Socrates, then, there was a harmony between his espoused values and actual practices that enabled him to speak freely.

Historically, and in different contexts, certain traveling performers have played a role in sustaining this tradition of fearless speech, ironically sometimes without even using words. An English clown spoke about being influenced by Kelly the Hobo, a figure from the Great Depression in the United States in the 1930s, whom he regarded as his first model as a clown (EC1999). Part of Kelly's role was comically undermining and satirizing the comfortable middle classes who during the Depression had jobs and enough food. This role he identified with Kelly's idea of the core of truth, the clown, and the fool, analogous with the role of the court jester in challenging the power of authority in order to keep the wheels of society turning. If there were an unpopular measure, then people would go to the court jester and would say to him, "You need to tell the King that this is not working." And equally if the King knew that some people were trying to rebel against him or were getting restless, he would tell the jester. And in both cases, during *après-banquet* entertainments, the jester would show through comedy what was going on, and no words were ever said, but in each case the people picked up the messages very quickly. This insight recalls the important role of the fool in Shakespearean tragic dramas such as *King Lear*.

Implications for the Future Education of Mobile Learning Communities

The ideas that we have explored in this chapter concerning the multiliteracies and meaning-making processes of mobile learning communities certainly have implications for these groups' future educational experiences. It seems clear that these literacies and constructions of meaning will continue to evolve in response to the impact of changing technologies and lifestyle values upon these communities. What we have observed among these communities, to a greater or lesser extent, are both an attachment to traditions and a preparedness to adapt to change.

While the oral traditions of mobile communities create a rich tapestry of meaning on which to draw, it is evident that the challenges of the contemporary world have made the development of formalized educational literacies necessary for many traveling groups. This mixture of the formal and the informal, the traditional and the current, locates those groups at the interface of some challenging tensions that also contain the potential for some creative solutions to those tensions.

In respect of formal literacy, it is clear from the experience of certain traveling groups that a culture of illiteracy that has endured across generations cannot be remedied quickly. It takes time to engender a love of reading and writing and to create the conditions of possibility for their expression. Accordingly, the focus on literacy standards and performance relative to other demographics can be counterproductive for certain Traveler groups. Careful nurturing of Travelers' literacy and classes that involve adult members of these communities would seem to be a better approach (see for example Danaher et al., 2007, pp. 99-102).

Implications for Broader Educational Practice

It is evident that mainstream communities can learn much of value from the multiliteracies and values of mobile communities. We have explored how so many circus skills, for example, can be used across the curriculum areas of drama, animal husbandry, mathematics, physics, and other sciences. There would seem to be significant opportunities to incorporate circus arts into mainstream schooling. In this case, the class clown might have a certain degree of legitimacy. It has been the case that other performance-based traveling groups, such as touring drama, opera, and dance productions, have had an educational dimension: many people in regional and rural communities will recall being taken as part of a school group to watch such a performance. While there still seems a degree of resistance in some sections of the school system to conferring a similar educational value to other traveling groups, such as the circus and carnival, it is clear that they offer much to formalized learning and teaching.

The responses of circus school teachers explored in this chapter suggest that there is something very widely resonant in the language of circus arts that communicates across cultural differences and that is able to operate on a presocial level. As such, these arts might be employed in educational programs aimed at students diagnosed with autism or Asperger's syndrome, and might also be useful for learners with attention deficit and hyperactive disorder. Similarly, clowning can be extremely valuable in the treatment of very sick children.

More generally, the considerable benefit of the multiliteracies of mobile learners for broader educational practice might be in terms of inculcating the values of tolerance and openness. We have seen how mobile communities work closely together in assembling and taking down joints and in performing acts, which build up close bonds of trust and cooperation. Beyond that, the diversity of lifestyles and differences in cultural values, languages, and beliefs encountered through traveling can be a most enriching experience. This openness to others and to fresh perspectives is encapsulated in the remark of a Scottish show person: "It raises the very old question about the nomadic person and the settled person. The person who stays in one place and says, 'This is mine', and the person who just wanders round and says, 'This is everyone's'" (SS1999). In a world of increasingly complex interactions and challenges, drawing on the multiliteracies and meaning-making processes of Travelers to promote this perspective might be considered a laudable objective for education in general.

Questions for Reflection

- In what ways can new and emerging ICTs contribute to fostering the multiliteracies of mobile learning communities?
- How do the multiliteracies of mobile learning communities help them in sustaining their lifestyles both economically and culturally?
- What value can the multiliteracies of Travelers have for settled communities?
- In what ways does the concept of multiliteracies contribute to our understandings of the distinctions and connections between mobile and sedentary communities?

Suggestions for Further Reading

Bruce, B. C. (Ed.) (2003). *Literacy in the information age: Inquiries into meaning making with new technologies.* Newark, DE: International Reading Association.

Cope, B., & Kalantzis, M. (Eds.) (1999). *Multiliteracies: Literacy learning and the design of social futures.* London: Routledge.

Harreveld, R. E., & Danaher, P. A. (Eds.) (2004, June). *Multiliteracies and distance education: Diversities and technologies in contemporary universities.* Theme issue of the *Malaysian Journal of Distance Education, 6*(1), i-iv and 1-142.

Healy, A. H. (2000). *Teaching reading and writing in a multiliteracies context: Classroom practice.* Flaxton, Qld: Post Pressed.

Koschmann, T. (Ed.) (1999). *Meaning making: A special issue of" Discourse Processes".* London: Routledge.

Unsworth, L. (2001). *Teaching multiliteracies across the curriculum: Changing contexts of text and image in classroom practice.* Buckingham, UK and Philadelphia, PA: Open University Press.

7

Communities at Risk
Building Capacities for Sustainability

The notion of risk is often associated with mobile communities and derives from constructions of mobility as deficit and deviant. These constructions locate mobile communities outside the usual sources of capacity building and forms of capital. Accordingly mobile community members must create new and different approaches to building their capacities in ways that are individually and communally sustainable. This chapter traces the multiple means by which these community members embrace risk and build capacity, in the process maximizing sustainable learning outcomes.

Introduction

Risk, capacity building, and sustainability are three recurring themes in current accounts of social life. Forces as varied as concerns about global warming, terrorism, and (in the Christian calendar) the advent of a new millennium have combined to highlight uncertainties and instabilities in the contemporary world and in its possible future.

These uncertainties and instabilities give particular point to ongoing debates about educational policy-making and provision. This is because formal education is often posited as providing the basis for building capacity and developing sustainability that are needed as antidotes to the risks of an increasingly uncertain world. Yet paradoxically formal education can be both a contributor to and a vehicle for creating those risks, engaging productively with which suggests the creation of new and alternative educational futures, as this book proposes.

This paradox highlights, and derives from, a fundamental ambivalence about the three concepts framing this chapter. On the one hand, the linear and progressivist perspective portrayed in Figure 7.1 sees risk as a problem to be solved by means of capacity built and applied rationally and predictably in order to facilitate sustainability.

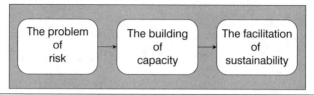

Figure 7.1 A progressivist representation of risk, capacity building, and sustainability

On the other hand, as Figure 7.2 below represents, a more organic and holistic representation of the same concepts sees their interrelationship as much more complex: at once chaotic and unpredictable and potentially complementary and/or contradictory, depending on context and the influence of other factors. This perspective sees risk as dynamic and generative rather than as necessarily threatening or constraining—a theme that is taken up in this chapter.

The chapter charts a course through this ambivalence to focus on how the three concepts are understood by and enacted in selected mobile learning communities. On the one hand, we eschew the progressivist representation of risk, capacity building, and sustainability, not least because it is too easily rendered complicit with constructions of such communities as deficit and deviant. On the other hand, we assert that recognizing, engaging with, and moving beyond those constructions is crucial if members of such communities are to create new educational futures for themselves and others. Furthermore,

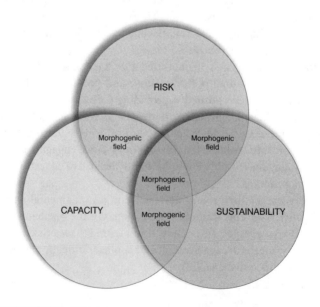

Figure 7.2 A holistic representation of risk, capacity building, and sustainability

we contend that the key to that creation is the application of the holistic conceptualization of the three concepts illustrated in Figure 7.2.

This argument is prosecuted by means of the chapter's five sections:

- Risk, capacity building, and sustainability in the literature about learning communities
- Risk, capacity building, and sustainability in the literature about mobile communities
- Examples of risk, capacity building, and sustainability in selected mobile learning communities
- Implications for the future education of mobile learning communities
- Implications for broader educational practice.

The chapter focuses particularly on the approaches that mobile community members adopt to embrace multiple types of risk and to build various forms of capital, in doing so maximizing their sustainable learning outcomes.

Risk, Capacity Building, and Sustainability in Learning Communities

We turn now to explore representations of risk, capacity building, and sustainability in selected literature about learning communities, in the process defining each term.

Risk

The term "risk" generally has a negative valence, especially when placed in front of words like "assessment," "averse," "avoidance," "management," "minimization," and "reduction" (Anteliz et al., 2004, p. 159; see also Bessant et al., 2003 on the origins and politics of "risk talk"). This positioning of risk as something to be feared and where possible circumvented shades in certain circumstances into what Swadener (2000) powerfully labeled "the hegemony of the risk rhetoric and ideology" (p. 118; see also Anteliz et al., 2004, p. 159; Danaher et al., 2007b, p. 214). Swadener and Lubeck (1995) had earlier contended that discourses of risk are ideological pressures involving the identification of posited causes of and potential solutions for various "problems" associated with specific groups considered "at risk" (see also Rowan, 2004, p. 22). Subsequently Swadener (2000) asserted a direct link between "the rhetoric of 'children of families at risk'" and "the currently popular language for describing those who are *socially excluded* or at risk of failure in various systems or concerns" (p. 117; emphasis in original). Moreover, she argued, somewhat provocatively, that "the term 'at risk' has become a buzzword, and is often added to the title of proposals in order to increase the likelihood of funding" (p. 118).

From this it follows that we are cautious and ambivalent about defining risk, which we characterize in an educational context as denoting properties or qualities perceived by some as potentially leading to reduced success. In doing so, we are certainly not wishing to depict "Traveller communities as sites of endearing and enduring happiness that are unproblematic because they have found the nirvana that permanently settled residents are seeking without success" (Danaher et al., 2007b, p. 214). We recognize, and have highlighted throughout this book, continuing examples of disjuncture between the mobility of these communities and their educational access. Yet to embrace uncritically "the hegemony of the risk rhetoric and ideology" (Swadener, 2000, p. 118)—for example, by accepting unproblematically the premise of "at risk learners"—is in turn to take the risk of making ourselves complicit with the forces that create that disjuncture and that hegemony.

There is support for this position in the learning communities literature, a prominent theme of which is that educational innovations, including effective— and sustainable—learning communities, encourage risk and provide a strong foundation for engaging with such risk. For example, Kilpatrick, Barrett, and Jones (2003) stated baldly, "Learning communities offer rich possibilities for dealing with some of the risks and dilemmas that education faces in the twenty-first century" (p. 3). In particular, "In the learning communities within educational institutions' perspective, respecting diversity fosters learning by building a climate of trust and encouraging risk-taking" (p. 9). One specific strategy proposed for this encouragement was by means of the creation of "… a professional learning culture that values professional development … , and a climate of openness that promotes sharing of knowledge, dialogue, inquiry and risk-taking, and gives constructive feedback to peoples at all levels …" (p. 10). This strategy is consistent with a view that learning in learning communities "… requires a degree of initiative and risk taking in the face of uncertainty. It is experimental by nature. The learner must be patient and forgiving because learning is a trial-and-error process, and mistakes are inevitable" (Wald & Castleberry, 2000, pp. 11-12).

Likewise Mitchell and Sackney (2000) averred:

> … professional learning is most likely to lead to profound improvement when individuals work collaboratively with supportive colleagues who are also engaged in continuous development. For this to happen, a culture of collegial relations and professional risk taking needs to be in place. (p. xv)

The specific strategies advocated by Mitchell and Sackney (2000) as a vehicle for developing enduring professional learning communities include "… visioning and purposing, team building, facilitating communication, encouraging experimentation and risk taking, promoting rewards and recognition, facilitating staff development, reculturing, modeling self-learning, and creating time and space for learning" (p. xvi). Although these strategies are likely to be less explicit and formalized in mobile learning communities, the underling principles of interdependence and mutuality are crucial—and they are crucial as well to engaging proactively with dynamic risk in ways that create new possibilities and futures.

At the same time, it is important to acknowledge that some of the learning communities' literature emphasizes the avoidance of risk rather than its encouragement. For instance, despite their overall position that learning communities welcome risk and provide a solid foundation for engaging productively with it, Kilpatrick, Barrett, and Jones (2003) asserted that "Learning communities can minimise risks for individuals in the increasingly complex world of the twenty-first century" (p. 11). This reflects the ambivalence noted above about how learning communities should understand and connect with risk, which in turn illustrates "the hegemony of the risk rhetoric and ideology" (Swadener, 2000, p. 118).

Capacity Building

Capacity can be understood as the ability to enact socially sanctioned behaviors. The socially sanctioned dimension becomes particularly important in relation to a community, where community continuity and viability depend on individual capacity being cultivated in ways that enhance the group's power. In the context of a learning community, this individual capacity can be presumed to be directed at demonstrating a person's capability of acting competently across a range of situations and of understanding and making meaning in the world, and simultaneously of contributing substantially to the community's survival and sustainability. Capacity building in learning communities is similarly the personal and communal development of socially sanctioned capacity among individuals and groups constituting those communities. Conceptualized in this sense, capacity building is clearly crucial to the likelihood of those individuals and groups embracing risk effectively rather than fearing and avoiding it.

Chaskin, Brown, Venkatesh, and Vidal (2001) synthesized what they saw as the main elements of capacity in relation to communities—with potential extrapolation to learning communities—in the following useful "summary definition" (p. 7):

> Community capacity is the interaction of human capital, organizational resources, and social capital existing within a given community that can be leveraged to solve collective problems and improve or maintain the well-being of that community. It may operate through informal social processes and/or organized efforts by individuals, organizations, and social networks that exist among them and between them and the larger systems of which the community is a part. (p. 7)

The learning communities literature generally assigns a prominent role to capacity as both an indicator of the functioning of such a community and a vehicle for generating and enhancing that functioning. Kilpatrick, Barrett, and Jones (2003) referred to "… community capacity to shape and manage its own future" (p. 3). Furthermore, they identified external networks as one driver with the demonstrated potential "… to improve the capacity of communities to learn to manage change …" (p. 9), and they affirmed that "Respect for diversity enhances the learning capacity of a community" (p. 9)—both these elements highlighting learning communities as open systems and dynamic entities. Kilpatrick, Barrett, and Jones synthesized the vital interdependence between learning communities and capacity in this way: "Learning communities can provide benefits to individual members and the community as a whole by developing the capacity or enhancing the potential of members … " (p. 10).

Examples of capacities considered necessary to underpinning successful learning communities include those related to student learning and instruction (Lieberman, 2000; Spillane & Louis, 2002), supporting social interactions (Swan & Shea, 2005, p. 6), learning from experience (Shulman & Shulman, 2004), dealing with uncertainty (Benner, 2003), community involvement in governance (Taylor, 2000), and a system's ability to innovate (Putman & Borko, 2001). Each of these capacities reflects a fundamental interdependence between the individual and the group and the convergence of separate and shared interests.

Capacity building also stands tall in the learning communities literature. Chaskin, Brown, Venkatesh, and Vidal (2001) referred directly to "… the possibilities and limitations of community capacity building as a tool to promote social change" (p. 3). Fullan (2000) posited a link between building capacity for learning skills and the elaboration of learning communities. Hopkins and Jackson (2003) identified "five elements which, taken together[,] contribute to what we understand by capacity" in contemporary learning communities, specifically schools (p. 90):

1. foundation conditions;
2. the personal;
3. the interpersonal;
4. the organisation;
5. external opportunities. (p. 90)

These five elements are certainly evident, in different combinations and with various manifestations, in the mobile learning communities considered here. So too with the inquiry process nominated by Copland (2003) as a vital plank of building capacity (in his case, for school improvement). This applies as well to the insights from a very different field with similar concerns, sustainable development and social-ecological systems, where "the concept of resilience–the capacity to buffer change, learn and develop–[is proposed] as a framework for understanding how to sustain and enhance adaptive capacity in a complex world of rapid transformations" (Folke et al., 2002, p. 437).

Thus capacity and capacity building emerge as inextricably linked with learning communities of diverse types. Several strategies are elicited in the literature as liable to foster the capacity building of community members, including the identification of needs, individual and group goal setting and reflection, and lobbying of those with the resources to address specific learning needs. Probably even more important than these strategies are the dispositions and values that accompany them, particularly the goodwill and sense of mutual obligation that are concerned about building personal and communal capacity. That goodwill and mutuality are also vital elements in the proactive mobilization of risk and in ongoing efforts to ensure the community's survival and sustainability.

Sustainability

Sustainability is focused on the long-term effectiveness and viability of organisms and organizations, implying a balance between meeting current and future needs and a potentially creative tension between continuity and change. Like risk engagement and capacity building, sustainability is central to the simultaneous fulfillment of individual and group aspirations within learning communities. At the same time, debate continues as to whether sustainability should be seen as an end in itself (toward which capacity building might be directed, for example) and/or whether other sociocultural goals can and should be attained by means of sustainability (Dillard et al., 2008).

The learning communities literature deals extensively with the presumed dependence of such communities on actions and attitudes aimed at their sustainability, with crucial personal and communal responsibilities for all members. Mitchell and Sackney (2000) "… see [learning] community building as an organic, evolutionary process that entails the deep involvement of each individual in pursuit of ways and means to promote sustaining and sustainable processes, structures, tasks, and commitments" (p. xii). Likewise Thorpe and Kubiak (2005) explained how, in networked learning communities in schools in England:

> Activists make strategic use of existing power relationships in order to facilitate networked learning, and develop skills in influencing and communicating across existing practice communities. Sustaining the network also depends on continuing intervention and strong support from activists' personal communities of trusted peers and colleagues with whom values and goals are shared. (p. 151)

Both these analyses highlighted learning communities as dynamic and fluid systems and the integral impact that individuals and groups have on those systems and their sustainability. This was also evident in accounts of efforts to resist constraints on community sustainability derived from the attrition of change (Giles & Hargreaves, 2006), to maximize the benefits for sustainability in virtual learning communities afforded by information accessibility and community adaptivity (Teo et al., 2003), to drawing on the lessons (as well as acknowledging the potential limitations) taken from a systems approach to design such communities (Castro Laszio, 2001), and to synthesizing multiple frameworks of indicators of sustainability to conduct holistic assessments of such sustainability in local communities (Reed et al., 2006).

Clearly working toward sustainability in learning communities is a highly complex process, requiring acting simultaneously on several fronts to attain multiple outcomes and to fulfill different and potentially conflicting interests. One site of potential conflict pertains to the utilization of resources for current members *vis-à-vis* future generations within a community. Sustainability principles suggest caution and careful thought in this regard—working out what should be consumed and/or invested today in order to ensure viability tomorrow. Another site refers to the appropriate balance between what should be retained and what should be changed in the basic elements of the community's way of life. Both of these sites are evident in the data analysis later in this chapter.

Risk, capacity building, and sustainability are certainly "hot topics" in current debates about educational policy-making and practice, encapsulating as they do broader sociocultural, economic, and ecological concerns at global, regional, national, provincial, and local levels. While each is a complex concept that does not admit of easy definition, and while their interrelationships are manifold, separately and in combination they have a close and ongoing connection with contemporary learning communities. Indeed, they constitute powerful theoretical lenses for interrogating claims about such communities, alerting us to the fundamental dynamism and fluidity that are vital to a community's longevity. They also remind us that many if not all community members would expect it to provide a facilitative and robust framework with which to engage and mobilize risk productively, build individual and communal capacity, and help to ensure survival and sustainability. Those are undoubtedly the expectations of most members of mobile communities.

Risk, Capacity Building, and Sustainability in Mobile Communities

Risk is a recurring theme of varying degrees of explicitness in historical and contemporary accounts of mobile communities. This is as true of Roma (both mobile and settled) and occupational Travelers such as barge, circus, and fairground people in Europe as it is of nomadic pastoralists in Africa and Asia as it is of migrant workers in the United States of America. This risk discourse is reflected in multiple statements linking mobility with various types of marginalization. As noted above, Lucassen, Willems, and Cottar (1998) observed "the inclination to view itinerant groups predominantly as down and out riff-raff" (p. 2)—or, equally baldly, "Historically, Gypsy Travellers have been universally stigmatised and treated with hostility by the majority culture" (Derrington & Kendall, 2004, p. 2). Similarly, Jordan (2000) remarked:

> Travellers have been identified as the most marginalized, illiterate group that underachieves in European state schools … They are today the subjects of some of the most overt racism and discrimination and, where mobility is a factor, they suffer the added disadvantage of discontinuity in attendance and curriculum experience. (p. 255)

Dyer (2000) in turn noted about nomadic pastoralists in India:

> Migrant groups fall into a gap between the inclusive rhetoric of Education for All and the exclusive reality of the sedentary modes of educational provision. Consequently, these groups will not benefit in the foreseeable future from the expansion, consolidation and improvement of current Basic Education initiatives. (p. 242)

Likewise Henderson (2001) commented that in Australia "many of the recommendations" from education systems for engaging with learners' mobility "are framed in a manner that locates 'the problem' in the mobile children themselves and/or their families" (p. 1). Consequently, "… there has been a tendency, often an implicit one, to blame the children or their parents for their itinerancy and the negative impact on children's educational achievement" (p. 2). Furthermore, with reference to migrant workers in the United States: "Educating children from immigrant and ethnic minority group families is a major concern of school systems across the country. For many of these children, U.S. education is not a successful experience" (Garcia, 1996, p. ix). And for the same communities eight years later:

> It has been said you can tell the quality and humanity of a society by the way it treats its most vulnerable members. The migrant workers and their families who harvest our nation's food can certainly be counted among the most vulnerable … Though demographic data fail to put a sharply defined face on the migrant community, we can safely assume that migrants experience greater poverty than any other group in this nation. (Baca, 2004, p. ix)

Focusing on this close connection between mobility and perceived risk itself runs the risk of contributing to the ongoing marginalization of mobile communities (Danaher, 2000a). At the same time, that risk is significantly ameliorated by the counternarrative to this theme of mobility-as-marginalizing-risk that is also evident in much of the literature about such communities: that those communities actively engage with risk and use it to create new opportunities, both educationally and socioeconomically. As was also noted above, this counternarrative constructs risk as dynamic and generative rather than as necessarily threatening or constraining. For example, in their account of the education of Gypsy and Traveler children in the United Kingdom, O'Hanlon and Holmes (2004) devoted a chapter (pp. 15-35) to elaborating the "[c]ommunity values and experience" (p. 15) of those communities, in the process identifying the culturally diverse and resilient practices that frame their home lives and family learning activities. This framework was then used as the basis for eliciting a set of "educational continuity strategies" for "[s]upporting mobility" (p. 37) for those communities, some more radical departures than others from current systemic provision for settled learners. This approach reflected a view that mobile communities, like all human systems, are adaptable and organic, and moreover that individuals and groups within those groups exhibit varying degrees of agency instead of passive acceptance of their marginalized positions. That adaptability and agency were also manifested in Dyer's (2006b) synthesis of nomadic pastoralists' pragmatic yet also principled engagements with formalized schooling:

> There seems to be a wide-ranging consensus that nomadic families opt for formal schooling as a means of becoming equipped for life in other livelihood systems ... nomads see schools as an opportunity to develop multi-resource household economies ... For nomadic families, schooling for some appears a more sensitive aspiration than schooling for all. (p. 262)

This same interplay between marginalization and agency in relation to mobile communities was demonstrated in the literature's discussions of capacity and capacity building. For nomadic pastoralists in Africa and Asia, for example, capacity ranges from individual Bakkarwal children exhibiting the ability to take their place in the community as productive adults (Rao, 2006, p. 60) to the economic concept of carrying capacity applied to the animals herded by pastoralist communities (Ho, 2001; Nautiyal et al., 2003; Vetter, 2005).

Equally, many of the educational initiatives focused on mobile communities—at least some of them in close consultation with, and indeed at the instigation of, members of those communities—are concerned with building capacity among the communities at both individual and group levels. This is certainly the case with many of the projects associated with migrant education provision in the United States in America. Examples range from maximizing parental involvement in schools attended by migrant children (López, 2004) to exploiting technological advances to enhance family literacies in after-school programs (Carrillo, 2004) to drawing on current research into language and literacy to boost migrant children's in-school literacy outcomes (Alanís, 2004).

So too with the discourse of sustainability in the mobile communities literature. On the one hand, sustainability has been linked with risk management for nomadic pastoralists (Fratkin & Mearns, 2003) and with "some of the unprogressive aspects of the nomadic culture" (Torimiro et al., 2003, p. 185), suggesting at least some ambivalence about such sustainability. On the other hand, there is certainly evidence of efforts to promote sustainability through risky and innovative educational practices that seek to build community members' multiple capacities. These include a mobile preschool education project deploying the nomads' white tents and cars as mobile training centers in the summer months, with the teachers also functioning as nomads (Krätli with Dyer, 2006, p. 18), and the evolution of the Queensland School for Travelling Show Children (Fullerton et al., 2004; Fullerton et al., 2005). Despite these undoubted successes, as McCaffery et al., (2006) pointed out in a useful encapsulation of the challenges to sustainability that can be extrapolated to other contexts:

> There are also no guarantees of sustainability. This depends on the ability of state stakeholders ... to develop a concrete plan for taking over the responsibility of running established centres and building on project gains .... [E]fforts [need to focus] on scaling up the positive aspects of the project, advocacy to alert state stakeholders to the urgency of their intervention and supporting stakeholders in taking over full financial and management responsibility for continuing project activities. (p. 251)

This discussion raises the crucial issue of mobile communities being part of broader contexts and systems that can be favorable and/or hostile to the communities' efforts to mobilize risk, build capacity, and be sustainable. That location simultaneously creates the challenges faced by such communities, given the mobile–settled disjuncture that courses through this book, and contains the seeds to innovative and transformative engagements with those challenges. Yet that simultaneity constitutes a further and crucial challenge: can we explicate conceptual lenses for theorizing, and can we distill evaluative criteria for interrogating, situated factors that facilitate and/or inhibit mobilized risk, capacity building, and sustainability among mobile communities? And by means of that explication and distillation, can we distinguish rigorously between efforts to achieve those outcomes that resonate with the aspirations of mobile learning communities and those that are inimical to the sustainability of their diversity and difference? Mobile communities have to take up that question as a normal part of their everyday lives—and so must researchers into the educational dimensions of such communities.

Risk, Capacity Building, and Sustainability in Selected Mobile Learning Communities

There has certainly been considerable discussion of risk, capacity building, and sustainability among the mobile learning communities represented in this book, and sometimes of the intersections among those three key concepts. Not surprisingly, understandings of those intersections varied widely according to the material circumstances and the philosophical dispositions of the respondents. What they had broadly in common was their reflection of the perceived challenges linking mobility and formal education and also of the possibilities in engaging with those challenges afforded by risk mobilization, capacity building, and measures to promote sustainability.

Some of those challenges definitely pertained to the complexities and rigors of earning and learning while traveling on the respective itineraries of the different mobile communities, which from one perspective constitute significant risks that must be mastered. For example, a member of a Scottish show community spoke about the necessary cost of public liability insurance, whose premiums were so large that they could be afforded only by organizations such as the Showmen's Guild of Great Britain (SS1999). Similarly, a member of a Dutch show community referred to the expense of buying and maintaining equipment: "When you're traveling five years, you must do new carpet and everything" and "... that attraction ... costs a lot of money" (DS1999). Yet the same interviewee commented that persistence sometimes yields dividends in terms of promoting understanding between mobile and settled residents of communities that can help to engage with the risk of mutual misunderstanding:

> In the early days the local people here decided we are very strange people ... I think there are not so many problems any more ... The same with the community here. They say it in the [news]papers—how we work; how we live. That's better. (DS1999)

A similar mix between realistic assessment of possible threats and determination to demonstrate resilience in the light of those threats was evident in a statement by a member of an English circus community:

> Every business struggles; this is not an exception. Recessions and whatever hit every type, and the first type of thing is [that] entertainment suffers first. Everybody eats, everybody dresses, but not necessar[il]y to go to the circus. That is the problem. Normally our audiences are the working class, and the working class suffers all the time. [If] there is a financial problem in the world, then our class of audience is the one who first suffers. Therefore our business suffers. But, as I say to you, there's always a space. Circus is never going to go. It changes, yes, like everything else, but it is not going to be finished. (EC1999)

The proposition outlined earlier in the chapter, whereby mobilizing risks is an integral element alike of mobile communities and educational innovations, was confirmed by an interviewee associated with the Australian show community. This respondent reflected on the crucial role of a group of women from the community in lobbying for the establishment of their own school, and on how in doing so they took considerable personal and group risks for the perceived benefits to flow to the community: "The women were risk takers; that's why I always thought that they were like Rose Kennedy, the power behind the throne" (AS2003). And again: "It was the women who wanted school for the kids. It's always been the women who were the risk takers" (AS2003).

It follows from the earlier posited link between risk-taking and educational innovation that Traveler teachers needed to mobilize risk effectively if they were to assist the mobile communities whose interests they were committed to serving (see also Danaher et al., 2007a, chapters 9 and 10). One such teacher provided an evocative account of bringing these two imperatives together:

> ... if you look at the finances around Traveler education, and how you have to be careful about delivering on even the smallest resources, it actually doesn't allow you to be innovative, or to take risks, or to take chances, or to make mistakes. Yet in order to find solutions to these really complex issues we've got to do all of those things. I'm a firm believer [that] if all we do is what we do then all we have and all we'll ever have is what we have [now]. (TT1999)

With regard to building capacity, a member of a Dutch bargee community identified a key difference between them and the settled community that in turn created a potential difference in the strategies available for that building (although in this respect many mobile learning groups are closer to the settled than to the bargee community):

> What now is different is that when I work with [bargee] children they're not so used to playing in a group. When I was at school it was normal that the children played in a group and played with each other and listened to the stories of other children. Now what they're doing now is always an adult and child. A big difference. (DB1999)

The same respondent exhibited an individually developmental approach to building capacity, working with individual bargee children to build their multiple capacities:

> ... sometimes [they are gifted and talented] in one way, and then there are so many other things still to develop. So when a child already can read, I don't have to stimulate reading, so we do other things. But we help the child one step further. We don't say to the child, "You already

know that; we [will] stop teaching you." We always go one step further or go deeper into the subject. (DB1999)

Capacity building understood as individual development also underpinned some of the comments by interviewees associated with a Dutch amateur circus group attached to a local school whose members traveled varied distances to perform their acts:

> Together we organize the whole circus when someone is calling us and asks if we want to come and perform. Then we go outside with the children and we go to another city or another school—it doesn't matter where. There we give a performance. (DC1999)

For these respondents, this capacity building of young circus performers took the form of individualized accountability within a collaborative framework:

> In our lessons, when we train them, everyone has to do it. Some are very good and some are very shy and [don't] want to perform. But everyone has to do it in their own group, in their own way, on their own level. So we know so much about circus and acrobat[ic]s that there is always something to do for the student who is very good and for the student who has less capacity to do it. But all have to do it. Those children who want to do more than we do in our lesson, they can come on Friday afternoon when we train our circus group and children who want to learn circus activity. (DC1999)

A variation on this approach was articulated by a member of a Dutch circus community (already cited in chapter 5 for a different purpose), who in doing so identified other values such as balance and trust that were considered to help with building capacity for lifelong and life-wide learning:

> … teaching circus skills to other people, … helps people in a very simple way, because … acrobatics are [such] basic things in life. It's like if you are diving and you have a diving board, it's like … a diving board to your future … I divide it into three main things. It's working together because, if you don't do that well, or in a team[, there are difficulties]. It's being in balance yourself. And the third thing is trust. You have to trust each other to be able to [do] acrobatic things. It's [energy] going into your body, and that also helps in your mind. If you are really in balance, it also balances you in your head. (DC1999)

This view of capacity building as depending on individual accountability and self-reliance was echoed by a member of a Dutch show community who reflected on the skills needed to keep the show stalls operational: "I do it [my]self; most things I do [my]self. I can work with my hands. Other people bring it to special companies for painting or something. That's different. It's not so difficult to do painting" (DS1999). Or as another member of the same community expressed it succinctly: "It's learning for yourself. You watch other people, and then you have one idea. You begin" (DS1999). And also: "What you do on the fairgrounds, you have to watch and you can learn" (DS1999). Similarly, a respondent from the Venezuelan show community explained how important it was for him to make prompt judgments about people such as prospective employees and competitors, by looking at body language and the manner of dress (VS1999)—skills forged in the furnace of experience.

A broader view of capacity building was articulated by a respondent connected with the Australian show community, specifically in relation to the perceived long-term impact of the Queensland School for Travelling Show Children, whereby, in addition to the enhancement of growth of individual children: "... other results that we're achieving—the social cohesiveness that's building and the capacity that we're developing in a broader community" (AS2003). This speaker elaborated:

> I think we are in possession of something that is unique in the nation in terms of a mode of service delivery, and I think there's learning coming out of that [and] there's curriculum ... out of that. I think the community capacity coming out of that that we need to hook into those strategic elements and continue to promote them across a broader context. (AS2003)

With regard to sustainability and potential impediments to its attainment, several respondents confirmed the fundamental contradiction between forms of mobility and formal educational systems—the Gordian knot identified in Chapter 1. One participant articulated this contradiction in action for Dutch bargee people:

> ... when they are coming into a harbor, they were ordered for six [o'clock] in the morning. They don't call [the teacher] at night, but when they come in the harbor at six, then they get a telephone call, "It's not necessary at six o'clock; it's now 12 o'clock." Then they call [the teacher] at eight o'clock and say, "Will you come this morning?" (DB1999)

This kind of situation clearly disrupts not only the individual barge family seeking to organize a session with the teacher but also other families with whom that same teacher needs to liaise.

Various strategies have been implemented to enhance the sustainability of particular mobile learning communities, again dependent in part on the contexts in which their mobilities are enacted. A member of a Venezuelan show community showed the interviewer a plaque provided by the local Rotary Club in recognition of the show's contribution to building a new fire station (VS1999). This type of link between the show community and the broader community reflected their interdependence and in turn the vital role played by that interdependence in fostering the show community's sustainability.

The following statement, by a member of an English show community, encapsulated several of the ideas expressed in the research data about risk, capacity building, and sustainability:

> It's a very unusual experience. You'd have to live it for a year to begin to understand the complexities of it. The internal disputes we have—we have lots of those. It's like we're members of a trade association, a guild, like a club, but not everybody sticks to the rules. So we do have our disputes, but we still plod along. There's a business there for my son to go on with, as much as I would have loved to have seen him stay at school and have a good education, and go out [of] the business, because I think he had the ability to go in another profession a long way. I honestly think he did. He didn't want it. He's 18 now, and he loves the dodgems, he loves the business, and at that age it's a lovely thing because he's got such a wide range of abilities given to him to learn. This winter, he's been welding, painting, sign writing, doing electrical work, doing carpentry, all basic stuff that he's [been] taught from watching the rest of us and from doing, that nobody else outside our kind of community gets. So it's a lovely thing when you're 18; when you get to my age, there's so many uncertainties as you get older. At that age, money to him is no object. He says, "I'll have that," and I'm the one who says, "No, you can't do that. We just can't afford it." You don't think of that at 18 or 20. When you get to our age, then you realize that resources are very finite, and perhaps there is a better income, a better way of life, outside the business, but by that time it's too late. (ES1999)

Here we have references to risks to livelihood such as not all community members obeying the rules, as well as to an approach to risk mobilization encapsulated in the pithy understatement: "… we still plod along." We also have an account of building capacity by means of the myriad of skills being acquired with varying degrees of formality and credentialing by the participant's son. And we have the concerns about, as well as the shrewd investments in, the long-term viability of the individual family business as well as the show community as a whole—including the ongoing discussions of expending versus saving resources.

Or as a member of a Scottish show community expressed the potential benefits attendant on seeking to sustain the business through expansion: "Sometimes if you take the chance you get your fingers burned, but they're willing to have a go. It's a big step" (SS1999). This disposition to aspire to sustainability, despite the potential drawbacks, highlighted the community members' ongoing discussion of how much should be changed in the group's way of life and what should be retained, emphasizing the cohesiveness of a community well-versed in the strategies needed to conduct such reflexive and rigorous discourse—and with such high stakes (see also the discussion of reflexivity in Chapter 8).

This disposition was exemplified by a different member of an English show community (who is also cited in Chapter 8) musing on the "challenges and opposition" that attach to the business and on the attitude needed to engage with them:

> ... where it did used to be that fairgrounds were just traveling fairgrounds, there are now a lot of theme parks, but also a lot of stores or shopping malls—they also have things for children now, rides and amusements. So really I wouldn't say it's so much a threat, because I think there is something magical about a traveling fair. It's there one day; the next day it's gone. I think that holds a bit of mystery for people. (ES1999)

Implications for the Future Education of Mobile Learning Communities

This chapter has explored multiple means by which selected mobile learning communities have acknowledged and mobilized different types of risk, deployed strategies to build personal and communal capacity, and sought ways to ensure sustainability at group and community levels. The perspective adopted has been that of risk, capacity, and sustainability as dynamic and generative as well as interdependent and mutually reinforcing when conditions are favorable.

The single most significant factor rending such conditions unfavorable is the continuing marginalization of mobility as deficit and deviant. This applies to educational as much as to sociocultural and economic domains of life. The literature is replete with references to the divergence between what mobile communities need for earning, learning, and living and what sedentary communities and the state are willing and able to provide to them.

Yet the literature also contains several examples whereby members of mobile learning communities have succeeded in mobilizing risk in productive ways. Some of these ways relate to the diligent discharge of their occupations, requiring careful decision-making about locations and types of work, the balance between production and consumption, and short- and long-term decisions about future activities. Other ways of mobilizing risk pertain to formal, non-formal, and informal education, such as which forms of provision are most suited to their families' current and projected future circumstances and which agencies in settled communities are most likely to assist them in maximizing their educational access and outcomes. These types of risk mobilization lead in turn to opportunities to build capacity and to sow the seeds for sustainability—provided again that the constellations in the firmament are aligned appropriately.

From this perspective, risk, capacity building, and sustainability, far from being optional extras in the functioning of mobile learning communities, are actually crucial to the long-term survival and viability of those communities. At the same time, they cannot be centrally mandated or state imposed; instead they must evolve fluidly and be enacted strategically according to the contexts in which the communities are located and that they traverse. Given the diversity of the contexts of the communities represented in this book, this is no easy task.

The communities most likely to succeed in this regard are those accustomed to talking and working together to articulate individual and communal goals and interests that they seek collectively to attain. They are also experienced in identifying and negotiating with multiple stakeholders in settled communities, including those with the ability to secure much needed resources and support. Yet it is precisely these types of mobile learning communities that are most liable to mobilize risk, build capacities at multiple levels, and secure their own sustainability and contribute to that of other communities with which they intersect. Or as an insightful observer of the Australian show community expressed the elements that are also evident in many other mobile learning communities that mobilize risk, build capacity, and enhance sustainability: "Community, capacity, identity, esteem—all those intangibles" (AS2003).

Implications for Broader Educational Practice

So what does this chapter's emphasis on risk, capacity building, and sustainability mean for broader educational practice? Three specific implications appear worthy of consideration. The first focuses on risk. A burgeoning field of scholarship continues to explore the multiple discourses attached to formal education, young people, and perceived threats in the contemporary world (Brendtro et al., 2002; Dwyer & Wyn, 2001; Helve & Holm, 2005; Kenway et al., 2006; Leaton Gray, 2006; Welch, 2001). Many of these discourses position formal education and young people as being conjoined in a relationship of crisis, in response to both larger shifts in the global landscapes and personal angst as individuals experience lack and loss of meaning and purpose.

Yet, if we remember Swadener's (2000) articulation of "the hegemony of the risk rhetoric and ideology" (p. 118), we are liable to be skeptical about these kinds of discourses, asking instead in whose interests they are propagated and who is likely to benefit—and who not—from their proposed "solutions" to particular types of "problems." Moreover, we are inclined to see risk-taking as crucial to educational innovation and to efforts to create new educational futures (Ellis, 2005; see also Kahneman & Lovallo, 1993). This was evident, for example, in the call by Garrison and Kanuka (2004) for decision-makers in higher education to engage in the risk-taking and investment needed to achieve the full educational potential of blended learning technologies. Likewise Knight, Weir, and Woldehanna (2003) argued that schooling in rural Ethiopia has an important role to play in reducing risk aversion and thereby promoting innovation in agriculture there, with potential individual and communal benefits. Furthermore, as Sobel and King (2008) reminded us, there is a strong potential connection between schooling approaches to innovation and rates of youth entrepreneurship, underscoring the ongoing responsibility of schools in helping to prepare students for post-school life.

The second implication of the chapter for broader educational practice relates to building capacity. There is certainly much literature suggesting this as a prime function of formal education at individual, institutional, and community levels across a range of sectors in different countries (Mendoza et al., 2007; Seddon & Billett, 2004; Spoth et al., 2004; Stokes et al., 2006; Stanley & Tognolini, 2007). Yet there is a requirement as well to judge each learner individually and as part of a broader collective in terms of what s/he needs and wants to be able to learn. There is also clearly a balance to be struck between formal education as proto-training for the workforce and the economy that depends on it on the one hand and capacity building related to non-economic domains such as sociocultural life and spirituality on the other.

The third implication of the chapter is concerned with the sustainability of broader educational practice. This refers in part to ongoing debates such as public versus private funding of schools (Luis Bernal, 2005) and universities (Enders & Jongbloed, 2007) and the degree of effectiveness of declarations and targets like EFA (Carr-Hill, 2006, pp. 35-36). What is at issue—locally, nationally, and globally—is who has access to formal education, who pays for it, and how it can be sustained across multiple spaces and from one generation to the next. An associated question is how educational provision can be sustained while still exhibiting and enabling sufficient flexibility and responsiveness to engage meaningfully with the wide diversity of learners who are dependent on it to sustain their own lives and their communities.

A related focus is on formal education playing its part in enhancing community, national, and global sustainability. As with risk mobilization and capacity building, there is substantial scholarship advocating this role at school and post-school levels (Blaze Corcoran & Wals, 2004; Scheunpflug & Asbrand, 2006). Yet a key element of this kind of contribution is recognizing the complexity of sustainability as an aspiration as well as acknowledging the sometimes conflicting interests associated with its implementation, as with the example of teaching about climate change (Anteliz et al., 1997). This entails in turn highlighting the ongoing need for communication and dialogue within and across communities, which require dispositions of respect and trust and which would doubtless benefit from training in and application of formal skills in listening to others and considering alternative viewpoints.

In sum, then, risk mobilization, capacity building, and striving for sustainability have significant implications for broader educational practice gleaned from the experiences and opportunities of mobile learning communities. Those lessons are learned most effectively when these three concepts are understood as fluid, shifting, proactive, and resistant to stultification or cooption by narrowly conceived and homogenizing actions by the state and educational providers—much like the members of the mobile communities themselves.

Questions for Reflection

- What kinds of risk do you consider most significant in relation to contemporary education?
- In what ways can and should those risks be minimized and/or mobilized?
- What types of capacities in learners should formal education contribute to building? What are the prerequisites of such building being effective?
- What is your understanding of sustainability at local, national, and global levels? What do you see as the character of the relationship between sustainability and formal education?
- To what extent do you agree with the argument presented in this chapter about risk, capacity building, and sustainability as they relate to mobile learning communities? Why?
- What in your view needs to happen for such communities to be successful and sustainable?

Suggestions for Further Reading

Ale, B. (2009/in press). *Risk: An introduction: The concepts of risk, danger and chance.* London: Routledge.

Bekerman, Z., & Kopelowitz, E. (Eds.) (2008). *Cultural education–cultural sustainability: Minority, diaspora, indigenous and ethno-religious groups in multicultural societies.* London: Routledge.

Dillard, J., Dujon, V., & King, M. C. (Eds.) (2008). *Understanding the social dimension of sustainability.* London: Routledge.

Gray, D., Colucci-Gray, L., & Camino, E. (Eds.) (2009/in press). *Science, society and sustainability: Education and empowerment for an uncertain world.* London: Routledge.

Lewens, T. (Ed.) (2007). *Risk: Philosophical perspectives.* London: Routledge.

Whitehead, M. (2006). *Spaces of sustainability: Geographical perspectives on the sustainable society.* London: Routledge.

Wilkinson, K. (2009/in press). *Risk, vulnerability and everyday life.* London: Routledge.

8
Marginalization and Transformation

Marginalization and transformation are significant issues impinging on the nexus between mobilities and learning communities. Mobility in one form or another can lead to marginalization—lifestyles regarded as different from the norm and separated from centered patterns of settlement. Such lifestyles, however, can generate learning communities that engage their marginalized status constructively and proactively in order to transform their educational outcomes and life opportunities.

Introduction

It seems appropriate to devote the last chapter of a book on mobile learning communities to the themes of marginalization and transformation. These themes in many ways encapsulate the challenges and opportunities that Travelers experience in relation to their engagements with both settled communities and other mobile groups. In a sense Travelers experience a lifestyle characterized by quite literal marginalization in the way that they traverse the fringes of society, displaced from fixed settlement. It is the way in which this literal marginalization is transformed into official and unofficial practices of prejudice and exclusion, along with counteracting tendencies, that is the focus of this chapter.

Marginalization in some cases can be attributed to direct prejudice in the form of derogatory labeling, abusive treatment, and institutional racism. In other cases, the distinctive lifestyle routines and cultural values of traveling groups can be a source of marginalization in the sense that they are difficult to accommodate within the practices and protocols of mainstream, sedentary communities. However, in responding to these challenges, and in drawing upon the rich possibilities for empowering change and growth that travel affords, mobile learning communities offer a model for observing transformation in action.

The concept of marginalization has been subject to much discussion and debate within various fields of scholarship: sociology, cultural studies, politics, education, and psychology, among others (Ferguson et al., 1990). The idea of a margin tends to imply a center from which a group or individual is marginalized. Historically, such marginalization has been associated with various markers of identity: gender, race and ethnicity, religion, sexual preference, and so forth. In relation to mobile learning communities, the marginalized status tends to relate to the difficulty of sustaining educational access in the context of provision designed largely for settled or sedentary populations.

While marginalization is conventionally understood in deficit terms as a kind of lack (that is, if you are marginalized you lack the opportunities and access to resources that those at the center enjoy), this chapter also seeks to explore how a marginalized status can be understood more positively. The perspective from the margins can be fresh and free of some of the limitations and biases of those occupying the center. Indeed, the idea of mobility lends itself to shifting perspectives that might lead to transformation and empowerment for various kinds of marginalized groups.

The chapter examines various theories associated with marginalization and transformation and their applicability to the experiences of mobile learning communities. It draws upon interview data from different Traveler groups to explore the ways in which they have been marginalized. While not seeking to downplay the difficulties that such processes of marginalization have caused for these communities, we are also concerned with showing how creative and resilient responses to these forces help mobile learning communities in transforming their lives and perspectives.

The chapter is divided into five sections:

- Marginalization and transformation in the literature about learning communities
- Marginalization and transformation in the literature about mobile communities
- Examples of marginalization and transformation in selected mobile learning communities
- Implications for the future education of mobile learning communities
- Implications for broader educational practice.

Marginalization and Transformation in Learning Communities

An interest in education as a vehicle for transformation has been the subject of considerable debate. While scholars such as Bourdieu (Bourdieu & Passeron, 1977) have focused on the ways in which formal education tends to reproduce cultural distinctions and social class divisions within society, and thereby contributes to the ongoing marginalization of less powerful groups, other theorists have sought ways of conceptualizing the means by which learning communities can promote transformative outcomes.

Inspired by the work of critical intellectual Paulo Freire, Giroux (1992) drew on the idea of border crossing as a way of empowering hybrid postmodern identities to proclaim the arbitrariness of boundaries and to create the "opportunity for new subject positions, identities and social relations that can produce resistance to and relief from the structures of domination and oppression" (p. 18). In other words, while modernist institutions such as schools and universities acted as agents of marginalization in constructing borders between those with access to positions of privilege and those denied the opportunities or resources to access such positions, the commitment to change of thinkers like Freire and those influenced by them help to deconstruct such boundaries.

There has also been considerable attention within the literature to perspective transformation and transformative learning theory. Perspective transformation can be understood as:

> ... the process of becoming critically aware of how and why our assumptions have come to constrain the way we perceive, understand, and feel about our world; changing these structures of habitual expectation to make possible a more inclusive, discriminating, and integrating perspective; and, finally, making choices or otherwise acting upon these new understandings. (Imel, 1998, p. 1)

Mezirow (2000, p. 24) suggested that perspective transformation takes place when "individuals change their frames of reference by critically reflecting on their assumptions and beliefs and consciously making and implementing plans that bring about new ways of defining their worlds." So, while Giroux (1992) was attendant to the contextual forces and conditions of possibility that create opportunities for border crossing, and the role of cultural workers in promoting such a move, perspective transformation shifts the focus to the work that individuals do at the level of their frames of reference or habits of mind.

While transformational learning theory is often used interchangeably with perspective transformation, according to Mezirow (2000) it refers to:

> ... the process by which we transform our taken-for-granted frames of reference (meaning perspectives, habits of mind, mind-sets) to make them more inclusive, discriminating, open, emotionally capable of change, and reflective so that they may generate beliefs and opinions that will prove more true or justified to guide action. (pp. 7-8)

It is evident that a process of critical reflection and critical awareness is integral to such a process of transformation. In a related sense, Brookfield (1986) saw major personal learning occurring when the individual can "come to reflect on self-images, change their self-concepts, question their previously uncritically internalized norms, and reinterpret their current and past behaviours from a new perspective" (p. 216). And even while theorists such as Bourdieu (Bourdieu & Passeron, 1977) have expressed skepticism about the extent to which educational institutions facilitate transformative outcomes, he

(Bourdieu, 1998), like the theorists of transformational learning, emphasized the importance of a reflexive attitude in challenging the deep structures that have contributed to the marginalization of certain groups.

We might explore, then, the ways and means through which learning communities are able to generate critically reflective dispositions that play a part in transforming their perspectives. An issue for mobile communities is the extent to which their lifestyle affords opportunities for developing such reflection. For example, Bourdieu (1998) identified as a key to reflective practice the scholastic point of view, the universalizing and objectifying perspective offered a position within the academy. That is, the academy traditionally involved being sequestered from the everyday world of work and commerce in order to reflect upon it, rather as a person sitting on a hill high above a town can look down and make sense of the various activities taking place there. Given that Travelers, by contrast, are caught up in the routines and challenges of keeping "the show on the road" and of moving from place to place, such a universalizing and objectifying reflective practice would seem to be denied them.

Marginalization and Transformation in Mobile Communities

Scholars have generated a range of concepts to make sense of the marginalization of mobile communities, as was indicated in the introduction to this book. We find particularly useful McVeigh's (1997) term "sedentarism," referring to a "system of ideas and practices which serves to normalise and reproduce sedentary modes of existence and pathologise and repress nomadic modes of existence" (p. 9). Danaher (2001a) drew on other Traveler interview data in exploring the cumulative effects of the interested and objectifying gaze to which Australian traveling show people are subjected every time that they enter a new community in contributing to their marginalization. Similarly, Lloyd and McCluskey (2008, p. 331)) found that discrimination against Gypsy Travelers in the United Kingdom is still so widespread that it has been called the last respectable form of racism.

A related challenge is in terms of the type of educational provision afforded mobile communities. Is it better to provide a specialized service that is geared toward accommodating the mobile lifestyle of Travelers or rather to seek to incorporate such groups within the educational mainstream? While it might seem that placing mobile learners outside the mainstream would contribute to their marginalization and difference, the inability of many mainstream sedentary institutions such as schools and educational bureaucracies to cater adequately for Travelers has been a force for marginalization itself. Thus, while mainstreaming is positively associated with an inclusive approach, it can also act as a vehicle of alienation.

The issue of nomenclature is an important factor in this debate. Thus, while on the one hand "inclusion" has also been called "integration" and "mainstreaming" with reference to students identified as having special educational needs (Farrell & Ainscow, 2002; Stainback et al., 1992), on the other hand "specialization" has been named "segregation" in relation to different kinds of disabilities (Cooney et al., 2006), ethnic (Massey, 2006) and religious (Leonard, 2006) minorities, socioeconomic background (Oakes, 2005), and residential location (Brunello & Checchi, 2007). "Specialization" has also been termed "separatism" in particular contexts (see for example Doerr, 2004; Zine, 2007). These names often have positive or negative valences both for the educators and researchers who employ them and for the groups so designated.

Historically, special education provision in many Western countries initially took the form of separate special schools set up by religious or philanthropic organizations, which were eventually adopted and extended as part of national educational arrangements when the state took over responsibility for mass schooling. This was the situation until the early 1990s, when the appropriateness of such a separate system was challenged on the grounds of both human rights and effectiveness (Farrell & Ainscow, 2002, p. 5). In terms of the human rights perspective, the United Nations Convention on the Rights of the Child endorsed the move toward inclusion. This inclusive orientation was also agreed by 92 governments and 25 international organizations in the Salamanca Statement on Principles, Policy and Practice in Special Needs Education in June 1994 (p. 6). In terms of effectiveness, Booth and Ainscow (1998, p. 4) linked the move toward inclusiveness with the provision of appropriate and sufficient resources needed for learning.

It is evident that, even within the context of moves toward inclusive education, the issue of whether mainstreaming or special provision is the preferred option remains open. For example, the Tomlinson committee in its national inquiry into further education provision for students with disabilities and/or difficulties in learning in England in 1996 defined inclusion in terms of obtaining the greatest degree of match or fit between individual learning requirements and provision. It left decisions about whether such match or fit is obtained in mainstream or segregated settings to education and training professionals (Centre for Studies on Inclusive Education, n.d.). This suggests that it is possible to complement a commitment to inclusive education with a somewhat segregated environment.

Clearly, contextual factors such as geography and cultural traditions play a role in deciding whether mainstreaming or specialization is appropriate for particular Traveler groups. In the United Kingdom, the large number of schools within a geographically relatively small nation means that, regardless of where a mobile community might have moved to, a mainstream school is likely to be nearby. In the comparatively vast distances of the Australian outback, on the other hand, such ready access to schools cannot be assumed. Consequently, Australia has a rich tradition of specialized provisions through innovations such as the School of the Air, whereby lessons have been delivered by radio to families dispersed across the country's interior.

The Queensland School for Travelling Show Children can be understood as an attempt to reconcile mainstream and specialized provision (Fullerton et al., 2004; Fullerton et al., 2005). While this school consists of specialized mobile classrooms that travel with the show community on its annual circuits around Australia, that these classrooms are situated within the grounds of the local school of the community that the show is visiting and adopt the routines of that school exhibits a commitment to mainstreaming and normalizing the educational experience of the children. In this way, the show school is seeking to challenge tendencies toward marginalization associated with specialized provision, while acknowledging the distinctive needs of its stakeholder community.

Marginalization and Transformation in Selected Mobile Learning Communities

Marginalization and Mobility

Our data affirm the perception that it is the very mobility of Travelers that is the source of their marginalization rather than their occupation *per se*. This point is demonstrated by the case of sedentary fairgrounds in Caracas, Venezuela, where the proprietors were able to build up links with the local community that made them influential rather than marginalized (VS1999). Owing to having permanent residence in the city, they were involved in community organizations and civic clubs such as Rotary—positions that accorded them a certain prestige and respectability.

It might be contended that such respectability accorded to sedentary lifestyles is also connected with a certain attitude toward property and the sense of propriety that accompanies it. As we saw in the discussion of multiliteracies in Chapter 6, within Western capitalist nations the provision of individual property rights, along with the rule of law and civic institutions such as formal education, tends to be regarded as fundamental to ensuring effective and civilized models of citizenship. Settlement, then, is bound up with the acquisition of fixed property. A traveling lifestyle tends to militate against this value, and is therefore seen as threatening. As was also noted in Chapter 6, this distinction was encapsulated in the remarks of a Scottish fairground Traveler: "It raises the very old question about the nomadic person and the settled person. The person who stays in one place and says, 'This is mine', and the person who just wanders round and says, 'This is everyone's'" (SS1999).

Certain mobile communities, such as New Travelers, are motivated quite explicitly by a rejection of property values. Other lifestyle Travelers exhibit a communal approach to sharing resources, such as Roma. However, other mobile communities, like occupational Travelers, demonstrate an interest in getting on in the world and acquiring property, but also in reconciling that aspiration with a commitment to their mobile lifestyles.

However, in spite of this commitment to property values, there is a lingering association of mobility with threats to property. In the context of the United States of America, for example, this association is revealed in the image of the hobo from the 1930s Great Depression, the itinerant who rides the rattler (the trains coming into town) and who begs for food. The hobo was associated with being a tramp, a reject from "proper" society. And Australia's most famous song, "Waltzing Matilda," is about another itinerant figure, the swagman, who is represented as stealing sheep.

The very idea of a mobile lifestyle contributes to the suspicions that work to marginalize Travelers. Such suspicions were reflected in the words of an English Traveler educator: "They see Travelers somehow getting away with things because you can't pin them down" (TT1999). Images of fly-by-night operators, of transient lifestyles, of people with no fixed abode are all symptoms of this response. It contrasts with images of settled life as being based on solid foundations and firmly embedded values, with the home configured as the fixed center of family life. As an English circus teacher remarked: ". . . [S]ociety is predicated on fixed residence" (EC1999).

One manifestation of this predication is that, while most people in paid employment actually travel to and from work, they are not designated as Travelers. In certain cases people can commute a considerable distance for work or education, covering far more distance than people of previous historical eras were accustomed to moving, but because they are returning to a fixed residence they are distinguished from those groups labeled as mobile communities.

An example of this distinction was a hotel landlord in England who displayed a sign saying "No Travelers" (TT1999). Even though many of his clients were people who traveled, including tourists from other parts of England or abroad, it was understood that the sign referred to a particular group of Travelers. The sign was removed as it constituted a breach of the Race Relations Act of the United Kingdom.

Marginalization and Institutionalized Racism

In some cases traveling communities experience institutionalized racism, based on an idea of an institution failing to meet the needs of a particular group while satisfying the needs of other groups. While the focus of this book is directed partly toward the role of some educational institutions in practicing such racism, it is important to consider how a range of other institutions can be complicit: the police, media, businesses, and so forth.

There are historical examples where such racism has been overt and horrific in its consequences. Within Nazi Germany, for example, Gypsies faced open persecution and were sent to concentration camps and exterminated. A key issue with such institutional racism is that, even though the Romany are an ethnic category rather than a racial one, within the mindset of the Nazi ideology they were identified and treated as a separate race and persecuted on that basis. Thus the concept of racism applies when ethnic (that is, cultural) characteristics are treated as racial or physiological properties.

The legacy of such persecution is profound and affects subsequent generations of that culture in their dealings with various institutionalized authorities in the countries through which they travel. Thus establishing enduring bonds of trust is one of the profound challenges facing educators seeking to engage Roma and other Travelers who have experienced persecution. For example, an English Traveler educator mentioned that wearing a blue anorak on visits to families was an error of judgment as some Travelers thought that he was a policeman (TT1999). Another reported that the field of Education Welfare, responsible for dealing with such matters as truancy, was viewed negatively as involving a lot of people who were formerly police officers or members of the armed forces (TT1999). Rather than being perceived as an education profession, it was regarded as a policing role.

Marginalization, Ethnicity, Lifestyle, and Occupation

The issue of ethnic identity is significant in according recognition and rights to different mobile groups, and can lead to tensions among Travelers. In the United Kingdom, Gypsy Travelers are recognized as an ethnic group for the purposes of the Race Relations Act. Gypsy Travelers have accused New Travelers of devaluing the Gypsies' legal and ethnic rights. And there have been reported cases of English and Welsh Travelers not allowing Irish Travelers to use sites, on the basis that they have come from outside the country rather than being Travelers within it (TT1999).

Under the broad category of Traveler are many different groups. The ethnicity of the Roma can be traced to Sanskrit and India from around the eighth century A.D. (TT1999). They gradually moved west, with many settling in Eastern Europe. They reached Britain during the Elizabethan age in the sixteenth century. Irish Travelers have a Celtic ethnicity, and there are also Welsh and Scottish Travelers. In Europe, occupational Travelers include circus, fairground, and bargee workers, as well as hawkers and tinkers (SS1999). In other parts of the world, horticultural workers such as fruit pickers and maritime workers such as fisher people can be categorized as occupational Travelers. The armed forces and humanitarian aid workers are further examples of occupational Travelers who operate in very stressful environments.

In some cases the distinction between lifestyle and occupational Travelers is blurred. Backpackers, for example, travel for the richness of the life experience but tend also to seek work opportunities along the way. Such is the case with New Travelers in Britain and, in some cases, gray nomads (people who have retired and travel around the country in generally well-appointed camper vans) in Australia.

One mobile community found in many countries is caravan people. In the context of the Netherlands, caravan dwellers are people who are outcasts from the original population. Unable to prosper within settled communities, they have left houses and bought old caravans to reside in. Such people tend to live in groups, and a Dutch fairground educator observed that, although they are not Gypsies, they tend to live a similar lifestyle (DS1999). In the United States of America, the pejorative term "trailer trash" is commonly used to designate such outcasts.

Such diversity among mobile communities raises the issue of providing a catch-all name for the purposes of service provision such as education. In the United Kingdom, "Travelers" is the designated name. An English Traveler educator reported that, while some people were very happy to be identified as Gypsies, other mobile groups would be very upset to be described in this way (TT1999). Indeed, as another English Traveler educator commented, the very difficulty of categorizing a group's ethnicity can contribute to their marginalization (TT1999).

At the same time, mobile communities are not ethnically homogeneous. Indeed, their very mobility generates the conditions for interaction and marriages with other such communities. For example, many circus and show people's families, particularly in the southern part of Europe, trace their historical background back to the Gypsy communities. Similarly, there was an influx of Gypsy Travelers in England in the 1500s. A Scottish fairground Traveler traced her lineage thus: "You see, my ancestors on my mother's side were Gypsies, London Gypsies, not tinkers or hedge-creepers, proper Gypsies" (SS1999). And an English Traveler educator observed: "There is lots of contact between the various Travelers—certainly between traditional Romany and traditional Irish Travelers" (TT1999).

The association of mobility with an exotic lifestyle is a contributing influence to these groups' marginalization. Indeed, this association causes something of a dilemma for traditional and occupational Travelers. On the one hand, there is a perceived need to emphasize their exotic character in order to make them stand out and appeal to others. In the circus, for example, acts like the freak shows, although extremely problematic from today's perspective, have played on the appeal of the exotic. On the other hand, the exoticizing of Travelers tends to emphasize their difference from the mainstream and can lead to a romanticizing of the lifestyle that fails to engage adequately with the challenges that they face. As an English Traveler educator said of one sedentary teacher who had a romantic view of Travelers: "She must have seen *Carmen* too many times" (TT1999).

The values of certain traditional traveling communities mean that specific members of that community seem to have become marginalized, particularly when viewed from the perspective of other communities. The Romany Gypsy culture, for example, appears to be a patriarchal arrangement where the male member is regarded as the head of the household and responsible for making the significant decisions, while girls are regarded as being marriageable from the age of 13 (TT1999). Traditionally, Romany Gypsies have large families, in some cases as many as 15 children, so the focus for females becomes domestic service and childrearing. Intermarriage within certain traditional Traveler families—for example, between first cousins—can also lead to what some perceive as significant health problems and learning difficulties (TT1999).

Marginalization from School

One very significant issue for mobile learning communities with enduring consequences has been their marginalization from the school experience. Traditionally, Travelers' peripatetic lifestyles have not suited schooling systems that have developed to cater for mostly settled or sedentary populations.

There are particular aspects of Travelers' lifestyles that have militated against their successful achievement in formal educational provision. One is the late start to schooling. Increasingly, educational psychologists acknowledge the importance of the early years of children's lives in shaping their educational aptitudes and attitudes (Anning & Edwards, 2006). However, Travelers' peripatetic lifestyles, along with a tradition of child-rearing within the community, can mean that children miss out on the early years' formal learning that settled children experience. While sedentary families in many parts of the world are compelled to put their children into childcare centers while the parents work, a compensating factor is that in many cases these centers have an educational dimension, and assist the children in the transition into kindergarten or preschool. While it might be thought preferable that Traveler children are able to remain in the care of their families and other members of that community, it also means that their acculturation to formalized learning institutions is delayed in comparison with sedentary children. One English Traveler teacher called this "delayed learning" (TT1999).

One English circus family spoke about having their children put in socially deprived areas where the relative academic performance of the children was comparatively low (EC1999). These were schools that tended to cater for those labeled as "problem" or remedial learners. The parents formed the perception that because they were traveling children the higher attaining academic schools automatically declined to accept them. The schools to which they were sent would be characterized by lacking basic facilities such as computer equipment.

In certain cases, perhaps paradoxically, it was being made the center of attention that contributed to the children's sense of isolation. An English circus parent recalled her painfully shy daughter being made to stand up in the front of the class at schools in which she was newly enrolled and being made to talk about life in the circus. While this child didn't recall being bullied, she did recall feeling very lonely, standing on her own in the middle of the playground.

An enduring school memory for many traveling families is of being made to do coloring in while the other children were engaged in other activities. As traveling children might be at the school only for a few days or a couple of weeks, it was not considered appropriate or viable to supply them with the same projects and opportunities as the settled children. One Australian showground mother remembered being awarded prizes for her coloring in, even though other areas of her schoolwork were sadly lacking (AS2003). A similar experience was recollected eloquently by a Scottish fairground member:

> To be honest it was hard for the teachers because we were only there for two weeks, so we were basically given pencil and paper and told to do a drawing in the corner, because they couldn't teach us anything in two weeks. We really needed somebody to bring it all together in some way, but it was difficult obviously. (SS1999)

In certain cases the discrimination against Travelers at or by schools has been more overt. An English circus family recalled schools saying directly: "Sorry, we don't take Gypsies" (EC1999). And a Scottish fairground operator remembered his mother's experience: "Mam was once chased out of the school by the kids before she even got to class. They stoned and pelted her" (SS1999).

An issue that can contribute to the marginalization of mobile communities relates to the extent that schooling acts as a vehicle for standardizing and normalizing. The question of testing to measure aptitudes against a norm can be problematic for Travelers, who because of various factors such as delayed learning and an enduring culture suspicious of formalized education are at risk of falling below the norm. Indeed, the focus on basic aptitudes such as reading, writing, and arithmetic overlooks the other attributes that mobile communities tend to have inculcated in their children as part of their cultural heritage, such as dressmaking and hairdressing for Roma girls (TT1999) and gymnastic skills for circus children (EC1999). And a primary focus on measuring IQ cognitive skills overlooks the multiple intelligences that Gardner (1993; see also Gardner, 2006) regards as important, including emotional intelligence.

The role of these normalizing measurements can be to marginalize those who fall outside the accepted standards through labels, such as "gifted and talented" and "special needs." As a Dutch bargee educator commented, the focus is on labeling the child rather than measuring the norm of development within the child (DB1999). And, in the case of mobile communities, this labeling extends from the individual child to the culture as a whole.

Marginalization by Name-Calling

Name-calling and stereotyping play a significant role in creating margins between traveling and settled people, as well as among different mobile communities. They constitute another form of the boundary maintenance to which Levinson (2007) refers. This is a common experience among Traveler children, who have become accustomed to being labeled with terms like "carnies" and "Gypsies." As an English circus parent pointed out, such labeling is not necessarily based on a belief that children are actually Gypsies; rather the taunters are not able to articulate themselves any better and draw on any term that is convenient in order to exercise their cruelty (EC1999). In turn, traveling children develop their own pejorative terms for settled children. In Australia, show children have called others "mugs" because they have to pay to go on the sideshow alley rides (Danaher, 2001a, pp. 311-314).

Such name-calling in certain cases endures into adulthood. Among Scottish fairground families, settled residents are called "flatties" and are represented as being unclean, without manners, and lazy and with no sense of family (SS1999). So these negative stereotypes can be used to label both settled and mobile groups. The difficulty of overcoming such labels is evident in the experience of a settled man who married into a traveling family and was still known as a "flatty" 50 years afterwards, even though his children were accepted as Travelers (SS1999). And in England, New (or New Age) Travelers have been labeled "just like hippy dropouts" (TT1999).

However, names that were once used to vilify a community can be transformed in their meaning. As an English Traveler teacher commented: "A word suddenly becomes a word to celebrate, and 'Gypsy' tends to have reached that status, and perhaps 'tinker' will eventually ..." (TT1999). Such a transformation seems to occur when people of the marginalized community embrace the negative label as an affirmation of their shared identity. Indeed, an English circus performer was happy to be identified as a Gypsy because he considered that he was living the same lifestyle as that of Gypsies, not merely because of traveling through different countries but also because he and his family speak six or seven languages (EC1999).

Marginalization of Space

The marginalization of space in relation to mobile communities is a profoundly significant issue. Such marginalizing can be manifested in the sites that traveling groups are permitted to occupy. For example, a Roma site in London was located next to the noise and disturbance of a busy road and railway lines (TT1999), while a Traveler educator in northern England spoke of sites located next to the railway bridge, the gasworks, and the rubbish tip (TT1999). Such locations can contribute to health problems for the community. Indeed, an English Traveler educator reported that local authorities did not collect the rubbish at some sites for fear of being seen to condone the presence of families there (TT1999). More generally, these locations mark the community as dirty and impoverished, removed from the safe and secure sites that mark a prosperous and stable home environment. Furthermore, the ongoing threat of being evicted from such sites contributes to these communities' sense of marginalization. In educational terms, it makes it very difficult to arrange ongoing access to school.

The deployment of space as a potential mechanism of marginalization is also evident in the treatment of occupational sites such as the fairgrounds. Local councils, for example, might sell sites hitherto made available for fairs or circuses, or act to move fairs out of the town centers where they have the opportunity to attract most customers. Furthermore, as these fairground sites become marginalized by being located on the edge of communities they tend to be neglected and left in very poor condition. Within the fairground site itself, competition for the best space can be very intense. There is a tradition in long-established fairground cultures for handing sites down from generation to generation, and membership of the Showmen's Guild is understood as important as a means of ensuring that members will continue to be allocated favorable sites. Such is the cut-throat competition on the fairgrounds that in certain places there have been allegations of extortion, with stand-over men demanding a proportion of the takings (SS1999).

The particular location of a site within Travelers' occupational spaces can be used as a marker of the place in that community's hierarchy. An English circus teacher who had experience of performing commented on the hierarchy of sites in that environment:

> It's a bit like—the circus equivalent of being below the salt is being beyond the electricity. We knew we'd been accepted when we were allowed to plug into the electric box. But there is a hierarchy. There's the box office; then there's the Director's trailers; then we have the people who have been with the family a long time, almost like family retainers; then there were us and [our] acts, we were in the same sort of area; then there were the ring boys and the laborers. (TT1999)

Such marginalization can also be apparent in the place of the Traveler education system within the school bureaucracy. In some cases, Traveler education has been placed underneath the special needs umbrella, or physically located next to the special needs section, making it seem that Travelers by their very nature are defined as having such needs. Indeed, as one Scottish fairground person noted, having a designated support teacher can make it seem "like there's something wrong with you" (SS1999).

Marginalization of Traveler Educators

Traveler educators can also experience something of the marginalization that the mobile learning communities whom they serve undergo (see also Danaher et al., 2007a). Being peripatetic, Traveler teachers in the United Kingdom and elsewhere tend to be marginalized within the schools they go to. A Scottish Traveler educator reported her colleagues in the Netherlands who ran a mobile school saying: "You know, it's odd. We park our school in their school playground, and we never meet the staff" (TT1999).

That, unlike mainstream teachers, Traveler educators have lacked a clearly defined pathway for career progression has contributed to their sense of marginalization within the education system. A symptom of this situation in the United Kingdom was Traveler educations jobs in the *Times Educational Supplement* being advertised in the back under "Miscellaneous" (TT1999). Such a lack of career pathway might help explain why the field of Traveler education has been dominated by females. An English Traveler educator suggested that ". . . women would think, 'This is an interesting job' [while] men would think, 'But where would I go from there?'" (TT1999).

Marginalization by Balancing Work and Education

A profound concern for some occupational Travelers is balancing aspirations for education with maintaining their traditional work patterns. A Scottish fairground Traveler who was the first in his family to receive a university education expressed this dilemma in this way:

> I always felt guilty when I was away doing my homework. It got worse when I went to university because as a student I was taking up even more time. And I would feel guilty when I was in the library at nights and I wasn't helping out at work. I'd still feel guilty for it. I would get the time off, but I'd feel guilty. Traveling families tend to work. Once you get to a certain age you have to. My brother and sister were like second parents; I had to please them as well as my mum and dad, and they were often less sympathetic as far as educations goes. So I always had to be seen to do my part. It's quite important to be seen to be doing your part. (SS1999)

Such a focus on work has contributed to a sometimes disparaging view of education among occupational Travelers. This same Scottish fairground Traveler remembered education being seen as something that had to be done, not something that was worthwhile (SS1999). Thus the desire to exclude oneself was very powerful, and something with which the school system could be complicit. A Traveler teacher from England commented: "The Traveler children, particularly the boys, learn very quickly how to get excluded from the system. And the schools play along with the game, don't they? Because they don't really want them there either" (TT1999).

Marginalization and Cultural Values

In some cases, it is the process of normalization of school experience that can lead to Traveler children missing out on the opportunities that previous generations had experienced. One English circus parent lamented how regularized schooling had had a negative impact on her children:

> They're becoming so normalized, they're not getting the opportunity to mix with children, they're not getting the opportunity to mix with children of other nationalities, they don't go to other circuses, they don't get immersed in the culture any more. (EC1999)

This respondent was grateful for a section of the Education Act that enabled children to be taken out of school when it was part of their parents' work and socially and culturally important to them. This situation highlights the fact that normalization of educational provision is not always in Traveler families' interests.

Certain mobile communities, particularly traditional lifestyle Travelers such as Roma, have very real concerns about the effects of formal schooling in marginalizing children from their cultural heritage. From their perspective, the price of mainstreaming is perceived to be a loss of their heritage and identity. An English Traveler educator, for example, reported Gypsy Travelers not wanting to send their children to high school, as it was against their culture (TT1999). Certain parts of the curriculum were regarded as particularly problematic, such as sex education. Travelers, then, are afraid of losing their children who become acculturated by the mainstream and who therefore no longer value the different kind of culture that their parents and forebears have practiced.

Indeed, it is evident that becoming educated can inculcate values that alienate Travelers from their own kind. This circumstance was simply but eloquently expressed by a Scottish fairground Traveler: "You go to some parties with relatives, and all they talk about is diesel. And I think, 'What the hell can I talk to you people about?' It's a different world in some ways" (SS1999). Furthermore, becoming educated can challenge established work routines. There was a case where an educated fairground child in the Netherlands who knew his rights refused to go on working, while others continued to work (DS1999).

Traveler educators address the very real concern that schooling threatens the traditional cultural values of Travelers. One English Traveler educator articulated the role of the TESS in terms of ". . . explaining about how [parents] could use what an education will give their children. Not that it will take them away from their culture, but it could be used to reinforce their culture and continue it in a way" (TT1999). Education, then, is understood as a way of increasing the options of Travelers. As the same educator put it: "In fact, they wouldn't necessarily choose to live like we live; they would choose how they wanted to live. But that education would give them the choice" (TT1999). As Travelers' cultures change, as employment opportunities change, their children are hopefully equipped with the opportunities or options from which they are able to choose. As such, they engage in the border crossing (Giroux, 1992) and perspective transformation (Mezirow, 2000) alluded to in the literature review at the beginning of this chapter.

Laws enacted to regulate the movement of Travelers have played a role in their marginalization that is integrally related with their cultural values. The effect of the Criminal Justice and Public Order Act introduced in 1994 in the United Kingdom was to criminalize Travelers by making what had once had been a civil offense, trespass, into a criminal one (Danaher et al., 2007a). An English Traveler educator recounted the effect that this act had on a family trying very hard to facilitate their children's schooling:

> Imagine, these families are on the roadside, they haven't got any of the amenities that you and I take for granted. I still am amazed at parents who have their children up, washed, fed, ready for school at nine o'clock in the morning without any of those basic facilities. I'll just give you an example. Almost the first week when the Act was introduced, we had a youngster going into secondary education for the first time from the roadside and a youngster going into reception class. Imagine the importance of these events, particularly for that family; this was the first child who had gone into a secondary school. While the children were at school on that day, the Public Order Act was used and the families were moved. No problem. The families got the children back to school the next day. On the sixth occasion then the families started to say to us, "Listen, we've been doing our best. Basically, our main concern now is where are our wheels going to rest tonight. If we stop here, are we going to be moved?" We actually saw the undermining of that family security and the commitment that families had actually made to the education process. We were absolutely powerless in that situation, without any influence at all. (TT1999)

In other words, the authority of the law invested in the Act took precedence over the work between educators and families to get the Traveler children to school.

Transformation and Articulation

This example points to a broader issue governing the relations between settled and mobile communities: how one connects with the other. Given the asymmetrical power relation between Travelers and fixed residents, the former are often made to fit in with the routines and values of the latter. Essentially, this is a question of accommodating the marginal within the mainstream. When this accommodation involves suggestions of assimilating or integrating the marginal group, their interests and values tend to be compromised in favor of sustaining the interests of the mainstream. For example, an English Traveler educator contended that the effect of the Criminal Justice and Public Order Act was an assimilationist model (TT1999).

Rather than assimilation or integration, we argue that articulation is an approach that would enable Travelers to maintain their distinctive routines and life patterns in a way that is able to accommodate rather than disrupt the interests of settled communities. The *Oxford English Dictionary* defines "articulate" variously as "connect by joints," as in an articulated lorry, and "speak distinctly." Articulation evokes two complementary processes: the idea of giving voice to ideas and articulating a perspective; and the means by which pieces of equipment are provisionally connected, as in the case of a semi-trailer. Such articulation is part of the everyday life of Travelers: Scottish fairground people, for example, referred to vehicles being "coupled up" (SS1999), while an Australian education official, reflecting on the success of the Queensland School for Travelling Show Children, spoke of being impressed by the "loose coupling" that held everything together and kept the show on the road (AS2003). Such a metaphor suggests ways in which Travelers might loosely couple their lifestyle routines with those of settled society to the mutual benefit of each community.

In the case of the United Kingdom, for example, a network of permanent and transient sites would enable Travelers to take responsibility for their movements and to articulate their interests with those of the mainstream by looking after those sites and getting their children into the local schools. As an English Traveler educator contended, where Travelers are

> . . . forced into an assimilationist model of accommodation provision, or where they're without a legal stopping place then they're just prone to haphazard [and] erratic movement that really seriously undermines not only the family control of their own affairs but also . . . our ability as service providers to deliver. (TT1999)

The principle of articulation could also help address the marginalization of Travelers on the basis of language. This would acknowledge the right of traditional Traveler cultures to speak their own language at home to help conserve this linguistic tradition while being schooled in the language of the countries through which they travel.

This concept of articulation is consistent with the ideas of philosopher Kwame Anthony Appiah (2006) in his book *Cosmopolitanism: Ethics in a World of Strangers*. The term "cosmopolitanism" was coined by the Cynics in ancient Greece in the fourth century B.C. to refer to "citizens of the cosmos" in opposition to "citizens of the polis." The value of cross-cultural dialogue, according to Appiah, is not because it ends in consensus but because it leads to specific practices of coexistence. Continuing conversations between strangers create a common ground through nothing more exalted than curiosity and habitual accommodation. Appiah contended that we should learn about people in other places, and take an interest in their civilizations, their arguments, their errors, and their achievements, not because that will bring us to agreement but because it will help us get used to one another. Thus, while mobile and settled communities have distinctive and somewhat conflicting values, it is in both groups' interests to have some understanding of the other as a means of becoming accustomed to their ways.

One role that Traveler educators perform is to act as vehicles of articulation between the marginalized Traveler community and the mainstream settled community. This position raises ethical considerations about the extent to which it is appropriate that educators act as advocates on behalf of the Travelers. Certain English Traveler educators, for example, indicated that an important part of their role is to show to other teachers, including head teachers, along with authorities ranging from the county councils to the local village policemen, the true situation of Travelers as well as the cultural distinctions between different Traveler groups. On the other hand, these educators also recognized the responsibility to teach Travelers about mainstream culture, as a way of ensuring that the bridge crossing was a two way process.

Transformation and Constructing a Culture of Tolerance

While cyclical factors influence the manifestation of patterns of marginalization and prejudice, it seems also to be the case that particular historical movements and geographical conditions influence the degree to which a culture is tolerant and open to difference. The Netherlands, for example, is acknowledged by many to be among the world leaders in Traveler education, with a strong and enduring tradition of tolerance toward mobile communities. A Dutch Traveler educator attributed this to two factors: first, the influence of the Protestants, who began as a minority group who were discriminated against so they know what it was to experience prejudice; and second, that the Netherlands is a small country surrounded by others, which has made it open to different people coming within its borders (TT1999). The Dutch have long had a history of trading in products and ideas. Additionally, the fact that the Netherlands is a flat country means an absence of geographical barriers such as mountains and valleys that limit contact and communication among different groups and lead to different and conflicting ethnic identities emerging, as has tended to occur in places like the Balkans. These considerations emphasize the underlying point that Traveler education needs to be located in the national and provincial cultural, historical, geographical, and ideological contexts in which it is practiced for it to be understood properly. That implies recognizing the diversity of forms of Traveler education in different countries, and certainly not trying for a single model.

What these national and cultural differences also suggest is conditions of possibility that tend to a greater or lesser extent either to foster or to inhibit a culture of tolerance. The Dutch experience makes it a very congenial culture to support the learning of mobile groups with a multiplicity of language backgrounds. Thus they welcomed children with such diversity from a circus school in Moscow while other countries shunned them (DS1999).

An associated issue here is the relative visibility or invisibility of Travelers, and the extent to which their lifestyles conform to a fixed routine. Thus when a Dutch Traveler educator remarked of the Netherlands, "It is not possible to disappear in this country" (DS1999), on the one hand that indicates the effectiveness of maintaining educational provision for Travelers, but on the other hand it suggests a system of surveillance and monitoring, which Foucault (1977) identified as being characteristic of a disciplinary society. Travelers internalize such values. For example, a couple of Scottish fairground Travelers commented of Gypsies and hawkers, "They just go here, there and everywhere. They're here today and gone tomorrow" (SS1999) and "They could be here today and never be seen again. Go to England, Ireland, anywhere, and never be seen again" (SS1999). By contrast, the speakers' own movements were regularized through their belonging to a union, the Showmen's Guild of Great Britain, and they came back to the same place year after year. A different couple commented that they liked members of settled communities to see how they lived within their caravans, to challenge perceptions that "we're living in the dark ages" (SS1999).

One vehicle for overcoming prejudice toward mobile learning communities could be the attitudes of children. A Dutch bargee educator commented on the openness of children in playing together with those marked by society at large as being different: "I really believe when you start very young, at an age of three, four, five years, at this age children are very open [to] all influences" (DB1999). A Belgian circus teacher concurred with this view, describing how his circus school taught autistic children skills such as juggling (BC1999). He contended that training in such movement-related attributes was important for the physical wellbeing of people and their sociability. Having children with special needs in each class helped other children to appreciate them: "It's something different, but never mind; he is like he is. It's a kind of appreciation of people. All the differences of people, accepting" (BC1999). Thus, the therapeutic role of certain mobile learning communities like the circus can be very beneficial in overcoming marginalization.

Transformation of Space

Ultimately, perhaps, the transformative possibilities offered by mobile communities are articulated in the way that they negotiate space. We mentioned earlier how the theorists regarded a capacity for critical reflection as being integral to perspective transformation. While Bourdieu (1998) saw the academy as an ideal space to nurture such reflection through the universalizing and objectifying perspective of the scholastic point of view, we conjectured whether Travelers, caught up in the ongoing routines and challenges of maintaining their lifestyles, would have an opportunity to develop such a reflective disposition.

By contrast, the interview data cited in this chapter and throughout this book suggest, we argue, that Travelers do indeed develop tendencies toward critical reflection. The very act of travel affords a range of shifting perspectives and a capacity to transform roles in order to deal effectively with different situations. Furthermore, the universalizing disposition to which Bourdieu (1998) referred is evident in the micro-worlds that Travelers inhabit. The circus, for example, could be understood as a world in itself that is recreated with every performance, and that demands critical reflection upon the various roles that each member of that community performs.

Indeed, it is the ongoing recreation of these worlds and the transformation of the associated space that would seem to equip mobile communities with the means to sustain their lifestyles in the face of various challenges. This contention was eloquently expressed in the words of an English fairground Traveler (also cited in chapter 7 from a different perspective) who reflected on the competition provided by theme parks, stores, and shopping malls and concluded:

> So really I wouldn't say it's so much a threat, because I think there is something magical about a traveling fair. It's there one day; the next day it's gone. I think that holds a bit of mystery for people. (ES1999)

Described in this way, the fair, along with other Traveler sites such as the circus, can be understood as what Foucault (1977) referred to as a heterotopia, a space that offers a kind of contestation to the place in which we live (p. 179; see also Danaher et al., 2006b).

Implications for the Future Education of Mobile Learning Communities

With mobility among communities likely to be a continuing theme, issues relating to dealing with the marginalization of such communities will likewise be an enduring theme. It is evident that in certain cases prejudice toward these communities (and, it should be added, prejudice within these communities toward mainstream society) has endured across generations, and entrenched attitudes can be very difficult to transform. It is also clear that, while seemingly more positive, tendencies toward exoticizing and romanticizing mobile communities can also contribute to their marginalization. On the other hand, acknowledging the differences in lifestyle, values, and perspectives between traveling and sedentary communities seems fundamental to creating some degree of understanding and trust.

Increasing the portability of learning technologies and formalized educational systems will certainly play a role in combating the marginalization of mobile learning communities. Yet it would seem naïve to believe in some technological utopia where developments in online learning will fully ameliorate the educational challenges faced by these communities. Rather, it seems likely that formalized education will continue to be incorporated into the lifeworlds of traveling groups in complex ways that will oscillate between absorption and resistance.

In these terms, we might encapsulate the thematic implications of this chapter by conjecturing that formalized learning for Travelers takes place in a marginal or liminal space where accommodation and contestation are both evident. The different value systems and lifestyles of occupational Travelers would suggest a resistance to being fully captured by the forms of governance constitutive of formalized education institutions; at the same time, the benefits of authorization conferred by these institutions in the form of certificates, credentials, and degrees will mean some extent of acquiescence and acceptance.

From this perspective, marginalization and transformation might be regarded as enduring themes in the relationship between mobile learning communities and settled institutions rather than as issues to be resolved. Taken together, they provide a means of sustaining an engagement with these groups while maintaining the distinctions among them. Rather than focusing on the integration or assimilation of mobile communities into the values systems of governing institutions such as formal education, it might be better to explore forms of articulation between the two. Here, and as noted above, we can think of articulation in ways in which the different parts of a semi-trailer or an articulated lorry are joined for a journey. This enjoining is not permanent but serves a particular role in keeping the vehicle together. Similarly, we can think of a loose coupling rather than a fixed and rigid relationship between mobile learning communities and centralized institutions, such that marginalization and transformation are ongoing, culturally sustaining acts.

Implications for Broader Educational Practice

The experience of marginalization and transformation among mobile learning communities has important implications for broader educational practice. Prime among these is the ongoing debate about the relative benefits of inclusion versus specialization. We have explored both forms of education in this chapter (and we also take up this point in the conclusion). While the experience in the United Kingdom tends to favor including Travelers in schools with support staff available to help this transition (Danaher et al., 2007), the dedicated schools established for bargee children in the Netherlands (Scholten, 2000) and for show children in Australia (Fullerton et al., 2004; Fullerton et al., 2005) are examples of specialized provision. The appropriate mix between inclusive and specialized models of such provision continues to exercise educational policy-makers across the globe.

Another implication relates to the degree of control over and surveillance of students within educational practice in general. A theme relating to the learning and teaching of mobile groups is a concern that they might "slip through the cracks" and miss out on the provision experienced by sedentary populations. While the benefits of formalized education in empowering citizens and furnishing them with skills and aptitudes to be successful in life are clear, it is evident that certain Traveler communities are suspicious of the authority and control invested in these educational institutions. So too with all manner of individuals and groups, many of whom are similarly labeled deficit and "at risk" by educational authorities. Yet this labeling, enabled by state control and systemic surveillance, is likely to promote continued marginalization, not transformation.

Consider again the idea of a piece of land on the margins of a settlement being transformed into the exotic and entrancing world of the carnival or circus big top. Such processes of transforming marginalized space through spectacle and entertainment might act as models for broader educational practices. They suggest ways in which marginalized spaces within mainstream schools can be vehicles for transformation. For example, the art and drama departments within schools tend not to be accorded the same importance as English, mathematics, and science departments. The very marginalized status of art and drama might mean that they are relatively removed from the surveillance and monitoring conferred on curriculum areas regarded as more significant and therefore freer to promote transformative outcomes through creativity and play (see for example Elsden-Clifton, 2006).

Questions for Reflection

- What different forms of marginalization do mobile learning communities experience?
- What are the costs and benefits of such marginalization?

- In what ways can processes of marginalization contribute to transformation experiences in both mobile and settled communities?
- What are the relative benefits and costs of offering specialized educational provision for mobile learning communities in comparison with working to include them in the educational mainstream?

Suggestions for Further Reading

Christensen, C. A. (2001). *Transforming classrooms: Educational psychology for teaching and learning.* Flaxton, Qld: Post Pressed.

de Souza, M. (2008, February). Education for transformation: Meeting students' needs in changing contemporary contexts. *International Journal of Children's Spirituality, 13*(1), 27-37.

Lipka, J., with Mohatt, G. V. and the Ciulistet Group. (1998). *Transforming the culture of schools: Yup'ik Eskimo examples.* Mahwah, NJ: Lawrence Erlbaum Associates.

Longworth, N. (2003). *Lifelong learning in action: Transforming education in the 21st century.* London: Routledge.

McCall, C. C. (2009/in press). *Transforming thinking: Philosophical inquiry in the primary and secondary classroom.* London: Routledge.

Robertson, S. L. (2005, May). Re-imagining and rescripting the future of education: Global knowledge economy discourses and the challenge to education systems. *Comparative Education, 41*(2), 151-170.

Conclusion
Creating New Educational Futures

The book concludes by synthesizing the themes and findings of the preceding eight chapters and by eliciting several possible implications for creating new educational futures for both mobile and non-mobile learning communities. These implications derive from the suggestions of mobile community members and researchers.

Foreword

We have traversed a widely variegated terrain in the course of this book's analysis of specific elements of mobile learning communities. In doing so, we have encountered particular dimensions of that analysis, including emotional and intellectual, theoretical and methodological, practical, and substantive. In some ways this terrain has been a troubling one (Henderson & Danaher, 2008), because it has highlighted several ways in which members of those communities are routinely and often unconsciously marginalized and positioned as "the other" in relation to sedentary populations. Yet there is also much that is hopeful in the preceding chapters, and it is that hope that we take up and explore in greater depth in this concluding text.

Much of that hope and optimism derives equally from the three key terms framing the book's title and focus: that the people with whom we have conducted research, and the people who have participated in research conducted by other scholars reported here, are simultaneously *mobile, learners,* and *members of communities*. We have argued in the preceding chapters that this tripartite status gives members of mobile learning communities considerable potential cohesiveness and power. Certainly the instances in the data collected by us and other researchers where educational initiatives and innovations have been sought and/or generated by mobile populations have depended on strong individuals interacting with strong groups, putting their learning into practice for shared benefits, and exercising agency to attain specific goals and interests.

Before we take the discussion further, two caveats are required at this juncture in the terrain that we are traversing. The first is to remind ourselves of a crucial point made in the introduction: the need to avoid homogenizing and essentializing people who are mobile. The intervening text has demonstrated the considerable diversity both within and among mobile communities, and that mobility is only one of the multiple signifiers of the subjectivities of members of those communities. Reducing the range and scale of that diversity to a single denominator risks reinforcing the marginalization noted above.

The second caveat is that it is important that we acknowledge the limits— and the limitations—of learning communities as both a concept and an explanatory framework (see also Fischer & Sugimoto, 2006; Fox, 2005; Hodgson & Reynolds, 2005; Mann, 2005; Talburt & Boyles, 2005). While we have found the idea a powerful and generative lens for examining the selected topics in the preceding chapters, we recognize that not all members of mobile communities necessarily see themselves as learners or their groups as learning communities. We realize also that there are extensive differences in the forms of cultural capital and hence the levels of educational access and opportunity within and across mobile groups. For example, Hargreaves (2002) noted an apparent connection between "[s]ophisticated professional learning communities … and often affluent systems …" (p. 10), reinforcing that formal education generally gives most to those who already have, whether they are mobile or sedentary. Clearly it is just as false to depict all members of mobile communities as always and equally engaged in learning, however that is conceptualized, as it is to characterize their mobility as uniform and undifferentiated. From this perspective, the aforementioned risk of homogenization and essentialization is accompanied by the risk of superimposing on mobile populations narrowly conceived middle class values and attendant—*albeit* usually unconscious—value judgments about the necessity of particular kinds of educational provision. And of course the potential outcome of this second risk is the same as that derived from the first: the reinforced marginalization of mobile groups.

Our principal response to both these possible charges in this chapter is that it is focused explicitly on *creating new educational futures*. These futures have been gleaned from what members of mobile communities and the people who have provided education for them and/or conducted research with them have said about past, present, and projected educational provision. That is, these futures are intentionally situated in and emergent from the lifeworlds and worldviews of mobile learners, teachers, and researchers. Consequently they are likely to challenge existing and taken for granted assumptions about formal education and to propose ideas for alternative structures and strategies that embrace different types of mobility rather than ignoring or seeking to assimilate them.

This concluding text is divided into three sections:

- What members of the mobile communities with whom we have conducted research say about new educational futures

- What researchers into mobile communities say about new educational futures
- Implications for creating new educational futures more broadly.

What Mobile Community Members Say about New Educational Futures

Several members of the mobile communities with whom we conducted research spoke about "the future" in widely varied ways, many of which manifested their thinking about possible alternative forms of formal, non-formal, and informal education. This was hardly surprising: these respondents clearly discerned a direct and enduring link between the kinds of educational provision to which they had access and the projected viability of their ways of life. Once again, the convergence among earning, learning, and living was very much to the fore in these participants' consciousness and in their articulated aspirations for their fellow community members and themselves.

A number of interviewees spoke about the perceived likely future directions of their respective industries and what they felt about that. For example, a member of a Dutch bargee community reflected an ambivalence about those directions that resonated with that of many speakers from different mobile communities:

> [I feel] optimistic in the sense that [the] conjunction of the ways is often here in the long term, so a lot of cargo is going to the water. I think the shipping people are much better—the young ones are a lot better educated than in my time. I think it is more commercial. When you see the bigger ships, they work with two teams, so one team one week, the other team the other week, then they're that week in the house. So they have a lot more possibilities to build their life socially. What I am worried about is the little ships where the family lives, and when they have to find an economic way of living they haven't a social life. So I think that's a problem … I think that will disappear, I'm afraid, the family business. (DB1999)

There was something of a paradox underlying this speaker's discourse. On the one hand, there was an acknowledgment of the commercial benefits of a growth in size and critical mass, leading in turn to the social benefits connected with turn taking and team-based collaboration that our analysis associates with membership of learning communities. On the other hand, that same commercial success was seen as a potential threat to the family unit as a learning community, as part of which the broader economic enterprise was divested of its community dimension and positioned as an example of big business and uncaring capitalism. This paradox highlighted a particular challenge for creating new educational futures for mobile communities: such futures will need to encompass this tension between large- and small-scale economic activities in those communities and to build on the complex and sometimes contradictory networks and affiliations that constitute them.

A member of a Dutch circus community communicated the same kind of ambivalence, but in relation to the family rather than the industry level. In doing so, she demonstrated some of the strategies needed to balance patterns of mobility and educational access—strategies that are also crucial to creating educational futures that are more encompassing of mobility as a way of life. In referring to officials from an educational organization with whom she had been liaising about possible arrangements for educating her daughter, this speaker observed:

> They like it because, when we came there to give her up, then we've been talking about it. "Do you like to have a child like this because we don't know what's going to happen in [the] future?" It might be that she's sometimes not there, because I think we're going to work on little circuses. [If] We have [a] big circus, [we would have] more children and then they [would] have a teacher. But you never know—maybe we are going to work in a big circus, and she [would] get … education [in a different country]. (DC1999)

Clearly these strategies for juggling options for the speaker's daughter's schooling were inextricably linked with the family's economic and employment strategies. This complex connection also needs to be located at the center of any educational future if it is to be viable for mobile community members.

The complexity of that connection was manifested also in the following comments by two members of a Scottish show community in response to a question about perceptions of likely future formal education for community members:

> One of the things, obviously, that the Showmen's Guild and members of the Guild are doing, they're trying to chase up the educational authority into putting aside more places for traveling children and more assistance for them. So, providing we can keep on chasing that up, hopefully we will. Years ago, very few people had the opportunity [of schooling] in the traveling business … You've got to be prepared to do a lot of hard work. But I think the opportunities are getting greater; there [are] more opportunities out there for the traveling children to get an education, if they wish it. We've just got to keep chasing it up until every traveling child is entitled to that. (SS1999)
>
> I think even not in our business, people staying in houses, there's a lot of kids coming back to college and taking things now. Once they all came out just wanting to leave school and get a job. I think they're all starting to understand that this is the way to get on: to stay at school and get to college. It's turning round again that they want to go to college now. (SS1999)

This conversation was noteworthy for a number of reasons. First, there was mention of the strategy (and the associated necessity) of continually lobbying educational authorities for recognition of and assistance for this community's distinctive circumstances. Second, "You've got to be prepared to do a lot of hard work" can be read in at least two ways: as referring to the ongoing labor of this lobbying; and as denoting the expectation that individual learners will engage fully with such opportunities as they become available. Third, the second speaker's reference to "people staying in houses" articulated the integral connection between mobile communities and shifts in broader educational and sociocultural experience; in this case, that connection has created an opportunity for coalescing the interests and aspirations of people both who are and who are "not in our business."

Likewise a respondent associated with a Dutch show community linked changes in that community (which also reflected shifts in the broader population) with dynamic expectations by show parents for their children's future educational opportunities:

> ... the origin of the school is laid down in the ... actions of the parents. They are concerned about the future possibilities of the children because most of them 45 years ago were illiterate, and now the whole population can read and write and can manage and know about geography and biology, and read the [news]paper and understand it ... There's a category, and that's growing, who think that secondary education for the children is more and more important to give them a good start in life ... (DS1999)

Despite this general shift, this participant's acknowledgment that "... but that's not the whole population" (DS1999) was a timely reminder that new educational futures are inevitably understood in a broad spectrum of ways by members of mobile communities, reflecting different priorities and pressures.

A member of an Australian circus community emphasized a different aspect of creating new educational futures:

> I think we have a pretty good future actually. A few years ago I would have thought differently, because there were a lot of people believing— animal rights people—and basically we've tried to educate people to "Come and have a look for yourselves first, then make up your mind." And a lot of people have come here and said, "I was really believing them until I've now seen what you have on offer ... for the animals." And that's changed a lot of people and it has changed [the situation]. When you hear something enough, you do believe it. (AC1998)

This statement encompassed a view of education as changing mindsets and challenging taken for granted assumptions, a commitment to teaching by example, and a belief in long-term success resulting from resilience. We consider all of these essential ingredients of new educational futures for mobile and non-mobile learners alike.

An enactment of these ingredients by a different mobile group was expressed by members of an Australian show community:

> We have done a couple of computer courses with the teachers after school, and they went really well.
> A lot of us are getting laptops.
> I learned the basics from doing it with the teachers.
> We've got an email address and we can check our emails … (AS2003)

This discussion resonated with issues of adult literacy and generational change, and highlighted dynamic and effective partnerships between mobile communities and educational authorities as a key element of sustaining and transforming futures.

Finally, the urgent importance of creating new educational futures that are significantly different from the *status quo* was reinforced by an experienced Traveler educator:

> I'm not optimistic [about the future]. I have to say I'm not optimistic. I think there's an element of the Travelers not wanting to be socially integrated. They want the children to be integrated in school, but that's different. But the culture is so important to them that they've got to keep their identity by being isolated, if you like. I don't ever see the day. I think if you came back in 20 years' time I'd probably be saying exactly the same thing to you. That's quite demoralizing really, isn't it? (TT1999)

A different Traveler teacher had a somewhat more optimistic view of the long-term dimension of her work:

> It's not teaching this young person to read now. It's teaching these people to see what they can get from education, put their children through the school and learn as well, and maybe get even more from it. It has to be long-term. It's not something that might be two or three generations. If you think about it that the idea of success is going in and teaching that one little person there, you won't get it in this time. (TT1999)

This discussion has synthesized a number of strategies put forward by members of mobile communities as possible elements in the creation of new educational futures for those communities (and in some cases for non-mobile learners as well). Given the necessity noted above of acknowledging diversity among mobile communities and avoiding their homogenization, it is important to reinforce that these strategies and elements are as disparate and distinctive as the communities from which they derive. Nevertheless they have a central organizing feature: the desire to bring into alignment the economic and sociocultural foundations of the communities' ways of life and the formal, non-formal, and informal educational opportunities available to them. Some participants in the research were optimistic about the prospect of the realization of that alignment, while others were less so. Equally some respondents were more specific than others about the kinds of initiatives that would signify the attainment of that realization. Yet fundamentally the mobile community members were seeking the unraveling of the Gordian knot identified earlier in this book. So for them a new educational future would not be desirable unless it succeeded in positioning their mobility and their education as interdependent and dialogically reinforcing rather than as mutually exclusive and contradictory.

What Mobile Community Researchers Say about New Educational Futures

We turn now for some more specific ideas about how such a new educational future—one that is genuinely pro-nomadic and anti-sedentarist (Danaher et al., 2004)—might look. We do so by examining some of the propositions emanating from researchers into mobile communities. Again we note the diversity of those researchers, of the questions that they have posed, and of the contexts in which they have addressed those questions. That diversity notwithstanding, we have discerned a number of useful starting points for what is clearly a complex and longstanding set of educational issues that needs ongoing attention.

As with our own caveats outlined above, it is important to recognize at the outset some of the qualifications made by these researchers in relation to proposing alternative educational approaches for mobile communities. The first is a reinforcement of the diversity identified in the previous paragraph and a concomitant reminder that the kinds of new frameworks that are needed will require sufficient time and trust:

> There can be no simple set of guidelines, because for all the differences between teachers and schools, there are comparable differences in attitudes between Gypsy Traveler families themselves. For every family that refuses to let their children near secondary schools fearful of the erosion of their traditional culture, there are others who are quite happy to see the children go and are only disappointed if the experience does not do as much for them as they had hoped … There is no point in dealing in stereotypes and making generalised assumptions. There can be no substitute for time, sensitivity, talking and individual concern. (Kiddle, 1999, pp. 154-155)

Given our acknowledgment above of the possible limits and limitations of learning communities, it is important to ensure that they do not become a metanarrative—for example, by seeking to apply Western ideas about particular kinds of relationships to African and Asian nomadic pastoralists with very different kinship systems—and instead to keep open for consideration the ongoing counternarratives that celebrate the multiplicity of forms of learning communities (see also Danaher, 2008). This point resonates with a particularly telling critique of a key feature of contemporary educational practice: "The agenda of formal education—to produce modern citizens that conform with the state's notion of contemporary development—has been thoroughly exposed as the ideological project that it is" (Dyer, 2006b, p. 259)—a hegemonic metanarrative indeed.

Yet Dyer (2006b) contended that that same ideological project contained within it the seeds of change—the potential dismantling of the ideological apparatus that might provide the foundation for a more equitable and engaged approach to educating mobile communities:

> … appropriate educational provision for nomadic peoples is possible, providing that considerable time and energy is put into making their needs visible through consultation, ensuring full nomadic participation in planning, decision-making and execution of jointly conceived educational programmes. Stories of success, just as much as stories of failure, point up the fallacy of schooling systems' hegemonic notion that 'one size fits all'—and an important contribution they all make is to highlight the specificity of context, and how that shapes nomads' engagement with formal education … [I]nnovation within this very system … [i]s testimony to the possibility of reform of what is likely to remain the mainstream provider of education for the foreseeable future. (p. 260)

This last point signifies a broader debate within the scholarship pertaining to mobile communities: the extent to which proposals for new educational futures for members of those communities should be located within formal education provided, or at least sanctioned, by the state versus the degree to which that system is seen as fundamentally flawed and antagonistic to mobile groups and hence needs to be supplemented by other approaches. This is clearly a complex debate, positions in relation to which reflect the researcher's own ideological viewpoint as much as her or his stance on educating mobile communities. For example, while cautioning against "the tendency of reformers to look for a silver bullet to produce quick results" (p. 245), Cardenas (2004) contended that "The future paradigm for migrant education must … focus aggressively on the assets of migrant children, families, and communities" (p. 246), positing that "Migrant children's experiences create formidable assets; we must build upon these assets to help them break through and succeed in school" (p. 248) and reflecting a particular understanding of the relationship between mobile communities and school systems. So too with Salinas and Fránquiz (2004), who even more explicitly positioned themselves theoretically and hence ideologically as well as practically:

Our primary premise for creating and implementing worthwhile migrant education programs is rooted in the work of multiculturalists … To achieve a view of the United States that encompasses multiple perspectives, multiculturalists encourage us to *embrace culturally responsible or congruent teaching methods that address different ways of knowing.* (p. xiii; emphasis in original)

It is against this backdrop of the intellectual and ideological foundations of researchers' recommendations that specific strategies for creating new educational futures for mobile communities need to be understood and evaluated. For instance, several suggestions are elaborated by the authors contributing to *Traveller Education: Accounts of Good Practice* (Tyler, 2005), ranging from early childhood and primary school education to secondary education and supporting distance education. While these have considerable merit, and derive from the authors' extensive experience in Traveler education in the United Kingdom, they inevitably reflect those same authors' assumptions about mobile communities and educational provision. Moreover, their suggestions are unlikely to "travel well" across cultural and national boundaries to be applicable (except perhaps at a generic level) to other mobile groups— not that the originators of these suggestions would necessarily claim such applicability.

Turning to examples of these specific strategies for reimagining the education of mobile communities explicitly or implicitly endorsed by researchers in this field of scholarship, we find a considerable number and range, including:

- the provision by two educational researchers of a non-formal peripatetic literacy program for adult women among the Rabari nomadic pastoralists in Kachchh in western India (Dyer, 2000, pp. 245-247)
- fostering research specifically directed at influencing educational and social policy in relation to Nigerian nomadic pastoralists (Umar & Tahir, 2000, p. 235)
- adopting a participatory approach to organizing the Migrant Educational Technology program, an after school program introducing Latino migrant families in the United States of America to computing and educational software applications (Carrillo, 2004)
- the trialing by the National Foundation of Education for Young Children of Bargee Families in the Netherlands of "a system to provide every bargee family with a tutor" who would act "as a kind of case manager, following the child in his or her preschool career, …" (Scholten, 2000, p. 283)
- the elaboration of a partnership between the Devon Consortium Traveller Education Service and mobile fairground parents in the United Kingdom in implementing training sessions for classroom teachers

about distance education for fairground children (Kiddle, 2000, pp. 272-274)

- "... home learning and other out-of-school possibilities that will 'normalize' the specific needs of Travellers and offer them a quality educational experience ... " (Jordan, 2000, p. 261).

Clearly what mobile community researchers say about creating new educational futures for members of those communities varies widely according to the contexts and character of their research and the ideological perspectives framing their own worldviews. At the same time, some common underlying elements that traverse the heterogeneity of mobile communities and those who teach and research with them can be distilled as exhibiting a focus on:

- consultation and partnerships among stakeholders
- engagement with the diversity within and among mobile communities
- mobilizing counternarratives in opposition to metanarratives
- seeking flexibility and innovation in educational provision
- and in some cases challenging the state's hegemony in educational structures.

As Cardenas (2004) noted, there is no "silver bullet to produce quick results" (p. 245). On the other hand, these and other suggestions by mobile community researchers encapsulate a great deal of experience and understanding that—in company with the aspirations and ideas of the members of those communities outlined above—can provide the foundation of new and transformative educational futures for mobile learners and educators.

Implications for Creating New Educational Futures More Broadly

A key part of every chapter in this book has been the identification of possible implications for wider educational practice of that chapter's particular "hot topic." The intention has been to situate the book's exploration of mobile learning communities in broader contemporary debates about educational conceptualizing, policy-making, and practice. This is a really important point, not only because as we have emphasized mobility is only one part of community members' subjectivities and other parts are shared with non-mobile learners but also because challenges and potential opportunities related to the education of mobile communities are likely to find resonance with non-mobile communities as well. We see that resonance as a crucial building block in the ongoing project of creating new educational futures in every country and across every sector of provision.

This point was certainly recognized by Kiddle (1999) in the peroration to her call to give Traveler children "a voice for themselves":

I would make the same argument for all children—the necessity for parents and teachers to work together to let the children have the chance to learn from both and then move on to be truly themselves. I would argue for all children that we should listen to what they have to say, because they have to deal with a different world from the one their parents and teachers grew into. (p. 156)

Taking up this point, we acknowledge the substantial corpus of current scholarship that identifies fundamental inequalities in educational access and outcomes and that analyzes the causes of those inequalities. There is the work, for example, of educational researchers such as Apple (2006, 2010/in preparation), Freire (1972), Giroux (2008), and Peters (Peters et al., 2008). There is also much useful thinking around the educational implications of theorists like Bakhtin (1981, 1984), Bourdieu (1998; see also Webb et al., 2002), de Certeau (1984), and Foucault (1977; see also Danaher et al., 2000b).

As with the mobile community members and researchers cited above, these and other educational researchers have proposed—and sometimes enacted—a number of possible strategies for engaging with these inequalities, ranging widely in terms of radicalism. At one end of the continuum sits the idea of deschooling society associated with the work of Ivan Illich (1971) and others who have been concerned about institutionalized education replicating and even enlarging existing socioeconomic inequities. This idea resonates strongly with critiques of the sedentarist project of state-based educational provision that seeks to minimize the mobility of mobile communities. Fairly close to that end of the continuum sit intentionally radical and usually single educational institutions such as Summerhill, founded by A. S. Neill (1960) in the United Kingdom. While not necessarily radical in that sense, individual institutions such as St Kieran's National School for Travellers south of Dublin (Kenny, 1997) and the Queensland School for Travelling Show Children (Fullerton et al., 2004; Fullerton et al., 2005) focus on specialized provision for mobile groups but do not necessarily challenge the sedentarist mindset of the broader educational community. Toward the other end of the continuum sits the emphasis on inclusion of educational minorities in mainstream education that currently constitutes "the dominant … agenda" (Macleod, 2006, p. 125) in educational policy-making. While the intention of inclusion is to generate positive change on the widest possible scale, the risk is of the institutionalization of diversity and hence the neglect of the specialized needs and aspirations of particular groups of learners. The work of the English TESSs, for example, is posited on helping mobile learners to have successful learning journeys within schools, yet many head teachers in those services have expressed concerns about Travelers' interests being subsumed within a very large system (Danaher et al., 2007a).

Clearly this is a vast and variegated territory containing a great many overlapping and sometimes disjointed contours. Our purpose here is merely to signal our awareness of its existence and to establish a direct link between this wider educational scholarship and our discussion of creating new educational futures for both mobile and non-mobile communities.

Given the book's focus on mobile learning communities, we envisage that link as being centered on taking up more broadly the potential benefits and strengths of such communities. We have acknowledged above the limits and limitations of learning communities and certainly do not present them as a universal panacea. Nevertheless we consider that engaging wholeheartedly with some of the central premises of learning communities—such as learning through dialogue, interdependence, mutuality, cooperative community, and celebrating diversity—can contribute significantly to creating educational futures that are sustaining and transforming.

One specific way that we see learning communities making this contribution is by helping to negotiate what we have identified as three crucial sets of creative tensions. We have distilled these creative tensions from the data presented in the preceding chapters and the associated scholarship. By labeling these tensions "creative," we wish to signal both that they are enduringly complex challenges confronting educators and learners and that potentially they afford innovative and successful responses to those challenges. These tensions apply equally to mobile and non-mobile learners and are thus vital elements in creating new educational futures:

Inclusion versus specialization is an ongoing educational debate. On the one hand, changing curriculum, pedagogy, and assessment to cater for all learners is an admirable goal and one intended to have positive flow on effects for sociocultural transformation. On the other hand, the risk of hegemonic replication and the elision of difference is high.

Diversity versus dialogue highlights the challenge of engaging wholeheartedly with difference. From one perspective, acknowledging diversity is a prerequisite of valuing it educationally and socioculturally. From a different perspective, dialogue directed at identifying the commonalities among groups is equally—perhaps more—likely to generate mutual respect and trust across widely disparate communities. This resonates strongly with the principle of articulation advocated in Chapter 8.

Change versus continuity is a timely reminder that educational systems evolve and transform by means of a sometimes volatile mix of elements, and that interrogating the possible ingredients of new educational futures entails a close examination of what to retain from current and even to resurrect former provision as well as what to replace and regenerate. Likewise this is the kind of discussion that members of mobile communities have continually in relation to their ways of life and the economic foundations of their communities.

Afterword

In closing this book, let us return to the working definition of learning communities that we cited in the introduction:

> Learning communities are made up of people who share a common purpose. They collaborate to draw on individual strengths, respect a variety of perspectives, and actively promote learning opportunities. The outcomes are the creation of a vibrant, synergistic environment, enhanced potential for all members, and the possibility that new knowledge will be created. (Kilpatrick et al., 2003, p. 11)

Since we cited that definition, we have traversed extensive terrain in our exploration of mobile learning communities, ranging from networks and partnerships and lifelong learning to technologies and globalization to the knowledge economy and multiliteracies to risk, capacity building, and sustainability and marginalization and transformation. While acknowledging the limits and limitations of learning communities, we contend that this working definition and the associated conceptualization have proved to be powerful allies in understanding the multiple ways in which the members of widely divergent mobile communities earn, learn, and live. Yet we assert also that the intervening account has added significant breadth and depth to that definition and conceptualization—for example, by demonstrating how mobility's departure (and in some ways freedom) from fixed residence creates new opportunities for the expression and strengthening of community bonds, and by highlighting the complex relationships between mobile and non-mobile community members.

Each chapter, and this concluding text, have sought to maximize the links between the mobile learning communities discussed here and broader educational practice. In some cases the discussion affirms particular aspects of current practice; in other cases it suggests different and even radical alternatives to that practice. These affirmations and suggestions are a crucial part of the book's other focus: distilling from mobile learning communities possible strategies for creating new and more enabling educational futures, based on particular enactments of the creative tensions between inclusion and specialization, diversity and dialogue, and change and continuity.

Mobility—learning—community: separately and in combination, these three ideas speak evocatively and powerfully across place and time and have much of value to say about contemporary and possible future educational practice, if we are willing and able to listen and engage.

Glossary of Terms

Articulation: rather than being integrated or assimilated into mainstream settled society, we argue for the principle of articulation, through which Travelers sustain their distinctive lifestyles and values, but couple or join up with mainstream society to pursue certain interests, rather like their vehicles that are coupled up to keep the show on the road.

Autonomous and heteronomous values: these concepts from Bourdieu (1990) relate to a continuum of positions within different cultural fields. While autonomous positions measure value in terms of the particular field and its form of production, heteronomous positions measure value in terms of connections with other fields, especially the economic field. Within the artistic field, for example, an autonomous position would value art as something good in itself ("art for art's sake"), while a heteronomous position would value art in terms of the revenue that it generates.

Border crossing: a concept derived from Giroux (1992) to refer to ways in which people such as Travelers can challenge the arbitrariness of boundaries in order to create an opportunity for new subject positions, identities, and social relations that can produce resistance to and relief from the structures of domination and oppression.

Capacity: the ability to enact socially sanctioned behaviors.

Capacity building: the personal and communal development of socially sanctioned capacity among individuals and groups constituting communities.

Globalization: a world-wide phenomenon that has led to the exchange of goods, services, information, and ideas at an unprecedented pace. It is commonly regarded as having political, economic, technological, and sociocultural dimensions that, depending on context and perspective, are perceived as impacting positively and/or negatively on life, on educational prospects, and on educational futures.

Habitus: a concept derived from Bourdieu (1990) to refer to the enduring dispositions and attitudes that Travelers develop that shape their cultural values and practices.

Institutional racism: occurs when an institution fails to meet the needs of a particular group while satisfying the needs of other groups. Travelers have often been subject to this form of prejudice.

Knowledge economy: refers to the reform of economic practice characteristic of much of the world today, where forms of knowledge generated through ICTs and the globalization of business drive economic performance.

Lifelong learning: continuous learning that occurs throughout the lifespan and that is often conceived as being formal, non-formal, or informal. Delors' (1996) conception of the term describes *learning to know, learning to do, learning to live together and with others,* and *learning to be* as the main elements. The precise meaning of the term varies over time and from one context to the next.

Life-wide learning: has also been described as formal and informal, occurring not just in educational institutions and community organizations but also in the workplace and the home. Optimal progress in learning is regarded as being most achievable when the individual draws on all life-wide and lifelong learning experiences.

Marginalization: the process through which certain groups are distinguished from those occupying positions of central authority and are located on the margins of established institutional frameworks.

Mobile learning community: a group of people who are mobile for sustained periods of the year or of their lives and who recognize in themselves and others a common experience of mobility and a shared commitment to learning for themselves and other group members.

Multiliteracies: the range of communication practices in which Travelers engage, shaped by their cultural values and traditions as well as the diversity of media and communication technologies with which they engage.

Network: a generally informal and often extensive set of relationships among large numbers of participants.

Perspective transformation: a concept derived from Mezirow (2000) that takes place when individuals change their frames of reference by critically reflecting on their assumptions and beliefs and consciously making and implementing plans that bring about new ways of defining their worlds.

Parrhesia: a concept derived from Foucault (2001) to refer to frank or fearless speech. Throughout history, performing Travelers such as clowns and fools have exercised fearless speech to challenge forms of authority.

Partnership: a formalized and sometimes legalized association among participants.

Risk: denoting properties or qualities perceived by some as potentially leading to reduced educational success.

Sedentarism: a concept derived from McVeigh (1997) to refer to the system of ideas and practices that serves to normalize and reproduce sedentary modes of existence and to pathologize and repress nomadic modes of existence.

Society of control: a concept from Deleuze (1995) to suggest the ways in which control is exercised in contemporary Western societies. While the disciplinary society that Foucault (1977) explored is based on closed institutions that are monitored from within, we are now in a more open society predicated on constant movement in which forms of control are disseminated throughout social space. While the all-seeing prison tower or panopticon was a central metaphor of the disciplinary society, close circuit television surveillance of a city is a metaphor for the society of control.

Sustainability: the long-term effectiveness and viability of organisms and organizations.

Systems thinking: a concept from Capra (1996) to suggest an interdependent and interconnected thinking necessary to respond to the challenges of today. While mechanistic thinking functions by breaking things down to their component parts, systems thinking operates by exploring how something that occurs in one part of a system such as an ecology has implications for other parts of that ecological system.

Technologies: have been defined in this book as artifacts related to transport, other forms of movement, earning, and learning, particularly in the context of mobile learning communities. This understanding reflects a broader application of the term than is implied by ICTs, which generally refer to computer usage.

References

Advisory Council for the Education of Romany and Other Travellers. (Ed.) (1993). *The education of Gypsy and Traveller children: Action-research and co-ordination*. Hatfield, UK: University of Hertfordshire Press.

Alanís, I. (2004). Effective instruction: Integrating language and literacy. In C. Salinas & M. E. Fránquiz (Eds.), *Scholars in the field: The challenges of migrant education* (pp. 209-222). Charleston, WV: ERIC Clearinghouse on Rural Education and Small Schools/Appalachia Educational Laboratory.

Anderson, T. (2004). Teaching in an online learning context. In T. Anderson & F. Elloumi (Eds.), *Theory and practice of online learning* (pp. 273-294). Athabasca, AB: Athabasca University.

Anderson, T., & Garrison, D. R. (1998). Learning in a networked world: New roles and responsibilities. In C. Gibson (Ed.), *Distance learners in higher education* (pp. 97-112). Madison, WI: Atwood.

Anning, A., & Edwards, A. (2006). *Promoting children's learning from birth to five: Developing the new early years professional* (2nd ed.). Buckingham, UK: Open University Press.

Anteliz, E. A., & Danaher, P. A. (2000). *Carritos chocones* and dodgem cars: A preliminary comparison between Venezuelan and Australian fairgrounds. *Journal of Nomadic Studies*, 3, 12-17.

Anteliz, E. A., Danaher, M. J. M., & Danaher, P. A. (1997, September). Teaching global climate change. *Tiempo*, 25, 17-22.

Anteliz, E. A., Danaher, G. R., & Danaher, P. A. (2004). Mobilising spatial risks: Reflections on researching Venezuelan and Australian fairground people's educational experiences. In P. N. Coombes, M. J. M. Danaher, & P. A. Danaher (Eds.), *Strategic uncertainties: Ethics, politics and risk in contemporary educational research* (pp. 155-168). Flaxton, Qld: Post Pressed.

Anyanwu, C. N. (1998). Transformative research for the promotion of nomadic education in Nigeria. *Journal of Nomadic Studies*, 1, 44-51.

Appiah, K. A. (2006). *Cosmopolitanism: Ethics in a world of strangers*. New York: W. W. Norton & Company.

Apple, M. W. (2006). *Educating the "right" way: Markets, standards, God, and inequality* (2nd ed.). London: Routledge.

Apple, M. W. (2010/in preparation). *Global crises, education, and social justice: What can education do?* London: Routledge.

Baca, L. (2004). Foreword. In C. Salinas & M. E. Fránquiz (Eds.), *Scholars in the field: The challenges of migrant education* (pp. ix-x). Charleston, WV: ERIC Clearinghouse on Rural Education and Small Schools/Appalachia Educational Laboratory.

Bakhtin, M. M. (1981). *The dialogic imagination: Four essays* (translated by C. Emerson & M. Holquist). Austin, TX: University of Texas Press.

Bakhtin, M. M. (1984). *Problems of Dostoevsky's poetics* (edited and translated by C. Emerson). Minneapolis, MN: University of Minnesota Press.

Bartlett, V. L., Bigum, C., & Rowan, L. O. (1997, June 5). Globalisation: Politics by another name. Paper presented at the "Globalisation and education" symposium, Brisbane, Qld.

Beck, C., & Kosnik, C. (2002). Components of a good practicum placement: Student teacher perceptions. *Teacher Education Quarterly*, 29(2), 81-98.

Beck, S. A. L. (2004). The challenge of change: A gringo remembers tough choices. In C. Salinas & M. E. Fránquiz (Eds.), *Scholars in the field: The challenges of migrant education* (pp.

225-237). Charleston, WV: ERIC Clearinghouse on Rural Education and Small Schools/ Appalachia Educational Laboratory.

Beck, U. (2000). *What is globalization?* (translated by P. Camiller). Cambridge, UK: Polity Press.

Beddie, F. (2004). Learning communities: A catalyst for collective responsibility. In P. A. Danaher, C. R. Macpherson, F. Nouwens, & D. Orr (Eds.), *Lifelong learning: Whose responsibility and what is your contribution?: Refereed papers from the 3rd international lifelong learning conference Yeppoon, Central Queensland, Australia 13-16 June 2004: Hosted by Central Queensland University* (pp. 1-7). Rockhampton, Qld: Lifelong Learning Conference Committee, Central Queensland University Press.

Benner, C. (2003). Learning communities in a learning region: The soft infrastructure of cross-firm learning networks in Silicon Valley. *Environment and Planning A*, 35, 1809-1830. Retrieved September 16, 2008, from http://envplan.com/epa/fulltext/a35/a35238.pdf

Bessant, J., Hill, R., & Watts, R. (2003). *Discovering risk: Social research and policy making*. New York: Peter Lang.

Biggs, J. (2003). *Teaching for quality learning at university* (2nd ed.). Buckingham, UK: Open University Press.

Bigum, C., Fitzclarence, L., Kenway, J., Collier, J., & Croker, C. A. (1993). That's edutainment: Restructuring universities and the Open Learning Initiative. *Australian Universities' Review*, 36(2), 21-27.

Blaney, B. (2005). Towards success in secondary schooling. In C. Tyler (Ed.), *Traveller education: Accounts of good practice* (pp. 105-113). Stoke on Trent, UK and Sterling, VA: Trentham Books.

Blaze Corcoran, P., & Wals, A. E. J. (Eds.) (2004). *Higher education and the challenge of sustainability: Problematics, promise, and practice*. Dordrecht, The Netherlands: Kluwer Academic Publishers.

Boling, E. C. (2003, Winter). The transformation of instruction through technology: Promoting inclusive learning communities in teacher education courses. *Action in Teacher Education*, 24(4), 64-73.

Bolton, R. (2004). *Why circus works: How the values and structures of circus make it a significant development experience for young people*. Unpublished Doctor of Philosophy thesis, Division of Arts, Murdoch University, Perth, WA.

Booth, T., & Ainscow, M. (1998). In T. Booth & M. Ainscow (Eds.), *From them to us: An international study of inclusion in education* (pp. 1-20). London: Routledge.

Borko, H. (2004). Professional development and teacher learning: Mapping the terrain. *Educational Researcher*, 33(8), 3-15.

Borthwick, A. C., Stirling, T., Mauman, A. D., & Cook, D. L. (2003). Achieving successful school–university collaboration. *Urban Education*, 38(3), 330-371.

Bourdieu, P. (1990). *The logic of practice* (translated by R. Nice). Stanford, CA: Stanford University Press.

Bourdieu, P. (1998). *Practical reason: On the theory of action*. Cambridge, UK: Polity Press.

Bourdieu, P., & Passeron, J. (1977). *Reproduction in education, society and culture*. London: Sage Publications.

Brabazon, T. (2002). *Digital hemlock: Internet education and the poisoning of teaching*. Sydney, NSW: University of New South Wales Press.

Brendtro, L. K., Brokenleg, M., & Van Bockern, S. (2002). *Reclaiming youth at risk: Our hope for the future* (revised ed.). Bloomington, IN: National Educational Service.

Breier, M. (1997). Literacy strategies among unschooled workers. In S. Walters (Ed.), *Globalization, adult education and training* (pp. 201-212). London: Zed Books.

Brookfield, S. (1986). *Understanding and facilitating adult learning*. San Francisco: Jossey-Bass.

Brown, A., & Danaher, P. A. (2008, May). Towards collaborative professional learning in the first year early childhood teacher education practicum: Issues in negotiating the multiple interests of stakeholder feedback. *Asia-Pacific Journal of Teacher Education*, 36(2), 147-161.

Brunello, G., & Checchi, D. (2007, October). Does school tracking affect equality of opportunity? New international evidence. *Economic Policy*, 22(52), 781-861.

Burchell, G., Gordon, C., & Miller, P. (Eds.) (1991). *The Foucault effect: Studies in governmentality*. Chicago, IL: University of Chicago Press.

Burnett, N. (2008). The Delors report: A guide towards Education for All. *European Journal of Education*, 43(2), 181-187.

Capra, F. (1996). *The web of life*. London: Flamingo.

Cardenas, B. (2004). Breaking through in migrant education. In C. Salinas & M. E. Fránquiz (Eds.), *Scholars in the field: The challenges of migrant education* (pp. 239-248). Charleston, WV: ERIC Clearinghouse on Rural Education and Small Schools/Appalachia Educational Laboratory.

Cardini, A. (2006). An analysis of the rhetoric and practice of educational partnerships in the UK: An arena of complexities, tensions and power. *Journal of Education Policy, 21*(4), 393-415.

Carmeli, Y. S. (2003, Spring). Lion on display: Culture, nature, and totality in a circus performance. *Poetics Today, 24*(1), 65-90.

Carr-Hill, R. (2006). Educational services and nomadic groups in Djibouti, Eritrea, Ethiopia, Kenya, Tanzania and Uganda. In C. Dyer (Ed.), *The education of nomadic peoples: Current issues, future prospects* (pp. 35-52). New York and Oxford, UK: Berghahn Books.

Carrillo, R. (2004). Making connections: Building family literacy through technology. In C. Salinas & M. E. Fránquiz (Eds.), *Scholars in the field: The challenges of migrant education* (pp. 165-179). Charleston, WV: ERIC Clearinghouse on Rural Education and Small Schools/Appalachia Educational Laboratory.

Castro Laszio, K. (2001, September-October). Learning, design, and action: Creating the conditions for Evolutionary Learning Community. *Systems Research and Behavioral Science, 18*(5), 379-391.

Celedón-Pattichis, S. (2004). Alternative secondary mathematics programs for migrant students: Cultural and linguistic considerations. In C. Salinas & M. E. Fránquiz (Eds.), *Scholars in the field: The challenges of migrant education* (pp. 195-208). Charleston, WV: ERIC Clearinghouse on Rural Education and Small Schools/Appalachia Educational Laboratory.

Centre for Studies on Inclusive Education. (n.d.). *Inclusive further education: Summary of the report of the Further Education Funding Council Learning Difficulties and/or Disabilities Committee chaired by Professor John Tomlinson.* Retrieved September 27, 2007, from http://inclusion.uwe.ac.uk/csie/tmlnsn.htm

Chaskin, R. J., Brown, P., Venkatesh, S. A., & Vidal, A. (2001). *Building community capacity (Modern applications of social work).* Hathorne, NY: Aldine Transaction.

Chatty, D. (2006). Boarding schools for mobile peoples: The Harasiis in the Sultanate of Oman. In C. Dyer (Ed.), *The education of nomadic peoples: Current issues, future prospects* (pp. 212-230). New York and Oxford, UK: Berghahn Books.

Cleary, V., & Moriarty, B. J. (2006). When theory meets practice: Increasing the value of pre-service teachers' practical experiences through inter-systemic partnerships. In J. McConachie, R. E. Harreveld, J. T. Luck, F. Nouwens, & P. A. Danaher (Eds.), *"Doctrina perpetua": Brokering change, promoting innovation and transforming marginalisation in university learning and teaching* (pp. 102-114). Teneriffe, Qld: Post Pressed.

Cookson, P. S. (2002, January). The hybridization of higher education: Cross national perspectives. *International Review of Open and Distance Learning, 2*(2). Retrived September 28, 2008, from http://www.irrodl.org/index.php/irrodl/article/view/66/135

Cooney, G., Jahoda, A., Gumley, A., & Knott, F. (2006, June). Young people with intellectual disabilities attending mainstream and segregated schooling: Perceived stigma, social comparison and future aspirations. *Journal of Intellectual Disability Research, 50*(6), 432-444.

Cope, B., & Kalantzis, M. (1996). Putting multiliteracies to the test. Retrieved November 15, 2003, from http://www.alea.edu.au/multilit.htm

Copland, M. A. (2003). Leadership of inquiry: Building and sustaining capacity for school improvement. *Educational Evaluation and Policy Analysis, 25*(4), 375-395.

Csikszentmihalyi, M. (1998). *Finding flow: The psychology of engagement with everyday life.* New York: Basic Books.

Csikszentmihalyi, M. (2003). *Good business: Leadership, flow and the making of meaning.* New York: Penguin Books.

Currie, H., & Danaher, P. A. (2001, Spring). Government funding for English Traveller Education Support Services. *Multicultural Teaching, 19*(2), 33-36.

Danaher, P. A. (Ed.) (1998a). *Beyond the Ferris wheel: Educating Queensland show children.* Rockhampton, Qld: Central Queensland University Press.

Danaher, P. A. (1998b). 'Home' and the show people. In P. A. Danaher (Ed.), *Beyond the Ferris wheel: Educating Queensland show children* (pp. 29-41). Rockhampton, Qld: Central Queensland University Press.

Danaher, P. A. (2000a). What's in a name? The "marginalization" of itinerant people. *Journal of Nomadic Studies, 3,* 67-71.

Danaher, P. A. (2000b). Guest editor's introduction. In P. A. Danaher (Ed.), *Mapping international diversity in researching Traveller and nomadic education*. Theme issue of the *International Journal of Educational Research, 33*(3), 221-230.

Danaher, P. A. (2001a, March). *Learning on the run: Traveller education for itinerant show children in coastal and western Queensland*. Unpublished Doctor of Philosophy thesis, Faculty of Education and Creative Arts, Central Queensland University, Rockhampton, Qld.

Danaher, P. A. (2001b, September). Globalisation and open and distance learning: Possibilities and problems for nomadic and Traveller education. *Indian Journal of Open Learning, 10*(3), 299-307.

Danaher, P. A. (2008). Telling tales: Metanarratives, counternarratives and other stories in lifelong learning successes and futures. In D. Orr, P. A. Danaher, G. R. Danaher, & R. E. Harreveld (Eds.), *Lifelong learning: Reflecting on successes and framing futures: Keynote and refereed papers from the 5th international lifelong learning conference, Yeppoon, Central Queensland, Australia, 16-19 June 2008: Hosted by Central Queensland University* (pp. 6-15). Rockhampton, Qld: Lifelong Learning Conference Committee, Central Queensland University Press.

Danaher, P. A., & Wyer, D. W. (1997). Itinerant education as border pedagogy: The globalisation and localisation of show culture. In L. O. Rowan, V. L. Bartlett, & T. D. Evans (Eds.), *Shifting borders: Globalisation, localisation and open and distance education* (pp. 99-111). Geelong, Vic: Deakin University Press.

Danaher, P. A., Coombes, P. N., Danaher, G. R., & Anteliz, E. A. (2000a, December). Life imprisonment or learning for life: Re-opening the social control–social capital debate about lifelong learning. *Re-Open, 1*(1): 1–14

Danaher, G. R., Schirato, T., & Webb, J. (2000b). *Understanding Foucault*. St Leonards, NSW: Allen & Unwin.

Danaher, P. A., Moriarty, B. J., & Danaher, G. R. (2004, November). Three pedagogies of mobility for Australian show people: Teaching about, through and towards the questioning of sedentarism. *Melbourne Studies in Education, 45*(2), 47-66.

Danaher, G. R., Moriarty, B. J., & Danaher, P. A. (2006a, May). Riding waves of resonance: Morphogenic fields and collaborative research with Australian travelling communities. *M/C Journal, 9*(2). Retrieved August 24, 2008, from http://journal.media-culture.org.au/0605/06-danahermoriarty.php

Danaher, G. R., Moriarty, B. J., & Danaher, P. A. (2006b, July). Challenging heterotopic space: A study of the Queensland School for Travelling Show Children. *Studies in Learning, Evaluation, Innovation and Development, 3*(1), 40-51.

Danaher, P. A., Coombes, P. N., & Kiddle, C. (2007a). *Teaching Traveller children: Maximising learning outcomes*. Stoke on Trent, UK and Sterling, VA: Trentham Books.

Danaher, P. A., Danaher, G. R., & Moriarty, B. J. (2007b, September). Subverting the hegemony of risk: Vulnerability and transformation among Australian show children. *Educational Research, 49*(3), 211-224.

Danaher, P. A., Hickey, A., Brown, A., & Conway, J. M. (2007c). Exploring elements for creating an online community of learners within a distance education course at the University of Southern Queensland. In R. J. Luppicini (Ed.), *Online learning communities* (pp. 219-240). Charlotte, NC: Information Age Publishing.

Danaher, P. A., Gururajan, R., & Hafeez-Baig, A. (2009). Transforming the practice of mobile learning: Promoting pedagogical innovation through educational principles and strategies that work. In H. Ryu & D. P. Parsons (Eds.), *Innovative mobile learning: Techniques and technologies* (pp. 21-45). Hershey, PA: Idea Group

D'Andrea, A. (2006). *Global nomads: Techno and new age as transnational countercultures*. London: Routledge.

Daymond, L. (2005). It's all about me: Resources at Foundation and Key Stage 1. In C. Tyler (Ed.), *Traveller education: Accounts of good practice* (pp. 71-80). Stoke on Trent, UK and Sterling, VA: Trentham Books.

de Certeau, M. (1984). *The practice of everyday life* (translated by S. Rendall). Berkeley, CA: University of California Press.

De Jongh, M. (2002, June). No fixed abode: The poorest of the poor and elusive identities in rural South Africa. *Journal of Southern African Studies, 28*(2), 441-460.

De Jongh, M., & Steyn, R. (2006). Learning to wander, wandering learners: Education and the peripatetic Karretjie people of the South African Karoo. In C. Dyer (Ed.), *The education of nomadic peoples: Current issues, future prospects* (pp. 77-100). New York and Oxford, UK: Berghahn Books.

Deleuze, G. (1995). *Negotiations: 1972–1990* (translated by M. Joughin). New York: Columbia University Press.

Deleuze, G., & Guattari, F. (1987). *A thousand plateaus: Capitalism and schizophrenia* (translated by B. Massumi). Minneapolis, MN: University of Minnesota Press.

Delors, J. (1996). *Learning: The treasure within.* Paris: UNESCO International Commission on Education for the Twenty-first Century.

Delwiche, A. (2006). Massively multiplayer online games (MMOs) in the new media classroom. *Educational Technology & Society, 9*(3), 160-172. Retrieved November 6, 2007, from http://www.ifets.info/journals/9_3/14.pdf

Derrington, C., & Kendall, S. (2004). *Gypsy Traveller students in secondary schools: Culture, identity and achievement.* Stoke on Trent, UK and Sterling, VA: Trentham Books.

Dillard, J., Dujon, V., & King, M. C. (Eds.) (2008). *Understanding the social dimension of sustainability.* London: Routledge.

Dinero, S. C. (2004). New identity/identities formulation in a post-nomadic community: The case of the bedouin of the Negev. *National Identities, 6*(3), 261-275.

Doerr, N. M. (2004, June). Desired division, disavowed division: An analysis of the labeling of the bilingual unit as separatist in an Aotearoa/New Zealand school. *Anthropology & Education Quarterly, 35*(2), 233-253.

Donovan, J. (2005). Still Travellers? Housed Travellers in a London borough. In C. Tyler (Ed.), *Traveller education: Accounts of good practice* (pp. 135-145). Stoke on Trent, UK and Sterling, VA: Trentham Books.

Duckworth, C. (1994, May 4-5). The knotty problem of civilization. *Weekend Australian Review, 5.*

Dwyer, P., & Wyn, J. (2001). *Youth, education and risk: Facing the future.* London: Routledge/Falmer.

Dyer, C. (2000). "Education for All" and the Rabaris of Kachchh, Western India. *International Journal of Educational Research, 33*(3), 241-251.

Dyer, C. (Ed.) (2006a). *The education of nomadic peoples: Current issues, future prospects.* New York and Oxford, UK: Berghahn Books.

Dyer, C. (2006b). Afterword. In C. Dyer (Ed.), *The education of nomadic peoples: Current issues, future prospects* (pp. 259-262). New York and Oxford, UK: Berghahn Books.

Dyer, C., & Choksi, A. (2006). With God's grace and with education, we will find a way: Literacy education and the Rabaris of Kutch, India. In C. Dyer (Ed.), *The education of nomadic peoples: Current issues, future prospects* (pp. 159-174). New York and Oxford, UK: Berghahn Books.

Ellis, A. K. (2005). *Research on educational innovations* (4th ed.). Larchmont, NY: Eye on Education.

Elsden-Clifton, J. (2006, July). Constructing "Thirdspaces": Migrant students and the visual arts. *Studies in Learning, Evaluation, Innovation and Development, 3*(1), 1-11. Retrieved September 16, 2008, from http://www.sleid.cqu.edu.au

Enders, J., & Jongbloed, B. (Eds.) (2007). *Public–private dynamics in higher education: Expectations, developments and outcomes.* Bielefeld, Germany: Transcript Verlag.

Eneroth, B. (2008). Knowledge, sentience and receptivity: A paradigm of lifelong learning. *European Journal of Education, 43*(2), 229-240.

Farrell, P., & Ainscow, M. (2002). Making special education inclusive: Mapping the issues. In P. Farrell & M. Ainscow (Eds.), *Making special education inclusive* (pp. 1-12). London: David Fulton Publishers.

Ferguson, R., Gever, M., Minh-ha, T. T., & West, C. (Eds.) (1990). *Out there: Marginalization and contemporary cultures.* New York and Cambridge, MA: New Museum of Contemporary Art and Massachusetts Institute of Technology Press.

Fernandez, B., Mutabazi, E., & Pierre, P. (2006, January). International executives, identity strategies and mobility in France and China. *Asia Pacific Business Review, 12*(1), 53-76.

Ferro, A. (2006, April). Desired mobility or satisfied immobility? Migratory aspirations among knowledge workers. *Journal of Education and Work, 19*(2), 171-200.

Findsen, B. (2002). Older adults and learning: A critique of participation and provision. In K. Appleton, C. R. Macpherson, & D. Orr (Eds.), *International lifelong learning conference: Refereed papers from the 2nd international lifelong learning conference Yeppoon, Central Queensland, Australia 16–19 June 2002: Hosted by Central Queensland University* (pp. 172-180). Rockhampton, Qld: Lifelong Learning Conference Committee, Central Queensland University Press.

Fischer, G., & Sugimoto, M. (2006, March). Supporting self-directed learners and learning communities with sociotechnical environments. *Research and Practice in Technology Enhanced Learning, 1*(1), 31-64.

Flores, J. L., & Hammer, P. C. (1996). Introduction. In J. L. Flores (Ed.), *Children of "la frontera": Binational efforts to serve Mexican migrant and immigrant students* (pp. 1-18). Charleston, WV: ERIC Clearinghouse on Rural Education and Small Schools/Appalachia Educational Laboratory.

Folke, C., Carpenter, S., Elmqvist, T., Gunderson, L., Holling, C. S., & Walker, B. (2002, August). Resilience and sustainable development: Building adaptive capacity in a world of transformations. *AMBIO: A Journal of the Human Environment, 31*(5). Retrieved September 16, 2008, from http://ambio.allenpress.com/archive/0044-7447/31/5/pdf/i0044-7447-31-5-437.pdf

Foucault, M. (1977). *Discipline and punish: The birth of the prison* (translated by A. Sheridan). London: Penguin.

Foucault, M. (2001). *Fearless speech* (edited by J. Pearson). Los Angeles, CA: Semiotext(e).

Foucault, M. (2003). *Society must be defended: Lectures at the Collège de France, 1975-6* (translated by D. Macey). London: Penguin Books.

Fox, S. (2005, February). An actor-network critique of community in higher education: Implications for networked learning. *Studies in Higher Education, 30*(1), 95-110.

Fratkin, E., & Mearns, R. (2003, Summer). Sustainability and pastoral livelihoods: Lessons from East African Maasai and Mongolia. *Human Organization, 62*(2), 112-122.

Freire, P. (1972). *Pedagogy of the oppressed*. Harmondsworth, UK: Penguin.

Frost, M. (2006-2007). The impact of *VET in schools* on new certification of post-compulsory education and training in Australia. *VOCAL: The Australian Journal of Vocational Education and Training in Schools, 6*, 17-23.

Fullan, M. (2000, January). The return of large-scale reform. *Journal of Educational Change, 1*(1), 5-27.

Fullerton, C., Danaher, G. R., Moriarty, B. J., & Danaher, P. A. (2004). A principal's perspective on multiliteracies in an Australian show community: Implications for learning as rural engagement. *Education in Rural Australia, 14*(2), 69-81.

Fullerton, C., Moriarty, B. J., Danaher, P. A., & Danaher, G. R. (2005, Autumn). Let the show go on! *Prime Focus, 40*, 15-17.

Gaghan, S. (2005). *Syriana*. Warner Brothers.

Garcia, E. E. (1996). Foreword. In J. L. Flores (Ed.), *Children of "la frontera": Binational efforts to serve Mexican migrant and immigrant students* (pp. ix-xiv). Charleston, WV: ERIC Clearinghouse on Rural Education and Small Schools/Appalachia Educational Laboratory.

Gardner, H. (1993). *Frames of mind: The theory of multiple intelligences* (10th anniversary ed.). New York: Basic Books.

Gardner, H. (2006). *Changing minds: The art and science of changing our own and other people's minds*. Boston, MA: Harvard Business Press.

Garrison, D. R., & Kanuka, H. (2004, 2nd Quarter). Blended learning; Uncovering its transformative potential in higher education. *The Internet and Higher Education, 7*(2), 95-105.

Giles, C., & Hargreaves, A. (2006). The sustainability of innovative schools as learning organizations and professional learning communities during standardized reform. *Educational Administration Quarterly, 42*(1), 124-156.

Giroux, H. A. (1992). *Border crossings: Cultural workers and the politics of education*. New York: Routledge.

Giroux, H. A. (2008). *Against the terror of neoliberalism: Politics beyond the age of greed*. Boulder, CO: Paradigm Publishers.

Grace, A. P. (2006). Reflecting critically on lifelong learning in an era of neoliberal pragmatism: Instrumental, social, and cultural perspectives. In D. Orr, F. Nouwens, C. R. Macpherson, R. E. Harreveld, & P. A. Danaher (Eds.), *Lifelong learning: Partners, pathways and pedagogies: Keynote and refereed papers from the 4th international lifelong learning conference Yeppoon, Central Queensland, Australia 13-16 June 2006: Hosted by Central Queensland University* (pp. 1-16). Rockhampton, Qld: Lifelong Learning Conference Committee, Central Queensland University Press.

Grahame, K. (1961). *The wind in the willows*. London: Methuen Children's Books.

Hafeez-Baig, A., & Danaher, P. A. (2007). Challenges and opportunities in facilitating student engagement and empowerment: Perspectives from information systems and education courses at the University of Southern Queensland, Australia. In C. Montgomerie & J. Seale (Eds.), *Proceedings of world conference on education multimedia, hypermedia and telecommunications 2007* (pp. 459-468). Chesapeake, VA: Association for the Advancement of Computing in Education.

Haigh, M., & Ward, G. (2003, July). Metaphors, myths and models: Clarifying practicum partnerships. Paper presented at the annual conference of the International Council on Education for Teaching and the Australian Teacher Education Association, Melbourne, Vic.

Halliday, M. A. K. (1976, September). Anti-languages. *American Anthropologist, 78*(3), 570-584.

Hallinan, P. M., & Wyer, D. W. (1998). Peer group relationships and the show children. In P. A. Danaher (Ed.), *Beyond the Ferris wheel: Educating Queensland show children* (pp. 89-97). Rockhampton, Qld: Central Queensland University Press.

Hargreaves, D. (2002, October 13-26, November 24-December 7). Teaching in the knowledge society. Paper presented at the 2nd international online conference of the Technology Colleges Trust. Retrieved September 16, 2008, from http://jotamac.typepad.com/jotamacs_weblog/files/teaching_in_a_knowledge_soc.pdf

Harreveld, R. E. (2002, October). *Brokering changes: A study of power and identity through discourses.* Unpublished Doctor of Philosophy thesis, Faculty of Education and Creative Arts, Central Queensland University, Rockhampton, Qld.

Harreveld, R. E., & Danaher, P. A. (2006-2007). Editorial: Transitions in senior phase learning. *VOCAL: The Australian Journal of Vocational Education and Training in Schools, 6*, 6-9.

Hayden, M. C., Rancic, B. A., & Thompson, J. J. (2000). Being international: Student and teacher perceptions from international schools. *Oxford Review of Education, 26*(1), 107-123.

Helve, H., & Holm, G. (Eds.) (2005). *Contemporary youth research: Local expressions and global connections.* Aldershot, UK: Ashgate Publishing.

Henderson, R. (2001). Student mobility: Moving beyond deficit views. *Australian Journal of Guidance and Counselling, 11*(1), 121-129.

Henderson, R. (2005, July). *The social and discursive construction of itinerant farm workers' children as literacy learners.* Unpublished Doctor of Philosophy thesis, School of Education, James Cook University, Townsville, Qld.

Henderson, R., & Danaher, P. A. (Eds.) (2008). *Troubling terrains: Tactics for traversing and transforming contemporary educational research.* Teneriffe, Qld: Post Pressed.

Herrington, J., Oliver, R., & Reeves, T. C. (2002, December 9). Patterns of engagement in authentic online learning environments. Paper presented at the annual conference of the Australasian Society for Computers in Learning in Tertiary Education, Auckland, New Zealand. Retrieved August 24, 2008, from http://www.ascilite.org.au/conferences/auckland02/proceedings/programme.html

Himmelman, A. T. (1994). Communities working collaboratively for a change. In M. S. Herrman (Ed.), *Resolving conflict: Strategies for local government* (pp. 27-47). Washington, DC: International City/County Management Association.

Ho, P. (2001, February). Rangeland degradation in North China revisited? A preliminary statistical analysis to validate non-equilibrium range ecology. *Journal of Development Studies, 37*(3), 99-133.

Hodas, S. (1993). Technology refusal and the organizational culture of schools. *Education Policy Analysis Archives, 1*(1). Retrieved April 9, 2005, from http://epaa.asu.edu/epaav1n10.html

Hodgson, V., & Reynolds, M. (2005, February). Consensus, difference and "multiple communities" in networked learning. *Studies in Higher Education, 30*(1), 11-24.

Hoogvelt, A. (1997). *Globalization and the postindustrial world: The new political economy of development.* Basingstoke, UK and London: Macmillan.

Hopkins, D., & Jackson, D. (2003). Building the capacity for leading and learning. In A. Harris, C. Day, M. Hadfield, D. Hopkins, A. Hargreaves, & C. Chapman (Eds.), *Effective leadership for school improvement* (pp. 84-104). London: Routledge.

Houghton, J., & Sheehan, P. (2000, February). *A primer on the knowledge economy (CSES working paper no. 18).* Melbourne, Vic: Centre for Strategic Economic Studies, Victoria University of Technology. Retrieved September 24, 2008, from http://www.cfses.com/documents/Wp18.pdf

Hurworth, R. (2002). Building and sustaining learning communities: The case of the University of the Third Age (U3A) in Victoria. In K. Appleton, C. R. Macpherson, & D. Orr (Eds.), *International lifelong learning conference: Refereed papers from the 2nd international lifelong learning conference Yeppoon, Central Queensland, Australia 16–19 June 2002: Hosted by*

Central Queensland University (pp. 214-220). Rockhampton, Qld: Lifelong Learning Conference Committee, Central Queensland University Press.

Illich, I. (1971). *Deschooling society*. New York: Harper and Row.

Imel, S. (1998). Transformative learning in adulthood. *ERIC Digest No. 2000*. Retrieved November 19, 2003, from http://www.ed.gov/databases/ERIC_Digests/ed423426.html

Iñárritu, A. G. (2006). *Babel*. Paramount Vantage.

Jackson, S. (2006). Learning citizenship: Lifelong learning, community and the Women's Institutes. In D. Orr, F. Nouwens, C. R. Macpherson, R. E. Harreveld, & P. A. Danaher (Eds.), *Lifelong learning: Partners, pathways, and pedagogies: Keynote and refereed papers from the 4th international lifelong learning conference Yeppoon, Central Queensland, Australia 13–16 June 2006: Hosted by Central Queensland University* (pp. 151-157). Rockhampton, Qld: Lifelong Learning Conference Committee, Central Queensland University Press.

Jordan, E. S. (2000). The exclusionary comprehensive school system: The experience of showground families in Scotland. *International Journal of Educational Research, 33*(3), 253-263.

Kahneman, D., & Lovallo, D. (1993, January). Timid choices and bold forecasts: A cognitive perspective on risk taking. *Management Science, 39*(1), 17-31. Retrieved September 18, 2008, from http://www.som.yale.edu/faculty/keith.chen/negot.%20papers/KahnemanLovallo_ChoicForcastsRisk93.pdf

Kanuka, H. (2002, Spring). A principled approach to facilitating distance education: The Internet, higher education and higher levels of learning. *Journal of Distance Education, 17*(2), 70-86.

Kehrwald, B. A. (2007). *Social presence and learner support: Understanding learners' experiences with mediated social processes in text-based online learning environments*. Unpublished Doctor of Philosophy thesis, University of Southern Queensland, Toowoomba, Qld.

Kellerman, A. (2006). *Personal mobilities*. London: Routledge.

Kennedy, M. (2004). Knowledge management and workplace learning – changing perspectives, issues, and understandings. In P. A. Danaher, C. R. Macpherson, F. Nouwens, & D. Orr (Eds.), *Lifelong learning: Whose responsibility and what is your contribution? Refereed papers from the 3rd international lifelong learning conference Yeppoon, Central Queensland, Australia 13–16 June 2004: Hosted by Central Queensland University* (pp. 179-185). Rockhampton, Qld: Lifelong Learning Conference Committee, Central Queensland University Press.

Kenny, M. D. (1997). *The routes of resistance: Travellers and second-level schooling*. Aldershot, UK: Ashgate.

Kenway, J., Bullen, E., & Robb, S. (2004). The knowledge economy, the technopreneur and the problematic future of the university. *Policy Futures in Education, 2*(2), 330-349.

Kenway, J., Bullen, E., Fahey, J., & Robb, S. (2006). *Haunting the knowledge economy*. London: Routledge.

Kiddle, C. (1999). *Traveller children: A voice for themselves*. London: Jessica Kingsley Publishers.

Kiddle, C. (2000). Partnerships depend on power-sharing: An exploration of the relationships between Fairground and Gypsy Traveller parents and their children's teachers in England. *International Journal of Educational Research, 33*(3), 265-274.

Kilpatrick, S., Barrett, M., & Jones, T. (2003). *Defining learning communities (CRLRA discussion paper series discussion paper D1/2003)*. Launceston, Tas: Centre for Research and Learning in Regional Australia, University of Tasmania.

Knight, J., Weir, S., & Woldehanna, T. (2003, August). The role of education in facilitating risk-taking and innovation in agriculture. *Journal of Development Studies, 39*(6), 1-22.

Krätli, S., with Dyer, C. (2006). Education and development for nomads: The issues and the evidence. In C. Dyer (Ed.), *The education of nomadic peoples: Current issues, future prospects* (pp. 8-34). New York and Oxford, UK: Berghahn Books.

Krieg, S., & Sharp, S. (2003, February). Rethinking relationships in teacher education partnerships: Collaborative research: The possibilities and practices within the Compart Partnership. Paper presented at the annual teaching and learning forum, Perth, WA.

Kukulska-Hulme, A., & Traxler, J. (Eds.) (2005). *Mobile learning: A handbook for educators and trainers*. London: Routledge.

Kuzma, L. M. (2000). Face-to-face in cyberspace: Simulating the Security Council through Internet technology. In J. S. Lantis, L. M. Kuzma, & J. Boehrer (Eds.), *The new international studies classroom: Active teaching, active learning* (pp. 183-200). Boulder, CO: Lynne Rienner Publishers.

Lave, J., & Wenger, E. (1991). *Situated learning: Legitimate peripheral participation*. New York: Cambridge University Press.

Leaton Gray, S. (2006). *Teachers under siege.* Stoke on Trent, UK and Sterling, VA: Trentham Books.

Leonard, M. (2006). Segregated schools in segregated societies: Issues of safety and risk. *Childhood, 13*(4), 441-458.

Levinson, M. P. (2007, March). Literacy in English Gypsy communities: Cultural capital manifested as negative assets. *American Educational Research Journal, 44*(1), 5-39.

Lieberman, A. (2000). Networks as learning communities: Shaping the future of teacher development. *Journal of Teacher Education, 51*(3), 221-227.

Liégeois, J.-P. (1998). *School provision for ethnic minorities: The Gypsy paradigm* (translated by S. ní Shuineár). Paris, France and Hatfield, UK: Gypsy Research Centre, Université René Descartes and University of Hertfordshire Press.

Lincoln, Y. S., & Guba, E. G. (1985). *Naturalistic inquiry.* Beverly Hills, CA: Sage Publications.

Linklater, R. (2006). *Fast food nation.* Fox Searchlight Pictures.

Lloyd, G., & McCluskey, G. (2008, July). Education and Gypsies/Travellers: "Contradictions and significant silences". *International Journal of Inclusive Education, 12*(4), 331-345.

Longworth, N. (2006). *Learning cities, learning regions, learning communities: Lifelong learning and local government.* London: Routledge.

López, G. R. (2004). Bringing the mountain to Mohammed: Parent involvement in migrant-impacted schools. In C. Salinas & M. E. Fránquiz (Eds.), *Scholars in the field: The challenges of migrant education* (pp. 135-146). Charleston, WV: ERIC Clearinghouse on Rural Education and Small Schools/Appalachia Educational Laboratory.

Lucassen, L., Willems, W., & Cottar, A. (1998). Introduction. In L. Lucassen, W. Willems, & A. Cottar (Eds.), *Gypsies and other itinerant groups: A socio-historical approach* (pp. 1-13). Houndmills, UK: Macmillan.

Luck, J. T. (2004). Learning doesn't happen only in the classroom: Technology-assisted informal and formal learning. In P. A. Danaher, C. R. Macpherson, F. Nouwens, & D. Orr (Eds.), *Lifelong learning: Whose responsibility and what is your contribution?: Refereed papers from the 3rd international lifelong learning conference Yeppoon, Central Queensland, Australia 13-16 June 2004: Hosted by Central Queensland University* (pp. 224-229). Rockhampton, Qld: Lifelong Learning Conference Committee, Central Queensland University Press.

Luis Bernal, J. (2005, November). Parental choice, social class and market forces: The consequences of privatization of public services in education. *Journal of Education Policy, 20*(6), 779-792.

Luke, A. (1993, March 25-31). Writing off literacy's empowering role. *Campus Review, 13.*

Luppicini, R. J. (Ed.) (2007). *Online learning communities.* Charlotte, NC: Information Age Publishing.

Macleod, M. A. G. (2006). The place of separate provision in a policy climate of inclusion. *Journal of Research in Special Educational Needs, 6*(3), 125-133.

Mann, S. J. (2005, February). Alienation in the learning environment: A failure of community? *Studies in Higher Education, 30*(1), 43-55.

Marks, K. (2005). Developments in supported distance learning. In C. Tyler (Ed.), *Traveller education: Accounts of good practice* (pp. 121-134). Stoke on Trent, UK and Sterling, VA: Trentham Books.

Massey, D. S. (2006). Social background and academic performance differentials: White and minority students at selective colleges. *American Law and Economics Review, 8*(2), 390-409.

Matelski, M. J. (2005, November). Hungary's Roma Radio: Undeserving the undeserved? *Journal of Radio Studies, 12*(2), 256-269.

Mayhew, H. (1862). *London labour and the London poor* (3 vols.). London: George Woodfall and Son.

McCaffery, J., Samni, K., Ezeomah, C., & Pennells, J. (2006). Adult literacy and teacher education in a community education programme in Nigeria. In C. Dyer (Ed.), *The education of nomadic peoples: Current issues, future prospects* (pp. 231-258). New York and Oxford, UK: Berghahn Books.

McDougall, J. K. (2004, July). *Changing mindsets: A study of Queensland primary teachers and the visual literacy initiative.* Unpublished Doctor of Philosophy thesis, Faculty of Education and Creative Arts, Central Queensland University, Rockhampton, Qld.

McInnis, C. (2001, August 13). Signs of disengagement? The changing undergraduate experience in Australian universities. Inaugural professorial lecture presented at the Centre for the Study of Higher Education, Faculty of Education, University of Melbourne, Melbourne, Vic.

McVeigh, R. (1997). Theorising sedentarism: The roots of anti-nomadism. In T. Acton (Ed.), *Gypsy politics and Traveller identity* (pp. 7-25). Hatfield, UK: University of Hertfordshire Press.

Mendoza, E., Perz, S. G., Chávez, A., Cullman, G., Duchelle, A., Luzar, J., Marsik, M., Alarcón, G., Dueñas, H., Brown, I. F., Carballo, J., Aguilar, C., Chávez, J., de los Rios, M., Reis, V., Ehringhaus, C., Mayna, J., Muñante, A., & van Oosten, C. (2007, November). The "Knowledge Exchange Train": A model for capacity building for participatory governance in the south-western Amazon. *Development in Practice, 17*(6), 791-799.

Menzies, H. (1994). Learning communities and the information superhighway. *Journal of Distance Education, 9*(1), 1-16.

Meyertholen, P., Castro, S., & Salinas, C. (2004). Project SMART: Using technology to provide educational continuity for migrant children. In C. Salinas & M. E. Fránquiz (Eds.), *Scholars in the field: The challenges of migrant education* (pp. 181-191). Charleston, WV: ERIC Clearinghouse on Rural Education and Small Schools/Appalachia Educational Laboratory.

Mezirow, J. (2000). Learning to think like an adult – core concepts of transformation theory. In J. Mezirow and Associates (Eds.), *Learning as transformation: Critical perspectives on a theory in progress* (pp. 3-31). San Francisco: Jossey-Bass.

Mitchell, C., & Sackney, L. (2000). *Profound improvement: Building capacity for a learning community.* Lisse, The Netherlands: Swets & Zeitlinger.

Monsour, A. (2007, August 17). New century, old story! Race, religion, bureaucrats, and the Australian Lebanese story. Paper presented in the research seminar series, Division of Teaching and Learning Services, Central Queensland University, Rockhampton, Qld.

Moriarty, B. J. (2000). Australian circuses as cooperative communities. *International Journal of Educational Research, 33*(3), 297-307.

Moriarty, B. J. (2004). Inter-systemic research and collaboration: Ethical and political dimensions and elements of risk among cooperative communities. In P. N. Coombes, M. J. M. Danaher, & P. A. Danaher (Eds.), *Strategic uncertainties: Ethics, politics and risk in contemporary educational research* (pp. 143-154). Flaxton, Qld: Post Pressed.

Moriarty, B. J., & Gray, B. (2003, Winter). Future directions: A model for educational partnerships in Australia. *Journal of Research in Rural Education, 18*(3), 159-163.

Moriarty, B. J., & McDonnell, J. (1998, October 2). Co-operative communities and circus life. Paper presented at the annual conference of the Australasian Association for Co-operative Education, Sydney, NSW.

Moriarty, B. J., Danaher, P. A., & Rose, C. G. (1998). Margins, mainstreams and the show people. In P. A. Danaher (Ed.), *Beyond the Ferris wheel: Educating Queensland show children* (pp. 43-56). Rockhampton, Qld: Central Queensland University Press.

Moriarty, B. J., Danaher, G. R., Kenny, M. D., & Danaher, P. A. (2004, June). *Experiences and issues in implementing an educational innovation: Report on research conducted with children and parents in the show community and personnel in the Queensland School for Travelling Show Children and Education Queensland in Brisbane and Southport in August 2003* (50 pp). Rockhampton, Qld: Central Queensland University.

Morrow, W. (2005). *Education and the Romani (Gypsy) people: The Sikavni.* Unpublished Doctor of Philosophy thesis, University of New England, Armidale, NSW.

Nautiyal, S., Rao, K. S., Maikhuri, R. K., & Saxena, K. G. (2003, August). Transhumant pastoralism in the Nanda Devi Biosphere Reserve, India. *Mountain Research and Development, 23*(3), 255-262.

Neill, A. S. (1960). *Summerhill: A radical approach to child rearing.* New York: Hart Publications Company.

Noyes, J. K. (2000). Nomadic fantasies: Producing landscapes of mobility in German southwest Africa. *Ecumene, 7*(1), 47-66.

Oakes, J. (2005). *Keeping track: How schools structure inequality* (2nd ed.). New Haven, CT: Yale University Press.

O'Hanlon, C., & Holmes, P. (2004). *The education of Gypsy and Traveller children: Towards inclusion and educational achievement.* Stoke on Trent, UK and Sterling, VA: Trentham Books.

Pace, S. (2007, July). Play and flow: Implications for online learning. *Studies in Learning, Evaluation, Innovation and Development, 4*(1), 67-78. Retrieved November 6, 2007, from http://www.sleid.cqu.edu.au

Peters, P. F. (2005). *Time, innovation and mobilities: Travels in technological cultures.* London: Routledge.

Peters, M. A., Maurer, S., Weber, S., Olssen, M., & Besley, A. C. (Eds.) (2008). *Governmentality and beyond: Education and the rise of neoliberalism.* Rotterdam, The Netherlands: Sense Publishers.

Postman, N. (1993). *Technopoly: The surrender of culture to technology.* New York: Vintage Books.

Prensky, M. (2001, October). Digital natives, digital immigrants. *On the Horizon, 9*(5), 1-2. Retrieved November 6, 2007, from http://www.marcprensky.com/writing/Prensky%2-%20 Digital%20Natives,%20Digital%20Immigrants%20-%20Part1.pdf

Putman, R. T., & Borko, H. (2001). What do new views of knowledge and thinking have to say about research on teacher learning? In B. Moon, J. Butcher, & E. Bird (Eds.), *Learning professional development in education* (pp. 11-29). London: Routledge.

Rao, A. (2006). The acquisition of manners, morals and knowledge: Growing into and out of Bakkarwal society. In C. Dyer (Ed.), *The education of nomadic peoples: Current issues, future prospects* (pp. 53-76). New York and Oxford, UK: Berghahn Books.

Ravid, R., & Handler, M. G. (2001). *The many faces of school–university collaboration: Characteristics of successful partnerships.* Englewood, CO: Teacher Ideas Press.

Reed, M. S., Fraser, E. D. G., & Dougill, A. J. (2006, October). An adaptive learning process for developing and applying sustainability indicators with local communities. *Ecological Economics, 59*(4), 406-418.

Retallick, J., Cocklin, B., & Coombe, K. (Eds.) (1999). *Learning communities in education: Issues, strategies and contexts.* London: Routledge/Falmer.

Reynolds, B. (2002). *Becoming criminal: Transversal performance and cultural dissonance in early modern England.* Baltimore, MD and London: John Hopkins University Press.

Rifkin, J. (1995). *The end of work: The decline of the global labor force and the dawn of the post-market era.* New York: G. P. Putman's Sons.

Ritchie, G. (2004, January). Quantifying the effects of teacher movements between schools in New Zealand: To schools that hath, shall be given. *Journal of Education Policy, 19*(1), 57-79.

Rothwell, N. (2008, August 23-24). The way of all flesh. *Weekend Australian Review,* 8-9.

Rowan, L. O. (2001). *Write me in: Inclusive texts in the primary classroom.* Newtown, NSW: Primary English Teachers Association.

Rowan, R. (2004). (De)Constructing educational risk: A discursive and ecological approach to research. In P. N. Coombes, M. J. M. Danaher, & P. A. Danaher (Eds.), *Strategic uncertainties: Ethics, politics and risk in contemporary educational research* (pp. 11-25). Flaxton, Qld: Post Pressed.

Salinas, C., & Fránquiz, M. E. (2004). Preface: Making migrant children and migrant education visible. In C. Salinas & M. E. Fránquiz (Eds.), *Scholars in the field: The challenges of migrant education* (pp. xi-xvii). Charleston, WV: ERIC Clearinghouse on Rural Education and Small Schools/Appalachia Educational Laboratory.

Scheunpflug, A., & Asbrand, B. (2006, February). Global education and education for sustainability. *Environmental Education Research, 12*(1), 33-46.

Scholten, U. (2000). Dutch bargee families: Partners in early childhood education. *International Journal of Educational Research, 33*(3), 275-283.

Seddon, T., & Billett, S. (2004). *Social partnerships in vocational education: Building community capacity.* Adelaide, SA: National Centre for Vocational Education Research.

Sheller, M., & Urry, J. (Eds.) (2004). *Tourism mobilities: Places to play, place in play.* London: Routledge.

Sheller, M. & Urry, J. (Eds.) (2006). *Mobile technologies of the city.* London: Routledge.

Shulman, L. S., & Shulman, J. H. (2004, March). How and what teachers learn: A shifting perspective. *Journal of Curriculum Studies, 36*(2), 257-271.

Simon, B. (2005, March 20). Sea Gypsies saw signs in the waves: How Moken people in Asia saved themselves from deadly tsunami. *CBS News.* Retrieved May 23, 2005, from http://www.cbsnews.com/stories/2005/03/18/60minutes/main681558.shtml

Smith, M. K. (2001, July 14). Non-formal education. Retrieved October 8, 2003, from http://www.infed.org/biblio/b-nonfor.htm

Sobel, R. S., & King, K. A. (2008, August). Does school choice increase the rate of youth entrepreneurship? *Economics of Education Review, 27*(4), 429-438.

Soliman, I. (2001). Collaboration and the negotiation of power. *Asia-Pacific Journal of Teacher Education, 29*(3), 219-234.

Somekh, B., & Lewin, C. (Eds.) (2005). *Research methods in the social sciences.* London: Sage Publications.

Spillane, J. P., & Louis, K. S. (2002). School improvement processes and practices: Professional learning for building instructional capacity. *Yearbook of the National Society for the Study of Education, 101*(1), 83-104.

Spoth, R., Greenberg, M., Bierman, K., & Redmond, C. (2004, March). PROSPER community–university partnership model for public education systems: Capacity-building for evidence-based, competence building prevention. *Prevention Science, 5*(1), 31-39.

Stainback, S., Stainback, W., & Jackson, H. J. (1992). Towards inclusive classroom. In S. Stainback & W. Stainback (Eds.), *Curriculum considerations in inclusive classrooms* (pp. 3-17). Baltimore, MD: Paul H. Brooks Publishing Company.

Stanley, G., & Tognolini, J. (2007, August). Standards-based assessment: A tool and means to the development of human capital and capacity building in education. *Australian Journal of Education, 51*(2), 129-145.

Stokes, H., Stacey, K., & Lake, M. (2006). *Schools, vocational education and training, and partnerships: Capacity-building in rural and regional communities*. Adelaide, SA: National Centre for Vocational Education Research.

Strickland, K. (1999, December 18-19). Wizards of Oz off the funds tightrope. *The Weekend Australian*, 6.

Swadener, B. B. (2000). "At risk" or "at promise?" From deficit constructions of the "other childhood" to possibilities for authentic alliances with children and families. In L. D. Soto (Ed.), *The politics of early childhood education* (pp. 117-134). New York: Peter Lang.

Swadener, B. B., & Lubeck, S. (Eds.) (1995). *Children and families at promise: Deconstructing the discourse of risk*. Albany, NY: State University of New York Press.

Swan, K. (2001). Virtual interaction: Design factors affecting student satisfaction and perceived learning in asynchronous online courses. *Distance Education, 22*(2), 306-331.

Swan, K., & Shea, P. (2005). The development of virtual learning communities. In S. R. Hiltz & R. Goldman (Ed.), *Asynchronous learning networks: The research frontier* (pp. 239-260). New York: Hampton Press.

Swick, K. J. (2001, May-June). Service-learning in teacher education: Building learning communities. *Clearing House, 74*(5), 261-264.

Talburt, S., & Boyles, D. (2005). Reconsidering learning communities: Expanding the discourse by challenging the discourse. *Journal of General Education, 54*(3), 209-236.

Taylor, M. (2000). Communities in the lead: Power, organisational capacity and social capital. *Urban Studies, 37*(5/6), 1019-1035.

Teo, H.-H., Chan, H.-C., Wei, K.-W., & Zhang, Z. (2003, November). Evaluating information accessibility and community adaptivity features for sustaining virtual learning communities. *International Journal of Human–Computer Studies, 59*(5), 671-697.

Thorpe, M., & Kubiak, C. (2005, Autumn). Working at community boundaries: A micro-analysis of the activist's role in participatory learning networks. *Studies in the Education of Adults, 37*(2), 151-165.

Tilbury, D. (2004). Rising to the challenge: Education for sustainability in Australia. *Australian Journal of Environmental Education, 20*(2), 103-114.

Torimiro, D. O., Dionco-Adetaya, E., & Okorie, V. O. (2003, June). Children and involvement in animal rearing: A traditional occupation for sustainability of nomadic culture? *Early Child Development and Care, 173*(2-3), 185-191.

Tuijnman, A., & Boudard, E. (2001). *Adult education participation in North America: International perspectives*. Ottawa: Statistics Canada

Turner, W., & Sharp, S. (2006). Evaluating the effective relationships and participation in teacher education partnerships. In J. Gray (Ed.), *Proceedings of the 2006 Australian Teacher Education Association conference* (pp. 286-288). Fremantle, WA: Australian Teacher Education Association. Retrieved August 24, 2008, from http://atea.edu.au/ConfPapers/ATEA2006.pdf

Twomey Fosnot, C. (1996). Constructivism: A psychological theory of learning. In C. Twomey Fosnot (Ed.), *Constructivism: Theory, perspectives and practice* (pp. 8-33). New York: Teachers College Press.

Tyler, C. (Ed.) (2005). *Traveller education: Accounts of good practice*. Stoke on Trent, UK and Sterling, VA: Trentham Books.

Umar, A., & Tahir, G. (2000). Researching nomadic education: A Nigerian perspective. *International Journal of Educational Research, 33*(3), 231-240.

Urry, J. (1999). *Sociology beyond societies: Mobilities for the twenty-first century*. London: Routledge.

Van Blerk, L. (2005, April). Negotiating spatial identities: Mobile perspectives on street life in Uganda. *Children's Geographies, 3*(1), 5-21.

Vetter, S. (2005, July). Rangelands at equilibrium and non-equilibrium: Recent developments in the debate. *Journal of Arid Environments, 62*(2), 321-341.

Vick, M. (2006). "It's a difficult matter": Historical perspectives on the enduring problem of the practicum in teacher education. *Asia-Pacific Journal of Teacher Education, 34*(2), 181-198.

Vickers, M., Harris, C., & McCarthy, F. (2004). University–community engagement: Exploring service-learning options within the practicum. *Asia-Pacific Journal of Teacher Education, 32*(2), 129-141.

Vygotsky, L. S. (1934/1962). *Thought and language.* Cambridge, MA: MIT Press.

Vygotsky, L. S. (1978). *Mind in society: The development of higher psychological processes.* Cambridge, MA: Harvard University Press.

Wald, P. E., & Castleberry, M. S. (Eds.). (2000). *Educators as learners: Creating a professional learning community in your school.* Alexandria, VA: Association for Supervision and Curriculum Development.

Warmington, P., & Murphy, R. (2004). Could do better? Media depictions of UK educational assessment results. *Journal of Education Policy, 19*(3), 285-299.

Watkins, C. (2005). *Classrooms as learning communities: What's in it for schools?* London: Routledge.

Webb, J., Schirato, T., & Danaher, G. R. (2002). *Understanding Bourdieu.* Crows Nest, NSW: Allen & Unwin.

Welch, A. R. (2001, November). Globalisation, post-modernity and the state: Comparative education facing the third millennium. *Comparative Education, 37*(4), 475-492.

Wenger, E. (1998). Communities of practice: Learning as a social system. Retrieved February 16, 2007, from http://www.co-i-l.com/coil/knowledge-garden/cop/lss.shtml

Wild-Smith, K. (2005). Improving access to early educational opportunities for Traveller children. In C. Tyler (Ed.), *Traveller education: Accounts of good practice* (pp. 61-70). Stoke on Trent, UK and Sterling, VA: Trentham Books.

Williams, R. (2005, February 1). *The science show.* ABC Radio National.

Wright, G. (2008, September 6-7). Planet Google. *Weekend Australian,* 14-19.

Zeichner, K. (2002). Beyond traditional structures of student teaching. *Teacher Education Quarterly, 29*(2), 59-64.

Zine, J. (2007, March). Safe havens or religious 'ghettos'? Narratives of Islamic schooling in Canada. *Race Ethnicity and Education, 10*(1), 71-92.

Index